finding this place

Marcia Breece

BOOK PUBLISHERS NETWORK

Book Publishers Network
P.O. Box 2256
Bothell • WA • 98041
Ph • 425-483-3040
www.bookpublishersnetwork.com

10 9 8 7 6 5 4 3 2 1

Printed in the United States of America

LCCN 2009907832
ISBN10 1-935359-20-7
ISBN13 978-1-935359-20-3

I based this memoir on my struggle to find emotional truth. It's how I remember the included events and may not match the memories of all concerned. I changed the names of people and places and combined some characters to protect privacy. I also compressed or estimated dialog to convey substance.

Editor: Vicki McCown
Cover Designer: Laura Zugzda
Cover Image: Marcia Breece
Typographer: Stephanie Martindale
Photo of Author: Winifred Whitfield

acknowledgments

Thanks to Kimberly King, actor and singer extraordinaire, who not only patiently read an early version of this book, she read it aloud as only an actor could. Thanks also to the members of the North Kitsap Book Club and Bainbridge Island Journeys with Words writing group for helping me bring this book alive.

introduction

Finding This Place recounts my healing journey. I hope it illustrates potential beyond limits and encourages each reader to fully experience her environment and listen to her heart. I believe unimagined possibilities exist for everyone, whether you live unconsciously or perceptively. Many talented authors, such as Shakti Gawain and Dr. Wayne Dyer, have created prominent works on healing, finding spirituality, and effecting change. Their influence on my journey is immeasurable.

While exploring petroglyphs in the Mojave Desert, I photographed the image on the cover. The wind had whipped a secure stem of grass, which had scratched circles in the loose sand. Depending on topography, wind direction, and the sturdiness of the grass, wind circles like this one can be faint or conspicuous. If the stem had not been secure, the circles would be faint or the grass would have blown away. With the stem secured and the ground smooth, the circles got deeper with each twist in the wind.

To me, each score in the sand represents knowledge. With experience, the knowledge gets deeper. As a child, I was unable to hold my footing. My knowledge seemed fleeting but with maturity came stability. As my emotional footing became more secure, I began to recover intrinsic wisdom and gained deeper understanding. Motivation, sometimes at hurricane force, caused changes I couldn't have imagined.

Like animals in a forest, infants and children know things—just know. Their lungs breathe. Their fingers clutch. Their heads bob in search of food, and they suckle. Memory embedded in their cells guides them to sense fear, happiness, joy, and danger. They see, but not with eyes; listen, but not with ears; and understand, but not with intellect. As they mature and develop communication skills, however, they learn to distinguish appropriate from intuitive knowledge because they realize how threatening their inexplicable wisdom is to the inhabitants of our planet. Therefore, children mistrust their native gifts and forget. The lucky ones, like me, unconsciously persist. Then, as if by escort, unimagined possibilities emerge.

chapter one

I laughed out loud, a big throw-your-head-back guffaw. Scooping llama manure isn't that hilarious, of course, but it's not as disgusting as it sounds. Llamas make little piles of pellets I fondly call llama beans, and they don't stink—really. When I bought this three-acre farm, about an hour from Seattle, I escaped my corporate façade. I scoop with alacrity because I realize at least I'm shoveling the real thing.

An echo of love for my grandparents and their dairy farm brings joy to this three-acre llama ranch. Their herd of black-and-white Holsteins produced milk while my five cinnamon and white llamas are mostly yard-art, but the energetic sensations endure, allowing the rediscovery of childhood thoughts and dreams before the judgment and restriction of our patriarchal planet obscured the light.

Granddad's burly hug squeezed the breath out of me while Grandma hugged firmly but gently. Their love was unconditional. I spent weeks every summer on their dairy farm near Columbus, Ohio, where I arose with the sun and a child's light-saturated spirit.

After the morning milking, Granddad brought raw milk to the house in a narrow stainless steel bucket. Grandma skimmed the cream and put the bucket on the stove. I climbed onto an old stool and stirred with a long wooden spoon. The steam made my face sweat, and I switched hands as one arm got tired. When Grandma proclaimed the milk "pasteurized," she carefully ladled it into a jar and moved it to the refrigerator.

Granddad drank hot coffee at every meal using the cream Grandma skimmed from fresh milk. "Please, can I have some too?" I begged. Grandma heated a pan of milk slowly on the stove, filled a mug, and added just enough strong coffee to change the color. I thought *I'm drinking coffee too*—like Granddad. Years later, I ordered my first latte at Starbucks in Seattle's Pike Place Market and realized I'd been drinking lattes all my life.

When afternoon sun scorched the rolling fields and it was too hot to bake, Grandma taught me to sew while my brother Craig helped Granddad in the barn. Grandma didn't buy Simplicity patterns at the dry goods store; she drew outlines on newspaper. The cotton pieces we cut looked nothing like clothes that would fit my doll. I stood in front of her, rocked the treadle, and she helped me hold the fabric under the presser foot. A doll dress materialized. Thirteen years later, I enrolled in Principles of Flat Pattern Design at Ohio State University and realized I'd learned flat pattern design before I was five.

Early morning air cooled the kitchen while sunrise filtered through the peach tree by the window. "Let's bake this bread before the sun gets too hot," Grandma said as she put on the apron that covered the front of her housedress. Although she'd made bread hundreds of times, she asked, "Can you find the recipe?"

I opened her wooden recipe box, and she waited while I searched for the card then sounded out, "Milk, sugar, salt, shor-ten-ing, and yea-st dis-sol-ved in warm water," thinking I was grown up.

We mixed the ingredients in a big green bowl, added flour with our hands, then dumped the mixture onto the flour-dusted counter. As we kneaded, the soft, sticky mixture became firm and resilient.

Flour lingered on Grandma's hands and forearms, but I looked as if I'd gone for a swim in the flour sack. "Look at you!" She didn't really mind. "While our dough gets bigger, let's dust you off outside." The weathered, green screen door clapped behind us.

I giggled as she dusted the flour from my eyelashes with the corner of her apron and the breeze brushed a white cloud from my hair. Back inside, she let me wipe the floor around my wooden stool with soapy rags. I probably made a bigger mess that she cleaned up later, but her patience felt like love.

I filled the sink with bubbly warm water and washed my four toy bread pans, then shaped tiny loaves with the dough Grandma had set aside for me. I waited on the floor by the oven.

"Are they done yet?"

"Now are they done?"

At last, Grandma removed one pan at a time, holding the precious golden bread high at arm's length and placed each loaf on the window-sill. "Look what a wonderful cook you are," she said. "Your little loaves are prettier than the big ones." Once they cooled, we wrapped all of the loaves in aluminum foil and found a basket to hold my little ones.

My mother arrived with three-year-old Rob and our baby sister, Lili. They were still too young for the farm. I told my mother my plans, "I'm going to make little peanut butter and jelly sandwiches for my dolls' tea party." I don't remember my mother being part of those days on the farm, but I remember the two-hour drive home in the back seat of her green 1952 Pontiac. It had big whitewall tires and a white roof. I sat between my brothers on a beige leather seat watching telephone poles pass by. Lili's baby chair hooked over the front seat, and Mom's arm flew sideways to hold her steady whenever we stopped or turned. On my lap, the former Easter basket lined with a yellow cloth napkin held four foil-wrapped loaves of my special bread.

After my bath, I readied the dolls' table with my china tea set, placing its pink cups and black saucers just so. Each doll waited on a little wooden chair. When my mother tucked me in, I reminded her, "Tomorrow I'm going to make sandwiches for my dolls."

Finally, at noon the next day, my mother placed the four tiny loaves on the cutting board. Barely able to see over the counter, I stood ready, sure I'd be invited to spread each tiny slice.

As though the big serrated bread knife cut my skin, I watched as she sliced a lengthwise gash in each loaf, reducing my culinary creations to hot dog buns.

"Why the tears?" she asked.

She knew my plans. I said nothing.

"Now stop crying and eat your hot dog. Do you want mustard?"

Wrongly forced into service, those perfect little loaves of golden crusty bread became a metaphor for my life, their destiny no longer my decision.

The horizontal gash signified the difference between fantasy and life. My mother could have said, "What a chef you are" or "How pretty they look" or "You must have worked very hard. Let's make hot dogs buns so we can all enjoy your bread." She could have recognized the importance of my spirit, my creativity, my talent perhaps. I could have learned a lesson of intent versus effect. Instead, she ignored me, assigning me to the periphery, as real as my dolls' repast. Any remaining spirit was set aside, like a condiment, waiting.

When I was nine, I drove the big John Deere tractor in the fields to spread manure. I helped feed the calves, herded the cows to the barn in the evening or to the pasture after milking in the morning. I helped plant the huge garden that provided crisp green lettuce, orange carrots, yellow sweet corn, long, full green beans, and big sweet Bermuda onions.

Granddad liked to pull an onion from the rich soil and eat it like an apple, so I did too. I bit, chewed, and ignored my burning eyes. If my mother had asked me to eat a raw onion, I'd have been appalled, but I wanted to be like Granddad. In fact, sometimes I wanted to *be* him.

A small incline, too steep to mow, separated the house and garden. A thick tangle of variegated ivy and morning glories covered the slope. While Grandma weeded the garden, I tugged at the morning glory vines. I loved the pale pink trumpet-shaped flowers and the light scent, strongest at sunset. I couldn't understand why Grandma considered them weeds. It seemed there was no way to disentangle the two vines, as if the ivy had found a way to bloom.

In 1954, I sat on the floor by Granddad's chair. He let me hold his camera in the brown leather case as he recounted his trip to Wilder, Montana. As required by the Homestead Act, starting in 1918, he'd spent three years on his land where cattle grazed on the drought-ravaged plain. To earn extra cash, he skippered on the Wilder Ferry, crossing the Missouri River with horses and buggies, stagecoaches, and cowboys on horseback.

Granddad was a descendent of Scottish hoodlums banished to Ireland by King James in the 1600s. His ancestors had come to America in 1713 and settled in Ohio in 1799. In 1921, he sold his 320 acres in Montana for $1.25/acre, returned to Ohio, married my grandmother, and began farming.

He was also a talented amateur photographer and semi-professional musician. His parents gave him the treasured bellows camera, "my Kodak," he'd say, for graduation. The black-and-white photos he sent to his sweetheart from Montana told his story. There were images of cottonwood trees, landscapes of the ice-covered Missouri River, cattle grazing in the open prairie in spring, horses harnessed to an enormous sleigh in deep snow, the bunkhouse, and his coworkers with huge mustaches hiding their lips, eyes shadowed by cowboy hats.

My favorite photo, a black-and-white faded to sepia, captured him in dappled sunlight, sitting in the elbow of a huge cottonwood tree with his companion, Rover, a brown-and-white collie lying in the weeds below him. "Who took this picture, Granddad?" I asked.

"I attached this-here wind-up timer gadget to the camera." He demonstrated. "Then I ran like hell to jump into that old tree before the shutter went off! Good thing that big old branch was so low, by jingo." He laughed that hoarse laugh that was uniquely his.

⚘ ⚘

Granddad often told the story of his daughter's birth. Mary Lucile, my mother, was born in January a year and a half after Granddad returned from Montana. She was a strikingly beautiful infant with black hair like Granddad's, long black eyelashes, and heart-stopping hazel eyes. Grandma developed a uterine infection a few days after the home birth. Penicillin could have cured her quickly but didn't become available until after WWII, twenty years later.

Granddad had to get her to the hospital twenty-five miles away. The packed-dirt roads were solid ice, and a thick, cold fog blanketed the rolling countryside. They decided not to take a horse and buggy; she'd be more comfortable and safer in the new Model-T Ford they called "the machine." They hoped to make better time. Grandma lay wrapped in wool blankets on the imitation leather seat; her sister Lucile crouched on the floor beside her. Leroy, Grandma's nineteen-year-old brother, drove the black car, leaning as far forward as he could to see the treacherous road—the new Model T had no windshield. He had no idea how fast he was going—there was no speedometer either. Granddad and a friend rode the fenders like broncos, giving Leroy directions for keeping the narrow tires on the road, nearly invisible in the thick murk. "... a little left ... hard right ... Turn! Turn!" They grasped either side of the fender as the tires slid on the ice. It took hours to get to Columbus, normally less than a one-hour drive in the new Model T. When they arrived, Grandma's temperature was 104 degrees, and she was delirious. The nurses rushed her away.

I imagined Granddad standing, hat in hand, in a dimly lit corridor. He'd endured three years in Montana, saving his money so they could be married.

Fortunately, guardian angels watched over them. As the pale purple crocuses pushed through wet snow, Grandma came home to her husband and their new baby girl. Lucile stayed with them for another month to help with the baby until Grandma got her strength back. My middle name was for Aunt Lucile.

"Luci," Granddad said, using one of his nicknames for me, "let's wash this smelly muck off our boots an' have some supper." Milking the cows was a twice-daily ritual, and I loved it, especially when I was four and Granddad still milked some of his herd by hand. He stood in the grass and used a strong blast from the hose to dislodge the muck from his black boots. When it was my turn, I pressed my back against his legs, and he bent over me. I curled my arms around his, and one at a time, extended my red plastic boots into the stream of water. Then he turned off the hose and lifted me out of the boots and onto the dry sidewalk. I wish I had a color photograph of my wet boots on the step next to his tall shiny black ones. A pool of water darkened the concrete and ran down to the step below with the weathered, hunter-green screen door behind.

Our stockinged feet climbed six wooden steps to the area near the kitchen where wooden pegs waited for Granddad's hat and coat. Tired from his strenuous day, he still had the patience to lift me high enough to hang my own coat and hat.

It was a light supper, usually leftovers from the big noontime meal. From my stool, I helped Grandma do the dishes, then she played the piano, and Granddad played whatever instrument matched his mood: saxophone, drums, or spoons. He could make music with anything, including his deep baritone voice.

His harmonica was my favorite. He could make any tune sound happy or sad. When he played "My Old Kentucky Home," I imagined him in Montana in 1919, beneath the shade of a big tree where the Missouri River rushed by and the tall prairie grass swayed with the rhythm of his lonely tune. His horse grazed, and his collie, Rover, sat beside him while he missed his sweetheart, my grandma.

Throughout the 1920s, Granddad and Grandma performed together when dance bands were the rage, Edith on piano, Cecil usually on drums. They played "Red River Valley," "Golden Slippers," and many tunes that have become politically incorrect, such as, "Ching Chong Chinamen" and "Dark Town Strutter's Ball." Number one on Granddad's hit parade was a playful rhythmic tune, "Sing Song Kitty Won't You Ki Me Oh." I only remember bits of it that he sang while he tapped the rhythm with spoons held bowl to bowl or with his palm on a steering wheel:

Well I tied my horse to a hickory stump
Sing song kitty won't you ki me oh
Me oh my oh dear oh me
Sing song kitty won't you ki me oh

Years later, when my children were preschool-age, the old couple created music, and we danced. By then his tunes melted into one another, and we had to listen carefully to hear the end of one and the beginning of the next. Hoedown songs, such as "Old Suzanna" dissolved into "Lil' Liza Jane" and then became "The Old Pine Tree."

By the time I was five, Granddad and Grandma slept in separate rooms. Granddad snored loudly, and Grandma's back required firm support. Granddad's walnut bed, with a soft feather mattress, occupied most of his small bedroom and left little space for the walnut dresser with acorn handles that held his clothes. At night, I snuggled next to Granddad's weary frame, cradled by his deep voice and clean musky scent. Reading aloud from Zane Grey novels about the railroad and Indians in the wild American West, he smoothed my golden hair still damp from my bath over the big feather pillow as he read:

> A dreamy murmur of running water arose from the green depths. Wade heard wild turkeys clucking. He was glad to get back to Smoky Hollow.
>
> Zane Grey, *Shadow on the Trail*

In the morning, I woke under a thick homemade quilt in the closet-sized guest room across the hall. Granddad had been working for hours. I padded down the stairs in my bare feet and found Grandma at her desk, her blond hair glowing in the morning light, as she made a pencil drawing of a calf born the day before.

At the turn of the twentieth century in rural Ohio, it was unusual for women to go to college or have a career, but in 1917, at only eighteen, Grandma graduated from Normal School, a two-year program for elementary teachers.

When my grandparents married in the spring of 1921, it was inappropriate for Grandma to continue her teaching career. Together, they built the dairy business. She kept meticulous financial records, made drawings of each new calf, cooked farmhand meals, and never considered another path. When I got older, I began to appreciate the sacrifice she must have made to be on the farm with Granddad.

One of Granddad's nicknames for me was "Sugar," and when he used it, I felt as sweet as the sound of his voice. Grandma brushed my long, blond hair into a ponytail and told me I was beautiful and smart. I knew I could be whatever I wanted to be.

Soon enough, *Training to be just a girl* would begin.

My brothers and I ran barefoot over the rolling green pastures, all three wearing nothing but shorts. I loved the wind in my straight hair and the warm sun on my pale, bare back when I hunched, clutching my knees, by the fishing hole. Then just before I started first grade, everything changed. My mother insisted I wear a shirt.

"Good little girls don't go running around half-naked," she said.

"Why don't Craig and Rob have to wear one too?" I asked.

She slipped a blue T-shirt over my head. As with most important decisions in my young life, there was no discussion.

It's not that I wanted to go topless all my life. I began to realize that the difference between girls and boys extended beyond the physical features I knew about. It was a complicated lesson. On the farm, our grandparents treated my brothers and me equally, but I learned to cook and sew just because I was a girl. I also helped with chores, played in the hayloft, and did all the things the boys did. I began to see that my life would not be as it was on their farm.

Training had begun.

I was nearly forty when Grandma died. I missed her funeral in Plain City, Ohio. Granddad died a year later, and I managed to get away from my new job in Seattle. My sister, Lili, and her family also came. I heard my uncle say, "They'll always be with us in spirit." That phrase would hold new meaning for me in the years to come.

After the funeral, we drove back to Mom and Dad's for an early supper.

When we'd finished the dishes, Mom gave Grandma's wooden recipe box to Lili. I thought she might toss out the dirty old paper inside, refinish the outside, and fill it with her own recipes. She was a skilled chef, a much better cook than I.

It should hold memories not recipes, I thought, but said nothing.

I missed Granddad and Grandma and their unconditional love. I missed the way I'd felt on their farm.

Lili found me sitting on the floor in our dimly lit bedroom, my legs held tight to my chest, my forehead resting on my knees. "This probably means a lot to you," she said, holding out the box. "You spent more time at their place than I did."

"I just miss them so much," I said, unable to look at her. "It's not the recipe box."

"You should have it." She put the box on the bed, leaned down to pat my shoulder, and left me alone with my memories.

I touched the box and felt Grandma in the room with me.

The fragrance of a blooming peach tree lured me from my room to my parents' orchard where the sunset was as pink as the blossoms.

Sitting on the grass, I touched an imaginary floury thumbprint and studied the collection of recipes stained by years of service. The box held our family history, written in the formal pen-and-ink script common in the early 1900s.

Devil's Food Cake, Mary Watson, Home Ec Teacher, 1916

Lemon Cookies—Mrs. Leonard Blumenschein, 1917 (Grandma's great-aunt)

French Loaf Cake, Nillie Hilbert, August 2, 1919 (her sister)

Mother's Cookies, 1921 (from my Great-Grandma Hilbert, her mother)

Whipped Cream Substitutes, clipped from the *Farm Journal*, January 1927

Elderberry Blossom Tea—June 28, 1929, written on the back of a Valentine's Day card, signed in child's script: Mary Lucile—my mother when she was six.

Irish Stew, clipped from a newspaper, March 28, 1930

Dried Beef, my favorite, called for: *one gal rainwater, 1½ lb salt, and ½ oz salt peter. Let boil. Pack in jars when brine is cool. Set for 3 weeks then rinse with warm water and scrub toroly. Hang over stove. After dry toroly - about 2 weeks - wrap in newspaper.* The curly script belonged to my great-grandma whose spelling matched her German accent.

In the wooden recipe box, I found a blurred cookie recipe imbued with my own history. I'd spilled vanilla on the card when I was five. Grandma never rewrote it. Sitting under the peach tree thirty-five years later, I brought the card to my face. Vanilla, real or imagined, wafted around me. I saw myself standing on that old wooden stool. Grandma and I were kneading bread, rolling dough, washing mud from fresh-dug potatoes, and husking yellow sweet corn. I smelled peach pie on the windowsill, bread in the oven, and freshly plowed dirt in the fields. I heard the purr of the sewing machine and felt the sweat tickle my neck.

No matter what happened, they would always be with me.

chapter two

"In the Book of Genesis, it is written that God made woman from Adam's rib," Reverend Swinehart bellowed to his Lutheran congregation, his bat-sleeves waving. "God intended for men to be in charge of women."

My black patent-leather shoes barely reached the edge of the pew beneath his angry pulpit as he told the story of Adam and Eve in the Garden of Eden. From my limited perspective, it seemed he blamed women for all the suffering in the world.

We sat in the second row. My tow-headed brothers, with Woody-Woodpecker haircuts, wore white shirts, bow ties, and jackets like Dad's. I wore a flowered cotton dress and yellow cardigan sweater that matched my hair. Our mother's mid-calf coat camouflaged her pregnancy while rhinestones woven in the grey tweed caused entertaining rainbows to dance on the pew in front of us. Perfectly dressed, perfectly behaved, a perfect façade.

Although I had no evidence to the contrary and had no capacity of articulation, something in my embedded cell memory, even at age four, knew that no Divine intention put men in charge of women.

In my version of the Garden of Eden, Eve knew the apple was forbidden. She probably told Adam, "I'm not tryin' it; you try it," so he did.

Then he loudly blamed her. "*She* made me eat it! She *made* me!" Even if you accept the theory that Eve tempted Adam to bite into the forbidden fruit, thus causing their banishment from paradise, you can't ignore Eve's ability to persuade him and his inability to resist.

⎯⎯⎯ ⎯⎯⎯

Birdsongs and laughter filled the woods as my brothers and I rode cardboard sleds down muddy ravine walls to the creek that trickled below. We constructed little sludge dams to make minnow pools and found crawdads and black salamanders under rocks in the soft, cool mud. We didn't know girls were supposed to be afraid of crawdads and salamanders.

Gramps and Grandma B, my father's parents, taught us to identify the abundant species of Midwestern birds that inhabited the deciduous woods around their house. They fed suet and seeds to chickadees, woodpeckers, and nuthatches.

Gramps cut a meandering path to a picnic area near the edge of our private water park. A canopy of maple, alder, walnut, oak, and redbud leaves shaded our Sunday parade to the big weathered picnic table and fire pit. The sound of the crackling wood fire, the smell of smoke and beef, hamburgers for the kids, steaks for the adults, were accompanied by baked beans, potato salad, and red Jell-O that I helped Grandma B prepare with marshmallows and canned fruit cocktail.

During one fall picnic, a great horned owl swooped down from a nearby golden maple to grab a piece of meat Gramps secretly pulled through the dry leaves with a string. He and the owl had practiced for weeks. In spring, a raccoon crawled out of the woods and onto Gramps' lap and found a lump of sugar in his shirt pocket. Gramps was magical with the animals that inhabited his property. All creatures were safe there.

My mother and Grandma B were close friends. "How are you today, Mrs. B?" my mother would say.

"I'm doing fine. How about you, Mrs. B?" Grandma would respond.

Then they'd laugh.

Gramps and Grandma B were married in 1919, when she was nineteen and he was twenty-two. For as long as I could remember, he would giggle and pinch her generous derriere while we did the dishes. I pretended not to notice. She'd scold, "Now, Marvin, stop that!" but I knew she loved his attention. Gramps and Grandma B slept in separate rooms except on Friday nights, which I thought curious. When he died in 1973, I heard Grandma B tell my mother, "Friday nights will be the hardest."

Grandma B taught me to be frugal. My mother said she was "tight with money." Grandma B didn't like to spend it. She'd save a leftover tablespoon of applesauce or five green beans in small Pyrex cups, cover them with elasticized plastic tops that resembled shower caps, and serve them at our next meal. I'm sure there were days in her youth when she would have given anything for a dab of applesauce and five green beans.

Once she saved the mushy cornflakes I didn't eat for breakfast. I hated cornflakes, crisp or soggy. I tossed the sloppy mess into the woods and told her I'd eaten them, but she found me out and ordered me to sit on a stool in the corner of the kitchen for what seemed like forever until I "learned to appreciate things."

On rare occasions, Gramps took me fishing without my brothers. The rowboat waited by a weathered dock on Little Darby Creek. He held my hand while I stepped in and sat in the bow facing the back. He untied the rope and jumped in, causing the boat to rock while he settled into the middle seat, facing me. Silently, the oars cut the calm water as he rowed to his favorite fishing hole. He dropped the anchor, a bucket filled with concrete, and we floated for hours, listening to rural Ohio: woodpeckers hammering dead trees, chickadees chirping, and water trickling from the farmland into the creek. I listened to the hum of unwinding fishing line, the plunk of Gramps' favorite lure, a Johnson-spoon, the click of the spinning reel, and the purr of the sparkling wet line pulled back into the belly of the reel. Then he'd cast again, hum-plunk-click-purr, hum-plunk-click-purr. I was content to listen for hours but delighted when a gleaming wet bass actually took the lure and danced on its tail, reluctant to become our dinner. Sometimes I was sure the fish danced just for fun, then spit out the lure and disappeared into the deep cool water laughing at us.

Gramps gave me a bamboo fishing pole and showed me how to attach the cork. "Push the red button on the white side and a wire loop comes out on the red side. The fishing line goes through that loop," he said. "When you let go of the button, the cork is attached to the line." I thought putting the worm on the hook was a lot like sewing except fabric didn't resist like the squirmy worm. I dropped the cork, hook, and worm into the water and waited for the cork to roll from red to white. Usually, when the cork flashed a change in color, the fish had avoided the hook and stolen my worm. When we ran out of worms, Gramps made dough-balls for bait; Wonder Bread worked best. "Pick the soft white part from the middle and roll it in your palms." He demonstrated, throwing the unnecessary crust into the water. I attached the dough ball to my hook and dropped it overboard. Fish liked dough balls. We caught bluegills, catfish, and an occasional little bass. Gramps stowed them in his wicker creel. Back at their home in the woods, we cleaned our fish. Grandma B and I dredged the fillets in flour before we fried them in butter, and I carried the precious feast to the supper table.

Gramps said I could be anything I wanted to be, and I believed him. I knew he was right in those idyllic days before *Training*, before I learned what girls were *supposed* to be. The old wicker creel sits on my bookshelf, reminding me still I can be what I want to be.

When I was five years old and starting first grade, my mother bobbed my sun-streaked hair, but it was hopelessly straight and stringy and hung in my face. My teacher, Mrs. Scarberry, insisted, "Can't you do something with that awful hair?"

Mrs. Scarberry was nasty. The other kids asked each other, "Why is she so mean?" I asked, "Why is she so unhappy?"

No matter how cruel or sad she was, I was eager to please her. Thus began the series of frizzy home permanents called Tonettes that chemically burned my fragile, sun-bleached hair. Once a week, in an attempt to create soft, manageable curls, Mother wound my clean wet hair onto pink rubber Spoolies, a new invention that was supposed to replace pin curls, and a predecessor to rollers. She left them to dry overnight. Inevitably, some of the Spoolies popped open and unraveled before my hair was dry, leaving frizzy wisps among smoother curls. This wild, over-cooked coiffure lasted throughout first grade.

My baby sister, Lili, had naturally curly, pale blond hair that waved perfectly around her perfect face. As my mother twisted my wet hair onto the shocking-pink spindles, she lamented, "Why couldn't you have beautiful hair like Lili?" I felt it was my fault.

In the summer of 1955, I was seven, Rob was five, Craig was nine. We built a fort in Gramps' woods. I dragged leafed-out branches as big as I could manage. The boys rolled logs from the woodpile into the shelter for our seats, but I felt the need to make it more comfortable. I spread old towels over our log chairs, and Grandma B helped me make peanut butter and jelly sandwiches.

While I nested, the boys prepared to attack like marauding invaders. They fashioned swords and shields from scraps of lumber they found behind the garage and attacked just as naturally as I nested. My brothers labeled me "invader," and they banned me from their boys-only forest hideaway. I dropped the basket of sandwiches and stomped angrily through the trees to the house.

"I don't even wanna play in your stupid ol' fort."

No one taught my brothers this behavior, and they didn't have TV "heroes" to emulate. Was their conduct the consequence of visceral patriarchal memory embedded in their cells? It made no sense to me. Perhaps my embedded memory was far more ancient. I hadn't yet discovered the powerful feminine symbols that predate swords and violence, but I was quite sure that the dominance of boys over girls had not always been the natural state of humanity, no matter what Reverend Swinehart said in church on Sunday.

"You can help me with the laundry," Grandma B suggested when I found her in the dark damp basement. I pulled wet socks from the tub of rinse water, pressed them into the wringer, and dropped the squished socks one by one into the basket ready to hang on the line. It never occurred to her to instruct the boys to include me, and it never occurred to me to ask her to do so. The males were in power, even at ages nine and five.

As our family grew, the four of us, Craig, Rob, Lili, and I shared a bedroom on the second floor of the big Victorian house that was also our father's medical office. Our father didn't allow us to play in our room. He believed that children's noisy activities would disturb the sick and injured in his office below.

I doubt that my parents enjoyed the music of their children's laughter, even when no patients waited.

Once, when I was three or four, I spilled my milk at lunchtime. My father, agitated as usual by midday, shouted at me, "You moron!"

I wriggled down from my seat, walked around the table and crawled onto his lap. I took the prickle of his shaved cheeks in my palms. Eyelash to eyelash, big nose to little nose, I said, "Daddy, those people in the office are driving you crazy!" With no comment, he put me down on the linoleum floor. My stoic mother cleaned up the milk and served his lightly grilled cheese sandwich, made with Oleo, Velveeta, and Wonder Bread. Standing by the chrome-and-red vinyl chair, I watched his chin moving as he chewed. The slight bump on his throat bobbed as he swallowed. Then he returned to his patients.

As I grew older, I forgot the cause of his rage and began to accept his judgment of me.

chapter three

June's nursing uniform glowed in the late afternoon sun as she marched toward us, freshly cut grass staining the toes of her white shoes. Her mid-calf straight white skirt and stiff nurse's hat contrasted with a hedge of tall hollyhocks and abundant red poppies. "Your dad wants you two in his office, now," she said. Craig and I slid from our swing seats. We'd never been in the office. In my haste, I scraped the back of my bare legs on the rough wooden swing. Rubbing the scrapes, I hopped on one foot to keep up. We followed Dad's nurse up the concrete steps and into the secret rooms of the office.

Mr. Klopenstein sat on the examining table. His dirty, grass-stained bib-overalls stretched tightly over his generous belly. His arms were big, but the skin hung loosely under his sleeveless, sweat-stained undershirt. The scent of fresh cut grass, blood, and soapy antiseptic filled the examining room.

Mr. Klopenstein's bare feet dangled at eye-level. Two bloody toes hung by thin ribbons of skin. Blood and grass caked the remaining three toes. His thick, yellow toenails needed trimming. Dad announced, "This is what happens when you aren't careful around lawnmowers." There was no space to retreat in the small examining room. My bare back pressed against the cold plaster wall. We watched Dad's white gloved hands drop the two severed toes and mounds of blood-soaked gauze into the stainless steel pan June held at his side. When June cleansed the wound, Mr. Klopenstein moaned and hissed air between his crooked yellow teeth. Then she poured the bright red water with bits of floating grass into a white porcelain sink. Red droplets splashed in a beam of sunlight from a window far above my head. Dad used tiny stitches to close the gaping space where Mr. Klopenstein's toes once wiggled. He wrapped yards of gauze around the stitches and remaining injured toes.

That night, Mr. Klopenstein limped through my red and white dreams, "Fix it, Doc, fix it, fix it." I awoke soaked in sweat, standing in a corner, attempting to escape the bedroom I shared with Craig and our baby brother. For many years, the smell of fresh cut grass evoked fear, and I froze at the sound of a lawnmower, too frightened to hide. When my children were small, I couldn't bring myself to wiggle their tiny toes and recite "This Little Piggy."

Mr. Klopenstein was only the first lesson.

When a six-year-old accidentally shot his teenage brother in the eye with a BB gun, we assembled like miniature medical students. This time our younger brother Rob was included. "See what happens if you play with guns?" June unrolled a bundle of white fabric, revealing shiny instruments. We stood at stoic attention while Dad used long tweezers to extract the shot from the muscles near the outer edge of Scott's eye. June moved silently as they worked, her stark white uniform intermittently blocking and exposing my view of the bloody socket, the eye staring at the ceiling, the lips grimaced over exposed teeth, hands clasped with white knuckles. Finally, we heard the clink in June's metal pan. I watched as the bloody gauze piled higher and higher above my head. The boy's shallow, gravelly breathing was the only reminder he was human and the only sound in the room. Again, I tried to back against the cold, green wall, but Rob hid behind me, pushing me closer to the blood and gauze and fear.

Dad put a patch on Scott's eye and told his mother, "He may or may not have normal vision in this eye," in the same tone he might have said, "He may or may not want crackers with his soup." On his white pad, in unreadable script, he wrote out prescriptions while ignoring the pain in the mother's eyes, the dreadful realization that her oldest son's vision might have been destroyed by his little brother. Dad had no white pad or salve for that kind of ache. I suspect he felt her pain but lacked the emotional strength to comfort her. Still, she worshiped him, my father, the doctor with a confident demeanor.

That night, my back pushed against a closet wall under out-of-season clothes as I tried to escape the growing mountain of bloody bandages. The mothball smell was comforting compared to the smell of antiseptic and blood. I awoke in that small closet the next morning and many mornings thereafter.

Tommy, a boy in my first grade class, broke his arm jumping from a hayloft. While June mixed the plaster, Dad washed the dirt from Tommy's skin. Tommy cried. Dad pulled a hose-shaped bandage over Tommy's fingers past his bent elbow, wrapped that with white gauze, then strips of cloth dipped in the thick plaster mixture June had prepared. The smell reminded me of the plaster of Paris praying hands we made at Bible School.

The next day, Tommy stepped from the yellow bus with his arm in a clean white sling, his elbow immobilized by the cast. Standing by the classroom door, I said, "Hi, Tommy. Is your arm feeling better?" The gaze of his blue eyes sliced past me. His jaw set. His face flushed. He walked into our first grade classroom. Why did I feel responsible, as if I'd personally pushed him from the hayloft?

Dad never considered how Tommy felt about observers and disregarded the consequences on his patients and children.

Steve and Les, boys we knew, were hit by a car while riding their bicycles on Main Street near our house. My brothers and I heard the screeching tires and watched from behind the hedge of red poppies. People came running from their homes. Dad's white lab coat and June's uniform reflected the mid-afternoon sun. They seemed to glow among the others. Without looking at us, Dad shouted, "Stay there."

When I think about that awful day, I wonder why Dad didn't tell us to go into the house. That's what I would have done for my children. Instead, we saw Steve's scraped and bleeding face. His blood-soaked white T-shirt exposed a deep cut on his shoulder. His leg was obviously broken. Although Steve was badly injured, he would recover. Les lay still on the street, one leg tangled in the bent frame of his green Huffy bicycle. He was dead.

As we gathered around the dinner table that night, Dad said, "See what happens if you ride bicycles?" He never allowed us to have bicycles.

I bought my first when I was forty-eight.

In real life or nightmares, Dad's mutilated, disfigured, and sickly patients marched through our lives like characters in a horror film, our personal parade of life lessons. I quit dreaming or having dreams. Life was too frightening for dreams.

Dad didn't grow up with dreams of healing the world or even these small-town folks. He loved music. Gramps was a factory worker, and Grandma B had no education beyond elementary school, but they supported Dad's cello and voice lessons. Grandma B had a 45-rpm recording of Dad's Carnegie Hall debut. When she placed the old hi-fi needle on the discolored record, I sat on the floor by the speakers. Static further distorted the poor quality recording, but the magnificence of his performance came through. Singing a cappella, his tenor voice held high notes longer than I could hold my breath. As I listened, her body became bent and soft, her voice low and inaudible. It was the only time I saw my Grandma B allow strong emotion other than anger. I could feel her pain in my chest. "Why doesn't he sing now, Grandma B?" I asked, but she could only shake her head and wipe her puffy eyes. It was a secret she would never reveal.

Dad sang in church when I was small, the only time I heard him. I stood on the pew next to him, his blond head still higher than mine. I was careful not to step on his brown felt hat, pinched on both sides and creased lengthwise down the crown. The brim tipped down in front, and he never left the house without it unless he was going fishing.

I held my side of the hymnal as though I could read the music and words. I only pretended to sing so I could stand close and listen.

Praise God from Whom all blessings flow. Praise Him all creatures here below. Praise Him above ye heavenly host. Praise Father, Son, and Holy Ghost.

His tenor notes floated above the parishioners, reached the stained glass walls, and filled the small-town streets. I knew even the birds longed to sing like my daddy.

The small-town congregation cared less about his musical contributions than his availability after the service. "Mornin', Doc," they'd say. "My knee's really been actin' up. What should I do?"

"I cut my hand a few days ago. Ya s'pose it needs stitches?"

He quit going to church with us.

He quit singing.

He quit playing his cello.

He became angry and rarely displayed another emotion. Dad's intelligence provided for the requisite medical knowledge, but he was emotionally ill-prepared for patients or for his growing family. Without the war, he might have immersed himself in a laboratory, but the United States needed MDs in the 1940s so he became an MD. I knew at age five that my daddy didn't like being a doctor, but I also knew that he preferred the company of those strangers to the company of his family.

My mother bobbed along in the current of her life, disappearing under pressure, going wherever the flow took her with no desire to control the direction or outcome except to ensure someone else met all of her needs.

One of my mother's favorite expressions was "Wait until your father gets home!" It was her worst threat. It took me years to realize my feelings for my father were largely due to her manipulation of his fury. Like a matador waving a red cape, she focused his ire on his children, disassociating herself from the responsibility of discipline and from the possibility that his wrath would turn on her if not quickly diverted. In a row, we the guilty leaned over to receive the yardstick. The growl from deep in his throat frightened me more than the anticipation of pain. As I stood bent at the waist, hands on my knees, bracing for my turn, I couldn't remember my offense, but I remembered to fear him.

He administered punishment just before supper. Since children were to be seen and not heard, no family discussion occurred at our evening meal. Usually we sat in silence while our father recounted details of his gory, frustrating day, administering his wasted talent on the "idiot" patients who rotated through his office. As he talked, his aura grew larger, as if disparaging others delighted him.

Sometimes I wonder if I actually remember the patients or just his graphic descriptions.

Dad's glow, usually red, changed dramatically with his mood. The ability to see his changing aura helped me avoid his rage.

My second grade teacher glowed with dull yellow light, mainly when I was inattentive.

I asked my mother, "Why does Mrs. Blank have colored lights over her head?"

"What on earth are you talking about?" she asked.

"Sometimes Mrs. Blank has yellow light around her."

She drove me to Shelby, fifteen miles away, to visit an optometrist for an eye exam. I crawled into the chair in a small dark examination room and scrutinized the doctor in a white lab coat. With my insides churning, I put my chin in the little cup. I'm not sure if I was more afraid of the dark room, the doctor, or the necessity to read aloud. Using one eye at a time as instructed, I recited the letters on his chart. He blocked my escape route with a scary contraption that he placed so close to my face my eyelashes tickled. He asked, "Which is clearer, A or B? B or C?" Finally, he diagnosed the problem as weak eye muscles. "She can exercise her eyes by stretching a foot-long string beyond the tip of her nose," he said to my mother as though I had left the room. "Have her focus her eyes on the knots up and down the string." I did the exercises every day for months, as instructed. The colors began to fade, except for Dad's red glow, and I never mentioned them again.

◦◦◦

After dinner, my mother often escaped into the knitting project that waited by her chair. Some of her projects were complex patterns that required many needles and many colors of yarn. She cast black, tan, and white yarn to build diamond shapes on socks she knitted for Dad, but I never saw him wear argyle socks. Sometimes she worked on a soft pink or blue cable-knit baby sweater for a new niece or nephew. If she discovered a mistake, she disengaged one stitch at a time until she reached and corrected the error. If the error was too far down, she slid all of the stitches off the needles, carefully unraveled the garment, gently rolled the yarn into a ball, and started over.

She tried to teach me, but I got impatient with the tiny stitches, and she got impatient with me, so I never learned to knit. "Why can't you sit still like Lili?" she asked. Even when Lili was five or six, she could sit for hours, controlling each stitch, "Knit one, purl one. Yes, that's right."

Lili was about four when Granddad installed an electric fence to contain his growing herd of Holsteins. While she was napping, Uncle Bob showed me how to determine if the fence was hot. "You take a tall stem of grass, hold one end, and put the other end on the wire like this." He demonstrated. "You can feel the electricity, but it won't shock you. Try it."

I pulled a tall stem from a nearby clump and lightly touched it to the wire. "It tickles!" I shouted. Later that afternoon, with the wisdom of experience, I demonstrated for Lili. Ignoring my instructions, she touched the wire with her hand, and it knocked her to her knees in the dirt. She got up and brushed off her knees. Then she grabbed that wire and shook it with both hands. It knocked her to the ground again, this time on her back. She was furious but didn't cry. She brushed off the dirt and stomped to the big white farmhouse where she found soap and a washcloth for her hands and legs.

When Lili and I played together in the huge sandbox under the kitchen window, I hauled a heavy, yellow, plastic bucket of cold water across the lawn, splashing my shorts and legs. I made mud pies and used our brothers' trucks to transport my concoctions. The sand was in my hair, down my shorts, and stuck to my wet knees. Proper female behavior never occurred to me. Meanwhile, Lili carefully poured dry sand from one bucket to another and stayed clean and pretty. I began to see that our parents recognized her as the superior female because of her lady-like behavior. I felt the chasm between what my parents and teachers thought I *should* be and who I really was.

Massive glass windows on either side of the L-shape house and carport camouflaged our new home in a four-acre woods three miles from Jensen Center. At night, it glowed like a monument to Dad's success. It had an unusual architectural design for 1956. A student of Frank Lloyd Wright had designed the house with low horizontal lines and a central chimney. Open spaces replaced defined rooms. Tiles covered most of the floors, and the furniture was mostly built-in. The only soft surfaces I remember were the beds and curtains in the bedrooms.

Frank Lloyd Wright intended to get American families out of their box-like structures, but our family's lifestyle was neither open nor modern. The layout of the house provided space for entertaining adult friends, but the inevitable clutter of a large family had no place there. Childish noise and laughter were as unwelcome as mud and forest debris.

The bedrooms had no space for toys and activities, as though we were to sit quietly and wait for life to include us. Kali was born eight months after we moved in and shared the room meant for Lili and me. Mom pushed our double bed into a corner to make room for her crib.

One night, ribbons of filtered moonlight illuminated my three-month-old sister breathing softly in her crib inches from my face. A chorus of tree frogs serenaded the stillness, croaking one over another until their sound became whole. Lili slept in the center of our double bed with her knees tucked tightly to her chest, sucking her thumb and encroaching on my small space. A strange, empty sensation, like a vacuum, shuddered inside me, and I could feel inner Self floating near the ceiling. Frightened, I touched my face and pillow. *"Am I still in my bed?"* I thought. *"Am I still alive?"* I felt as if my body occupied two places, one pinched between my sleeping sisters and the other floating, safe and calm. That strange otherworld dichotomy of numbness and awareness eventually subsided that night, but my true energetic Self stayed out of my body, safely floating beyond our unhappy family. It would take me nearly fifty years to connect to the earth and feel whole again.

chapter four

We left the modern house in the woods when Dad joined a medical clinic in Shelby, Ohio. Sheep herds, soybeans, and field corn surrounded our two-story farmhouse five miles out of town. A lone oak tree dominated the one-acre yard. Our escape to the outside world, the school bus, picked us up at seven-thirty in the morning and dropped us off at four in the afternoon. Kali, three by then, had our mother to herself and probably bonded with her more than the rest of us ever could.

While Kali was at home, bonding with Mom, I dealt with typical pubescent struggles. Parents as well as teachers sent confusing messages: develop social skills but don't be obsessed with friends, get good grades but don't appear "smart," have confidence in yourself but don't have a swelled head, and always let the boys win. *Training* required girls to be pretty, obedient, self-effaced, and coy. I hated coy. My grades suffered, but I was adjusting.

When eighth grade began, my mother enrolled me in a special class for struggling students—the loser's class. Regardless of her intention, the decision suggested I was stupid. My class schedule changed so much that I never saw my new friends, even at lunchtime. I tried to make the most of it but encountered obstacles that were out of my control.

I wanted to use the woodworking tools in Mr. Fazzinni's class, my new homeroom, but only boys could enroll. While the smart kids

were in language arts and beginning algebra, I sat in home economics reviewing the skills I'd learned before first grade. "This is a sewing
machine. This is the presser foot. This is the bobbin. Now girls, thread
your machines." Mind numbing!

Our history teacher didn't have a name. We called him "Coach."
He told bloody war stories of men killing other men and their wives
waiting at home. Then he attacked the boys' dignity, "You played like
girls Friday night." He didn't intentionally insult the girls, and we didn't
take it as such. I wondered why anyone would want to be a girl.

Christmas morning, my sisters and I waited in our room until summoned to discover Santa's bounty. We shared a gift that year, a pink
cardboard kitchen set, complete with an assortment of plastic cooking paraphernalia. Kali, four years old, prepared a pretend Christmas
breakfast, but Lili wasn't interested in make-believe cooking any more
than I was. She was nine. I was twelve and deeply insulted.

I talked to no one for the rest of the day, even when the neighbors
joined us for Christmas brunch. The adults drank mimosas, and my
mother served ham-and-egg strata, homemade cardamom bread, and
fried potatoes. I made the fruit ambrosia with canned mandarin oranges,
canned pineapple, marshmallows, coconut, and a sauce Mom had made
the night before. At least she let me do some real cooking.

A fire warmed the house, and condensation covered the windows.
I stared at my frowning reflection and scratched at the ice crystals on
the dining room windows while everyone found their seats.

I wanted my mother to acknowledge that I was growing up, but at
the same time I didn't want anyone to notice. I finished the dishes and
went outdoors. The snow crunched, and my coat smelled like cardamom
and ham. Solitude became my favorite companion.

My mother put sanitary supplies in my dresser drawer months
before I needed them, along with a small paperback book, *Growing Up
and Liking It*, which explained the whole mess. Menarche was an "in-
stride" occurrence. I told no one, but the laundry revealed my secret.
My mother came into the TV room, holding my panties at arm's length
like a dead rat. "You need to soak these in cold water so they don't
stain." Craig and Rob pretended not to hear.

Some cultures celebrate the threshold between girlhood and womanhood, but in our family, there was no commemoration. I began to respect the significance of that milestone when I turned the opposite direction, almost forty years later.

As my grandparents and I aged, we spent less and less time together. When I began middle school, no one reminded me that I could be whatever I wanted to be.

I stopped wanting to be anything, unaware that I'd been fully entrapped by patriarchal training.

I totally surrendered to a joyless existence. No sports, no art, no music, and I found the task of becoming an attractive woman uninteresting and hopeless. Mother cut my hair into a short, unflattering pixie, and I gained twenty pounds. I became the homely, dumb, fat girl I thought I was, sure no one would notice if I just faded away. Almost every day for the next forty years, I felt like I wanted to *go home,* confusing because I *was* home.

Reunited with my friends in ninth grade, I rapidly lost over twenty pounds. I put my lunch money into my savings account along with babysitting wages.

I was infatuated with Terry Tyler, also in ninth grade. I was thirteen. He was sixteen. He'd failed a couple of grades. His shiny black hairstyle was a cross between Elvis and James Dean. When he smiled at me through the volleyball net, my heart pounded—Sandra Dee looking into the eyes of Troy Donahue in *Summer Place.*

Terry Tyler could have been a double for John Travolta in the movie *Grease.* He walked with that strut, and he was just as handsome, cleft chin and all. My friends called him a "greaser," and my mother, had she known, would have called him a "bad boy" because he always wore a black too-tight T-shirt, tight black jeans, and came from the wrong side of the tracks, which triggered his appeal to me, I'm sure. Our relationship consisted of playing volleyball at lunch, nothing more.

At almost fourteen, I went to church dances on Friday nights, while older kids were at the football game down the street. I told Terry about the dance, but it never occurred to me that he would come. When his tall, thin frame appeared in the door, he looked out of place and uncomfortable. I quickly pulled him into the hall. "Let's go for a walk," he said.

I trembled below his gaze. "I'm not supposed to leave the dance but Mom and Dad will never know and I don't need to get my coat where should we walk it's not that cold out…" I babbled nervously. He held my hand, and we walked the chilly neighborhood streets for twenty minutes. I felt disappointed that Terry didn't try to make out with me. I thought I was ready. I probably didn't stop talking long enough to give him a chance. He walked me back to the dance and gave me a quick kiss in the parking lot. No one noticed that I had left, but my guilt was intense. I knew my parents would not approve of the handsome, sixteen-year-old bad boy, Terry Tyler.

A week later, Dad called me into the living room. My mother sat in her chair by the floor lamp with knitting needles and a ball of yellow yarn as she taught Lili to knit a cable stitch. Dad sat in his huge, dark-blue, leather chair. His chair, surrounded by *JAMA* (*Journal of American Medical Association*), *Time*, and *Field & Stream* magazines, sat like a throne in the living room. No one dared sit there even when he wasn't home. I remember that blue chair as the throne of God, the subject of Reverend Swinehart's tirade each Sunday. It was the archetypical symbol of authority and domination, the throne from which an infuriated God dispensed judgment and punishment for the sins of his servants.

Seated in the chair, Dad said, "Do you know Terry Tyler?" I stayed in the middle of the room, cautiously scrutinizing his aura, evaluating his mood.

"Yes, he plays volleyball with us at lunch sometimes." My mother looked up from the yellow scarf taking shape in her lap, surprised that I played volleyball at lunch. I knew a lecture about smelling bad, broken nails, and messing my new hairstyle would soon follow.

"He visited the office today. He told Dr. Jordan that you're his girl-friend." Dr. Jordan was a redheaded arrogant partner in Dad's medical clinic. His son, Robert, was an overachiever in my class. I could imagine their dinner conversation and dreaded the repercussions.

"Well … uh, I … uh, well, sort of … I, uh …" I thought, *Wow, Terry's my boyfriend? Do I really want a boyfriend?*

"He's got VD," Dad announced.

I stared at him, finally asking, "What's that?"

Scarcely lifting his chin from his *JAMA* magazine, he examined me with piercing brown eyes below his bushy blond eyebrows. "Well, it's what you get if you play around with boys like him." His aura remained pale. "Do we have any reason to be concerned?"

Did he know that I left the dance with Terry? "I ... I ... I ..." I didn't know how to respond. Concerned? What did he mean? Concerned? The kids at school didn't know that I liked Terry, but they would know if Robert Jordan blabbed. Terry had held my hand for twenty minutes and quickly kissed me; that's all. Concerned?

My virtue and confusion were obvious. Dad said, "Go finish your homework and stay away from that Terry Tyler."

It wasn't difficult; he stopped coming to the gym during lunch hour and never talked to me again.

As far as I could tell, Robert knew nothing about Terry and me. I realized that Dr. Jordan probably didn't discuss his work at the family dinner table as my father did. I began to recognize the inappropriateness of Dad's dinnertime discussions.

What's VD? Whom can I ask? I tried to look it up in the encyclopedia and the dictionary. And then, venereal disease became a topic in Mrs. Elsner's girls-only health class. "You get venereal disease, also known as VD, from contact with the opposite sex," she explained vaguely and read a list of symptoms. None of us listened. Once I knew that contact caused VD, I began to wonder if I could have gotten it from Terry's quick, closed-mouth kiss.

I raised my hand as nonchalantly as I could. "Can you get it from kissing?"

Every girl was listening now.

"No, you can't get it from kissing," Mrs. Elsner blushed. "You get it from sexual intercourse." She continued listing symptoms without looking at us, hoping no one would ask about sexual intercourse. Every girl in the room had been wondering the same thing, but I was sure no one else had kissed a boy who actually *had* VD. The other girls were glad I'd asked. Kissing was a popular activity among ninth graders.

In the spring, Darrell, captain of the JV tennis team, asked me to play tennis after school and walk to The Spot for a hamburger afterward. I'd learned to play tennis in gym class but borrowed his extra racket because I didn't have one of my own. When my mother picked me up, I told her, "I beat Darrell three times!"

As she drove her Ford Country Squire to the high school to pick up Craig at band practice, she said, "If you keep that up, you'll never get a date!" as though that would be my only goal in the coming years.

My first car date was the summer before sophomore year with Ryan, a lifeguard at the swimming pool. We went to the County Fair in the cutest car I'd ever seen, a fire-engine-red 1952 Pontiac convertible. It seemed small next to Dad's robin-egg-blue 1961 Chrysler Imperial.

Ryan won a fluffy pink teddy bear by hurling baseballs at a pyramid of concrete milk bottles, and we shared a cloud of pink cotton candy while we rode the Ferris wheel and merry-go-round. I avoided the tilt-a-whirl because it would mess up my hair. When Ryan brought me home at ten that night, he pulled me close to him in the front seat and kissed me on the lips, my first *real* kiss. I didn't count Terry Tyler's quick kiss in the church parking lot or the time James had kissed me under the stairs in second grade. This was a real kiss. For months, I proudly displayed the pink teddy bear on my neatly made bed. At fifteen, I still shared a room with my two sisters but had a single bed of my own. My mother frequently dropped me at the swimming pool that summer. I was too young to get a job and too old to play with my little sisters. She was happy to get me out of the house, I'm sure.

⁂

Dad's rage continued to be central to our lives. Seeing his anger as a red glow warned me to avoid him, and the out-of-body defenses I'd launched years before left me unnoticed. The angrier he got, the more invisible I became, and the less he noticed me, the better off I was.

My siblings weren't so lucky. They craved his attention, even if it was negative attention. Dad often released his wrath on Craig, tossing him around the living room. Rob was quiet and reclusive, so Dad called him "Rob-ina." Lili was his favorite. She could do or say almost anything without provoking his violence while Kali got more than her share of his cruelty and abuse. Kali was nine years younger than I was and soon the only sibling left to endure his dinnertime lectures. Like Craig, she told Dad what she thought even when he had that bright red glow. At fifteen, Mom shipped her off to boarding school on the East Coast, probably for her protection.

⎯⎯⎯ ⎯⎯⎯

With disregard for his maturing family, Dad hired the same architect to design a spacious and extravagant new house. Craig had a room of his own, even though he was a freshman at Ohio State. Lili and Kali still shared a small room. Mine was a mirror image of theirs, with built-in desk and dresser. I enjoyed the privacy after sharing with my little sisters for so many years. Eighteen months later, when I left for college, it became Lili's room. They built the house on a hill above a dense woods. The established orchard and well-maintained garden had been tended by the old man who lived next door.

I hung out with Suzie, the old man's granddaughter. She had a driver's license and her own car, which influenced my life even more than a room of my own. We often went shopping together.

"Can I help you?" said the young man, staring into my eyes. I was a junior at Shelby High School. He was starting his senior year.

"I'm looking for a pair of sandals," I said, staring back.

"Try on the red ones," Suzie said.

Paul was six feet tall and thin, with light brown hair. He wore horn-rimmed glasses like Barry Goldwater and Ho Chi Minh. Thick myopic lenses distorted his blue eyes, and he had small ears. For some reason I noticed his little ears. His brain, rather than his looks, attracted me.

He hauled out stacks of shoeboxes and sat on his stool as my long legs stretched before him. He supported my foot on the sloping surface as I wiggled into each style. Before we left the store, Paul invited me to the Putter Golf Dance on Tuesday night.

There was a concrete slab dance floor in the middle of the Putter Golf Course, and all the kids in the community were there every Tuesday night, including Suzie and her boyfriend and my best friends, Sharon, Barb, and Colleen. A DJ played current selections such as "I Want to Hold Your Hand" by the Beatles, "You Really Got Me" by the Kinks, and "I'm In for Something Good" by Herman's Hermits.

Paul dazzled me with vocabulary words. On the phone, he told me that he was interested in the juxtaposition of the orbicularis oris muscles. I looked up the words in the dictionary: *Juxtaposition: the act of placing two or more objects in a close spatial or ideal relation-ship. Orbicularis oris: a human facial muscle that is circular in shape and located around the mouth.* When he called the next day, I told him I was also interested in the juxtaposition of the orbicularis oris muscles and asked if he would demonstrate his understanding. It was our silly game. By Christmas, we were going steady. He gave me his class ring while parked on a deserted farm road several miles out of town. Like all the girls in our high school, I bought yards of angora yarn at the Five and Dime and wrapped it around his ring to make it stay on my finger. The big fuzzy wad of angora was a status symbol, and I wore it proudly.

In the fall of 1965, Barb, Sharon, Colleen, and I waved to the crowd from convertibles as the Homecoming Queen's court paraded around the running track. My mother made sure that my slenderizing outfit coordinated with the buff leather interior of the Cadillac I rode in. My good friend Johnny G. from history class was my escort while Dave, a friend from church, drove the car. Sharon was the Homecoming Queen. I knew I was included only because the four of us were good friends.

By then, Paul was a freshman at Ohio State and very jealous. I reassured him, "Johnny G. is just a friend from history class." During the football game, I sat with Johnny and my friends— after all, we were the queen's court. Paul lurked behind us. He thought I would join him if I knew he was waiting. "Will you excuse me for a minute, please?" I said to Johnny. "I'll be right back."

I approached Paul. "I'm going to sit with my other friends tonight," I told him. "You can call me in the morning, and we'll do something tomorrow if you want. OK?" Then I went back to my seat next to Johnny.

If I had demonstrated the same control and determination through-out our courtship, my life would have found a different path.

chapter five

After high school graduation, I joined Paul at Ohio State. While he finished his chemical engineering degree, I pledged a sorority, served tea, and graduated with a Bachelor of Science in Home Economics. My only career objective was wife and mother. The degree was strictly "fall back."

Chem E was a grueling five-year program. Paul didn't have money for dates, but in those days, he was nice to me, and I didn't question my orbit around him. Our safe and familiar relationship drew me in and kept me close. We studied together in empty classrooms or in the basement dining room of his fraternity house. When days were warm, we studied on a blanket near the Oval in the center of campus where crisscrossing sidewalks led passing students to surrounding buildings.

Training had smothered my feminine spirit. Reverend Swinehart had ranted about Adam and Eve, Mom had maintained boys always win, and high school teachers had suggested I attend cosmetology school instead of college. Somehow, I remained unconsciously aware of my feminine embers smoldering. It would take years for air to reach them.

Paul and I got pinned my freshman year. That meant I wore his fraternity pin connected by a tiny chain to my sorority pin, symbolizing we were engaged to be engaged.

We consummated our relationship on top of a dirty chest freezer in the basement of his fraternity house, a metaphor of flawed respect, mine as well as his. I felt committed and never considered another man until we divorced.

The university supported the secondary status of women. In 1966, we were required to wear dresses to dinner. Curfew was 11 p.m. on weekdays, midnight on weekends. Girls could stay out until 1 or 2 a.m. once each quarter, allowing for homecoming and formal events.

Men had no restrictions.

As Bob Dylan wrote, however, "These times, they are a changin'." When we graduated four years later, women wore whatever, wherever they wanted. Female students were burning their bras and going topless on the Oval in the heart of OSU campus. No one cared. The attention of the world was elsewhere. Kids were dying in Viet Nam.

I wanted desperately to be an adult, but in 1968, girls in rural Ohio weren't grown-up until they were married. When Paul proposed, I accepted. It never occurred to me that I'd assigned myself to a new warden.

Although I'd avoided church since confirmation at age thirteen, we visited Reverend Swinehart to ask if we could be married in the Lutheran church. Then I made a mistake. "I'd like for Reverend Stein to help with the service, if that's possible. He was very important to our family when we lived in Jensen Center," I told him. "Do you know him?"

"That's not possible!" bellowed Reverend Swinehart, furious. "Doctors don't see other doctors' patients. Why should I let Reverend Stein into *my* church?"

When I told Dad, he said, "That old fart. He got a prescription filled by Dr. Sparks and then came to me for something else. The drugs could have caused a problem if the pharmacist hadn't noticed."

I called Reverend Stein and asked if he would do the service at our house.

"What do you kids plan to do?" he asked.

Not sure what he meant, I said, "Well, first we'll finish up at Ohio State."

"Paul's Methodist and you're Lutheran. Which will it be?"

"Well, we haven't decided." He refused to do the service, and I never went to church again.

A justice of the peace officiated between the orchard and the garden in my parents' yard, with apple, peach, plum, and cherry trees on one side and bright red tomatoes, tall tender sweet corn, and curly-leafed green peas on the other.

The night before the wedding, I escaped the rehearsal dinner to drift alone in the garden. I took off my sandals and walked the row of rich soil between the tomato plants, then meandered through the fruit trees on the manicured lawn. Standing alone, inhaling the fragrances of late June, I remembered early morning walks when I ate sun-warmed tomatoes like apples. The juice ran to my elbow and dripped back into the rich soil.

"I'll miss you," I said aloud but had no idea what changes were ahead.

Paul and I briefly discussed our vows. I wanted "love, honor, and cherish," not "love, honor, and obey," but the rest was boilerplate "Do you take this man … blah, blah, blah." When the judge inadvertently included "obey," I robotically said, "I do." It took less than a few hours to realize my mistake.

After the reception, Paul and I dashed to our newly purchased 1962 Buick Special while aunts, uncles, parents, siblings, and friends showered us with rice. The money I'd saved all my life from birthdays, skipping lunch, and summer jobs paid for the car. I was only twenty, so my mother registered the white Buick Special in Paul's name. It was expected and consistent with *Training*.

✦

Paul's father, who'd worked in the same factory since he graduated from high school, thought Paul should get a job rather than go to school. Fortunately, Paul chose to finish studying for his engineering degree. As before, the money Paul earned at the shoe store and other odd jobs paid his tuition. Dad agreed to continue my allowance until graduation, which covered our rent and my tuition. I planned to work in a campus day care to help ends meet while Paul scheduled a heavy class load of thermodynamics, quantum physics, organic chemistry, and advanced calculus.

Now I was an adult—I thought—but I was grown-up only in the sense that I no longer lived in my father's house. I had a new master, and I morphed to meet his demands.

As we pulled off I-75 headed south toward a hotel in Cincinnati, Paul said, "There's a map in the glove box." When I found the map and the right section, I turned it upside down. I could think faster if the map was facing the same direction we were moving. "You idiot, turn the fuckin' map back over," he said. "Are you too damn stupid to tell right from left? Jeee-sssus Christ!" I got so flustered, we missed our turn and he shouted even louder. "Jeee-sssus Christ!"

I knew Paul had a temper. My friends on the Lutheran Church League basketball team didn't like to play against the Methodists because Paul was on the team, but he'd never directed that temper toward me. This was our honeymoon. I refused to think beyond that moment. Once we found our room, he acted as if nothing had happened, and I tried to pretend nothing had. If only I'd had the ovaries to say, "Wow, did I make a mistake! I'm going home," my life's path would have led elsewhere, but *Training* was too powerful. I was secondary. He owned me. Although not consciously aware, I knew my parents would support him, just because he was a "he."

We spent most of our two days in bed. After a while, it wasn't much fun for me, but I wanted him to think I was really into it, and I never dreamed of making suggestions. If I'd begun our marriage expressing my desires, sexually or otherwise, I would have diminished his control over me, but I had no idea what I wanted beyond pleasing him. *Training* had calcified the inner song of my childhood. I tried to be a "good wife."

After the two-day honeymoon, we left for Charleston, West Virginia, where Paul had a summer job. FMC was responsible for polluting the Kanawha River (pronounced K'naw). The river had recently caught fire, and FMC had hired Paul to do environmental engineering studies.

Our apartment was the size of a sailboat galley in the basement of a three-story Victorian house on the north side of the river. A tiny, wizened Southern Baptist, Mrs. White had lived there all her life. She was toothless on the top, making her hairy upper lip billow like a sail when she spoke. Her four bottom teeth protruded and reminded me of a Lhasa Apso puppy. I tried to avoid her Jesus discussions by walking the neighborhood, but inevitably she cornered me in the apartment or found me under the clothesline after Paul took the car to work. She read the Bible aloud and insisted that Jesus had visited her, leaving images of doves, stars, fish, crosses, and other Christian symbols on the walls of her bedroom. The marks looked like carbon deposits caused by a garish and troubled electric lamp, but I didn't say so.

Mrs. White inspected our apartment when I was out to make certain I defrosted the refrigerator and cleaned to her standards. Once she found too much accumulated ice on the freezer coils and scolded me fiercely about my responsibilities as a wife and homemaker. Thereafter, the apartment was always perfect so she wouldn't scold me again.

During our three-month stay, I laid out Paul's clothes each morning while he ate breakfast. I ironed his shirts, prepared his meals in the miniscule kitchen, and waited, but not just for him to come home to his meals. My feminine spirit patiently lingered while I tried to be a good spouse. I continued these wifely activities when we returned to Ohio State, finishing our last year. It was difficult to coordinate studies, a job, and being a wife, but Paul expected it, and I was well *Trained.*

On our first New Year's Eve as a married couple, we walked to a friend's apartment to welcome 1970, but after one drink, we were more interested in doing what newlyweds do and left before midnight. Back in our tiny ground-floor apartment, Paul stripped to his white T-shirt and jockey shorts and mixed us each a 7 and 7 (7-Up and Seagram's 7, popular in those days). I took my pale pink wedding nighty into the bathroom. In our haste, we'd failed to lock the front door. As Paul paced in anticipation, the door opened slightly. Paul thought the wind had blown it, but when he pushed to close it, the door pushed him back. A tall, husky man in a ski mask burst in and pointed a 48 revolver at Paul's face. From the bathroom, I heard the door close. Paul made a strange noise.

"What are you doing out there?" I asked. I heard voices and assumed that our mischievous best man Bill had followed us home to crash our private party. *That stinker would do something like this*, I thought.

Paul talked to me through the bathroom door. "Come on out."

"All I have in here is my nightgown," I said.

I heard voices again. The intruder asked Paul if I would scream. Paul had no idea if I would scream or faint or what.

Paul insisted, "Come out of the bathroom." Wrapping a damp bath towel around my sexy nighty, I peeked from behind the door. The cold barrel of a huge gun touched the skin between my eyebrows. I could see the bullets in the round chamber. "Don't scream or I'll shoot." His angry eyes said that he would. New Year's Eve noise permeated the college community. Even if the neighbors were sober, they wouldn't notice a gun blast.

The man in the black ski mask with red circles around his eyes and mouth held us hostage in the walk-in closet while he drank 7-Up and searched the apartment for money and valuables.

"Where's your purse?" he said from the kitchen.

"On the table in the living room," I said from the closet.

I whispered to Paul, "Glad we bought our books today. He won't get all of our Christmas money." My composure was bizarre. I took off my engagement ring and hid it between sweaters on the shelf.

I didn't suspect what he had planned for us.

The masked stranger directed us out of the closet. "Do it!" he said, jerking his head toward the bed while rotating the gun barrel.

"What?" we said in unison.

Louder he said, "DO IT!"

Arms and legs stiff with fear, I slid onto the bed, and Paul reluctantly climbed on top of me. The man shouted, "Take off your goddamn clothes." Awkwardly, Paul removed his underwear.

"Hers too," he demanded.

Hidden by Paul's body, I slipped out of my nightgown. We knew, to stay alive, we had to do whatever he demanded, and I hoped that my peculiar calmness was helping Paul.

We attempted to make love, or at least appear to do so, bouncing and moaning to put on a show for the perverted bastard. I cringed when he reached between my legs to see if Paul was finished.

Then he said, "My turn."

I braced for the intruder's response to Paul's hot temper, which I thought would be magnified with emotion, but Paul just moaned, "Ahhh … man, no … ahhh, man … ahhh, man … nnnooo."

Before Paul could move away, the burglar stood by the bed near my face, unzipped his jeans, and exposed himself. To my horror and the intruder's surprise, I robotically grabbed his disgusting, uncircumcised penis and held on tight, apparently guided by mysterious female instinct. "Can't I just jack you off?" I said, thinking, *Where the hell did I get that?* It was a phrase I'd never used or even consciously heard. With the weight of Paul's body still on top of me, I began pumping until I could feel the pressure build. I jerked my hand away just in time to avoid the mess.

Paul was too stunned to react.

Zipping up, the man said, "Stay there."

In the dark kitchen, he drank more 7-Up and dismantled our green plastic wall phone. He snarled, "If ya call the fuzz, I'll come back an' kill ya." With sixty dollars and Paul's old guitar, he slipped into the New Year's night.

Paul dashed to lock the door. I hurried to the bathroom to scrub my hands. Steam rose from the flowing hot water. I lathered the Zest for several minutes, knowing I would never cleanse the memory. Finally, Paul said, "Your hands are as clean as they're going to get." So I rinsed off the lather and found a clean towel. Then we sat naked beneath the blankets, silent for a long time.

My strange calmness vanished.

Adrenalin pumped.

I couldn't stop shivering.

After some discussion, we put the phone back together. Paul called the police and requested an unmarked car in case the pervert really was watching. The Columbus police officer arrived half an hour later in a black and white patrol car with its blue lights flashing. The officer looked down at me, shivering on the sofa in my gray sweats, my arms tightly locked around my bent knees. "You should go to the emergency room for an exam," he said.

"But he didn't rape me." I tried to describe my extraordinary diversion tactic. "When he took out his, well, you know, when he ... uh, exposed himself, I ... uh, sort of, well, I ... I ... I grabbed it, and, well, I ..."

Paul finally came to my rescue. "She jacked him off," he said, his voice stiff and clinical.

"She what?" said the officer, staring at me with wide eyes and lifted brows.

Without looking up, I said, "He wasn't circumcised," as if I was revealing important evidence in a Perry Mason episode.

The officer looked at Paul. "When he was busy, you shoulda grabbed the gun an' shot him."

During the next few months, two couples in our neighborhood were murdered in their beds.

At the time, I was so numbed by low self-esteem I didn't see my extraordinary achievement. While Paul's contribution was minimal at best, subservient cooperation saved us. *Training* had saved our lives—keep the man happy.

chapter six

Nostalgia had no place in our escape from Ohio State University. Paul's new employer, Dow Corning, hired Bekins to pack our secondhand belongings, and we headed north to begin adult life in Midland, Michigan. During the four-hour drive, we agreed to find a third-floor apartment with an inside entrance. When he realized that the rent was higher on the upper floors, Paul decided on a garden-level apartment with a view of vehicle license plates parked in front of our picture window.

I began looking for a job teaching preschool-age children even though Paul thought I should stay home. "Why should I sit around if I can be adding to our savings account?" I said. He agreed.

Daycare was a novelty in 1970. I wondered what the mommies did all day while I enjoyed their children. My favorite was Jeremy, a three-year-old. He had curly red hair and a fiery personality. Mr. Wiles, the daycare owner, demanded that the children be quiet and sit still during lunch, but every part of Jeremy's body touched his chair at some point during his meal. One day I guided the covey of three-year-olds into the bathroom where they had easy access to child-size toilets. Jeremy stood in front of the miniature urinal with his pants around his ankles. I noticed red welts on his legs and pale bum. I found more under his plaid shirt. He looked up at me and said, "I was bad."

I saw images of my father tossing Craig around the living room. After story time, when the children were napping, I spoke to Mr. Wiles. "Jeremy has red welts on his bum and back."

"Yeah? So what?" he said.

"Should we do something?" I asked, assuming Jeremy's father was like mine.

"Do what? The little brat wouldn't sit still at lunch, so I whopped 'im with my belt."

I was unable to speak.

When mothers began arriving, I hoped Jeremy's would see the welts and inquire. Mr. Wiles' behavior seemed so normal, it never occurred to me to report him to authorities, but I quit the next day.

A week later, I discovered I was pregnant. I began sewing maternity clothes and turning the extra room into a nursery.

Morning sickness plagued my entire pregnancy, so I always carried a little green bucket—just in case. Paul was thrifty but not a complete cad. On Valentine's Day, he gave me a homemade card, a little booklet really. He'd made pencil drawings of me carrying the bucket everywhere we went. Playing cards with the bucket. At the pool with the bucket. In the car with the bucket. At the grocery with the bucket. His efforts were touching.

One hot spring day, in my eighth month, a friend took me shopping. I purchased a huge fern to fill our sparsely furnished apartment. "You didn't ask if you could spend five dollars!" Paul said when he arrived home for lunch.

"This room is so empty, and they say that plants are good for the air. Anyway, it was on sale, half-off. I thought it would be good for the baby ..."

"You stupid idiot!" Paul screamed. "What a dumb-ass thing to believe, Jeeesssus Christ. I work my ass off all day, and you go out and blow it on crap. Christ!" He picked up our third-hand coffee table and slammed it to the floor. Then as if nothing had happened, he sat down to eat his lunch and went back to work. "I'll see you around 5:30," he said.

I took the pieces outside to the dumpster, thinking, *What if I'm his next victim?* I needed to talk to someone, but my friends were married to Paul's colleagues. Having no one else to confide in, I phoned my mother. Rates were higher during the day, but I hoped Paul wouldn't notice the bill.

First, I answered her questions about the baby. "The doctor says it will be at least another month."

"Is it as hot there as it is here?" she asked.

"It's really hot for Michigan in May. Yesterday it was over ninety. They say it'll be over a hundred next week."

"Doesn't your apartment have air conditioning?" she asked.

"Yes, we have a window unit, but Paul says it's too expensive. Sometimes I turn it on in the afternoon and then turn it off before he gets home. I don't want to make him mad. He thinks it's cooler because we're in the basement. He gets mad a lot these days." I described the smashing of the coffee table.

"Why did you spend the money without asking first?" my mother said. "You know how he is."

"His temper tantrums are escalating. Maybe he's under a lot of pressure at work, but ..." then I said it aloud to myself and to my mother, "I'm thinking about leaving him."

"Well, don't think you can run home to Mommy!" she said.

"OK, Mom, I'll call you on Sunday." I hung up.

On Mother's Day, I expected Paul to recognize my pending motherhood. "Why were you in such a bad mood all day?" he said as he dressed for bed.

"It's Mother's Day," I said. "You didn't even get me a card."

"You're not my mother," he said and turned off the light.

My life would inevitably change once the baby was born.

While the pregnancy dragged on, a moving van appeared outside our garden-level picture window. I heard activity in the hallway and opened the door. The new neighbors were moving in. I tried to hold the door while they carried in a chair, but my nine-month belly got in the way. The woman, whom I guessed to be about my age, was taller than I was. She was attractive with an easy-care short haircut that suited her. Her husband was very tall, about six-four, and even thinner than Paul. His hair was black, short, and neat, like Paul's—remember this was the early 1970s when most young men had long hair.

"Good morning," I said. "Looks like we'll be neighbors. I'm Marcia."

"Hi, I'm Cindy," she said, putting the chair on the carpet. "This is my husband, Dale." Our connection was instant.

"I guess I'm not much help with moving, but if you need anything, just knock. My only job now is waiting for this baby."

I shut the door and started a batch of cookies. Paul and I took a plate of warm chocolate chip cookies and a pitcher of cold milk across the hall to our new neighbors after lunch.

They had just graduated from Purdue University in West Lafayette, Indiana. Dale would be a chemical engineer for Dow Chemical. Cindy had graduated with a degree in home economics. She would be starting her teaching career at the high school in September.

"Paul's a Chem E for Dow Corning, and I applied for that teaching position too. I got pregnant instead of the job!" I said. "We graduated from Ohio State last spring."

We chatted a few minutes.

"Wanna come over for dinner tomorrow night?" Paul asked.

"That is—if I haven't popped by then," I patted my big over-due belly.

We all laughed.

During dinner, the men discussed whatever chemical engineers discuss. I heard something about a complex mathematical problem that intrigued them and tuned them out. Cindy and I discussed teaching, cooking, and sewing. She was excited about her new position. "I also applied for a job teaching an adult sewing class but haven't heard yet if I got that job."

Cindy and Dale grew up in a community similar to ours. Our educational backgrounds were ironically similar, but Cindy and Dale's marriage couldn't have been more different. On Saturdays, Cindy and Dale shared the household chores and grocery shopping. From my idealizing perspective, they had the perfect marriage. If she cooked, he did the dishes and vice versa. They had two cars, two incomes, and two voices in their marriage, but that marriage would end before ours.

Cindy and I were alike in many ways. Our parents had similar Midwest backgrounds, and her career as a home economics teacher was well within *Training*. Still, she built a teaching career while I mechanically conformed to Paul's demands. She seemed to know what she wanted while I felt I had no choice.

⚬⚬⚬ ⚬⚬⚬

During June's full moon, in the early morning hours, I gave birth to a baby girl. Paul did what he could to keep me comfortable and stayed with me until the actual delivery. Confined to the bed during labor, I couldn't walk off the cramps in my calves so Paul massaged each leg and encouraged me to push my feet against his chest to relieve the pain. The leg spasms were the worst part of the six-hour labor and he behaved with more kindness and caring than he'd ever shown. Breathing techniques I'd learned in Lamaze natural childbirth classes helped with the delivery. I didn't want to contaminate the baby, but in the end, the doctor insisted on a spinal block, and I didn't argue.

The maternity ward bustled with an overwhelming number of deliveries that June of 1971. Like it or not, we were rooming-in, a new term in the maternity ward. The baby would be in my room for the duration of our three-day stay. Paul brought me a Fostoria glass pitcher that matched our wedding china, full of painted daises. My favorite. The bridesmaids had carried daises at our wedding. I was surprised he remembered.

"You can have your baby now," said the nurse as she rolled the bassinette into my room at five in the morning, I'd been asleep only two hours.

"No, I already had my baby. It was a girl," I said. "Her name is Niki."

She pushed the button to raise my bed to a sitting position as I tried to wake up. She placed the swaddled baby in my hands and quickly left. I held the pink package at arm's length, waiting for the love to pour through me. Nothing happened. Terrified, I cradled her close to me, then unwrapped the blanket to expose tiny fingers and toes.

New-baby fragrance filled the air.

"Hi! You can call me 'Mommy,'" I said aloud.

She opened her eyes and locked onto my gaze with ancient intention.

I sensed mystic knowing but didn't understand.

Then she began to root toward my chest. I panicked and buzzed the nurse.

"What do you want?" I was an interruption.

"I think my baby's hungry," I said. "What do I do?"

"You feed her," she said and turned to leave, then at the doorway she asked, "Is this your first?"

"Yes," I replied as she walked to the foot of my bed.

"Are you going to nurse or bottle-feed?" rhetorically. She didn't listen to me. She just looked at my chart, as if I wouldn't know if I planned to bottle-feed or breast-feed my baby. "Do I need to bring formula in here?"

"I want to nurse, but I don't know what to do," I said. During birthing classes, we learned breathing techniques for delivery and discussed the benefits of nursing at length, but no one told me how get her on there.

In one swift move, the overworked night nurse pulled down my green hospital gown and stuck the baby to my breast as if hitching a plow to a tractor. She said, "You'll get the hang of it," and left the room.

I pulled the blanket over my nakedness. "Aren't we supposed to just know this stuff?" I asked my baby girl. Eventually we did get the hang of it, but it took weeks.

Niki and I formed a strong bond, even in the hospital, before I knew quite what to do with her. In spite of our first meeting, I loved Niki. By the time we came home from the hospital, I loved her so much Paul was jealous. I loved her so much the rest of my life became background noise. My Being revolved around her needs.

Mom came to help during those the first few days. She gave Niki a bath, kept me company in the night while I nursed Niki, cooked our meals, and went grocery shopping. I was grateful. It was as close as I ever felt to my mother.

Cindy came across the hall to congratulate me, meet Mom, and welcome Niki into the neighborhood. When Mom lifted my little bundle out of her bassinette and handed her to Cindy, I experienced my first high voltage surge of protective energy. It was involuntary, and I struggled to stay on the sofa. Cindy didn't see it, but Mom laughed at me later.

"You didn't like it when Cindy held the baby," she said.

"I couldn't bear it! It was weird. I know Cindy wouldn't hurt her; I guess it's hormones."

Cindy, Mom, and I made plans to attend a neighborhood Tupperware party.

"Can you watch Niki for a little while?" I asked Paul. "Or should I take her with me?"

"I can watch her," he said. "How hard can it be? She sleeps all the time, doesn't she? Give me the telephone number just in case."

About thirty minutes later, he called.

"You better come home," he said.

"Is everything OK?"

"Yeah, I just need a little help here." He didn't sound alarmed, just puzzled. "I tried to change her diaper—just come home."

Always a stickler for safety, he had strapped our five-day-old baby to her changing table before removing her diaper. He was concerned about the golden nuggets that newborns typically deposit. When he'd reached for a clean diaper, she'd tinkled. The changing table was wet. Her hair was wet. Her onesie was wet. He'd unfastened the safety strap and held her over his shoulder, and she'd done it again. His shirt was wet.

"Good thing she's not a boy," Mom chuckled when we got there. "You would have gotten it in the face."

"It just takes practice." I patted him on the back.

Normally, he controlled his environment and usually behaved as though he knew everything. Traumatized by baby urine, he rarely changed another diaper.

<hr>

Those first few months after Mom went home, Niki slept no more than two or three hours at a time. After her 2 a.m. feeding, I paced the floor. If I put her in her crib, she cried, so I sat in Paul's olive green Naugahyde recliner. I pulled the handle to elevate the footrest and pushed back so she could recline on my chest. We dozed. When I just *thought* about my marriage, Niki fussed, as if we both knew it was hopeless even then.

Her daily "fussy time"—all babies have them I discovered—was between four and six o'clock, when Paul wanted dinner. We ate casseroles in those days, meals I could prepare while she briefly slept. Paul complained, but I assured him these meals were economical.

One day I pricked my finger while replacing a button on Paul's shirt. Niki cried out as though I'd stuck her too. If I planned to leave her for an hour with a neighbor so I could run errands, she became fussy.

She seemed to know me inside out.

No longer in the womb but still part of me, I guess, quite literally, she did.

Due to an ineffective diaphragm, I got pregnant again when Niki was ten months old. Distraught, I resigned myself to a life of diapers and obedience.

The unbearable prospect of caring for two babies in our apartment kicked off my hunt for a house. Searching the classifieds, I found a split-level for eighteen thousand dollars. I researched the mortgage possibilities and found that our payment would be only slightly more than rent. Without telling Paul, I asked my parents if we could borrow two thousand dollars for a down payment.

One night when Paul was in a good mood, I fabricated a story. "On TV today they were talking about the rising values of real estate." He would think it was stupid if it was my idea. "Maybe it's a good time for us to buy a house—we could find something that wouldn't cost much more than rent."

"I've been thinking about that," he said, "but I haven't saved enough."

"I'm sure Mom and Dad would loan us the down payment." I didn't tell him Dad had agreed to a two-thousand-dollar loan.

"Guess it can't hurt to look," he said.

The next day while he was at work, I called the number in the for-sale-by-owner ad and arranged a Saturday visit. We looked at other houses too, but this one required no agent commission. I was nine months pregnant when we bought the house. The owners had time to move out while we endured another overdue pregnancy.

It was snowing when Paul drove me to the hospital that night in March of 1973. A neighbor cared for Niki. After the 1 a.m. delivery, Paul went home to get some rest. The next morning, when the nurse brought Matt to my room, she opened the curtains. Two feet of delicate snow balanced on a branch outside the window.

"It's going to be a wild day in here. None of the night crew can go home, and the day crew can't get here. Are you OK with your baby?"

"We'll be fine. I've done this before," I told her.

Paul called. "All the roads are closed. Maybe I can get in there tonight or tomorrow."

"No need to take chances; we're fine. I'll just sleep all day anyway."

I'm sure the hospital was total chaos, but I settled in, as if someone had hit the pause button on a high-action movie. My baby boy slept, and so did I.

The spring snow quickly melted, and life began again.

We moved into our new house when Matt was a week old.

Three weeks later, I sat on the sofa, nursing him while I looked out the picture window. I'd traded a view of license plates for a suburban sea of rooftops and TV antennas. Niki, almost two, was napping. Tears streamed down my face. I loved my babies more than I thought was possible, but I was so unhappy my insides ached. Paul refused to do any of the household chores and never got up in the night to help. With two in diapers, it was difficult to keep the house clean *and* the babies happy. I was exhausted. If they needed my attention, I didn't care if boxes went unpacked, his lunch dishes soaked in the sink or Niki's toys cluttered the floor. He didn't like the mess.

"What the hell did *you* do all day?" was usually his response to "Welcome home."

"Hi, it's me. I got that job at Central Michigan University," Cindy said on the phone. "I'll be commuting to Mt. Pleasant four days a week."

"Congratulations!" I said.

"There's more," she added. "I'm pregnant!"

"Wow, congrats!" I said. "That's good timing. When are you due?"

"Late May," she said. "School is out on the twenty-fifth so I'm hoping I don't deliver until I turn in the grades. One more thing, the high school wants me to teach that sewing class again, but I can't. I told them about you. Do you want the job?"

"Cindy, I don't know anything about making lingerie."

"It's easy. You know how to teach sewing; I can show you the tricks." She brought over her supplies and spent an hour showing me how to work with the flimsy fabric.

I taught ten thirty-something women how to make delicate panties, bras, and nightgowns from nylon knit fabric and lace. Paul allowed it because he said we needed the money. I enjoyed freedom for two and a half hours twice a week for six weeks. Before I left, I fed the kids and got them into their PJs. His dinner was on the table. Normally bedtime was 7:30 or 8, but he put them to bed at 6:30 pm so he could watch his favorite TV programs. He never changed a diaper while I was gone and by morning, their little bums were often raw. He called this inconvenience *baby-sitting*. I called it *parenting*, but he couldn't see it.

I cooked our meals, but his palate ruled. He preferred Miracle Whip and hated mayonnaise. He demanded creamy Jiffy, not crunchy, not Skippy. I never learned to make choices as a young adult. Why bother? I couldn't buy a houseplant or peanut butter without permission. I obeyed selflessly because I had no Self, no point of differentiation. When I was living at home, Dad's anger magnified if I didn't appear docile and obedient. Married life was no different.

I walked to a Saturday morning meeting of the La Leche League, a group of nursing mothers, while Paul played golf. I thought that Niki could play with children her own age and I could commiserate with other moms in my situation, but it turned out we had little in common beyond a new baby attached to a breast and one hand available to balance tea and cookies. The others were members of NOW (National Organization for Women). Their leader relaxed in an armchair, proudly naked to the waist. Her baby boy suckled on one huge brown nipple while his dimpled little hand stroked the other naked breast. Meanwhile I modestly covered the side I was offering, and my bra tightly supported the waiting, milk-filled breast beneath my sweater. I felt like an extraterrestrial.

I saw these women as half-naked, hostile she-gods, as patriarchal as any man I knew. They expounded the benefits of women working outside the home. I savored every moment with my babies. They were all that was right with my life. Why would I give up this magical pleasure just to prove I was *entitled* to give it up? Instead of rising up and joining the feministic call, I became Marabel Morgan's *Total Woman*, defending my position on motherhood, childrearing, inadequate daycare, and my daily banal activates as if I were a dull-witted robot.

NOW advocated an alternative version of women's potential, which I supported, but I was offended by their inability to champion motherhood or marriage free of complete compliance and humiliation. I knew their husbands were "yes, dear" repeaters, just like me. Their attitude was emasculating and demoralizing. If their position had been supportive rather than militant, I would have joined them, but becoming a hostile man-hater seemed counterproductive.

Women needed a venue that supported equality, mutual respect, and cooperation between the sexes, but, from my perspective, feminists had merely turned the tables against men. It was the same battle with genders reversed.

Meanwhile, ancient cell memory was shouting in my subconscious.

"It hasn't always been this way."

"Differences can be celebrated."

"Dominance is not required."

"Simultaneous happiness can be available to both genders."

I *knew* this to be true but couldn't hear my inner voice. I'd surrendered my life to my husband. Instead of gaining his love, I lost his respect.

Paul dismissed my needs as completely as I did.

Emotionally numb, I mechanically passed time with mundane housewifery with no cerebral activity. The following fall, Cindy needed daycare for her new son while she taught at the college level. "I hate to leave him with strangers all day," she said. "I'll pay you what I'd pay the daycare."

"That's a great idea." I loved the little guy. I put the money into our savings account.

One afternoon, when she came to pick him up, I served her a cup of tea. "Hot! Hot!" I said.

Cindy laughed. "You need to get out more." She shook her head in mock despair. I had few women friends in those days and depended on Cindy. Even though our *Training* had been similar, she became a college professor while I remained invisible.

I called home on Sunday as usual. Normally Mom always began the conversations with lots of questions but never listened to the answers. That day, her voice sounded strange. "What's going on?" I asked.

"Your father has a brain tumor," she said. "We're flying to San Francisco for his surgery."

Dad had suffered from severe headaches and dizzy spells but had lived in denial for years, which probably aggravated his constant irritability. When he reached fifty-two, and the pain became too intense for him to function, doctors in Dayton confirmed his self-diagnosis—acoustic neuroma. Symptoms included hearing loss, vertigo, nausea, and a high-pitched ringing in his ears as loud as roaring machinery. The tumor was beginning to press against the optic nerve.

He often stumbled. We thought he was drunk.

Many patients with this condition didn't survive surgery, and half the ones who survived became disabled for life. The surgical team in San Francisco had a reputation for achieving complete recovery.

At the end of the ten-hour operation, the surgeons told Mom that Dad would have no complications. The surgery was successful, but recovery would be slow. Confined to his bed for several days, he complained about "those goddamned nurses" controlling his every move.

They insisted on an enema.

He refused.

Pressure and bleeding in his brain, caused by straining on the bedpan, damaged his optic nerve and vestibular input, which controls balance and spatial orientation. He would never drive a car again. He developed tunnel vision, became deaf in his right ear, and drunk or not, forever staggered when he walked.

He never practiced medicine again.

He hated being a doctor.

I believe we get what we ask for.

⁂

Dow Corning transferred Paul to Flint, Kentucky, where chemical companies polluted the Ohio River. We traded the trendy, highly educated, high-income Dow Chemical community in Michigan for a town where the average resident had achieved less than a high school diploma. In my stupor of married isolation, I scarcely noticed.

When Niki was eight, she developed red dots on her tummy a few days before Thanksgiving. It was no surprise; she'd been exposed to chickenpox at school. Niki's case was mild, and though sprinkled with scabs, she soon felt better. By then, bright red spots covered Matt. He suffered from a high fever and wanted to sit on my lap most of the day. Paul wasn't enamored with baby-sitting sick children (or well ones for that matter), and household chores and grocery shopping were my responsibility, so I waited until Paul was home and the children were asleep to catch up on laundry, cleaning, and supermarket visits.

By my birthday in December, the day I turned thirty, Matt's ubiquitous red spots had transformed to ugly black scabs, and his rambunctious little boy behavior had returned. I'd been locked in the house for a month, except for the evening grocery excursions. I wanted to go Christmas shopping, but Paul wouldn't let me, saying, "It might snow, and anyway, I'd be stuck here without a car."

For nine years of marriage, I'd tried to do what was expected of me, but in that winter of 1978, the undertow was unbearable. Most days, while the kids were at school, I'd wander into the backyard to lean against a tree in my blue terrycloth bathrobe.

Standing like a blue heron stalking a frog, I privately considered my options.

Survival or suicide?

Independence or marriage?

Divorce or death?

If I'd been living in 478 BC, I could have been a goddess with property and wealth and men for servants. If I had been living in 1478 and had the audacity to consider independence, I would have been burned me at the stake, and in 1878, I would have been institutionalized for wanting to leave my husband. Fortunately, in 1978, when I chose independence over marriage, ironically, the feminine revolution had made that decision mainstream. Survival had been my choice as a child as well. When Dad's rage became unbearable, I became invisible, floating out of touch, unavailable for his torture.

I *knew* that women were not weak, ignorant, or frail, and I knew that there was no divine intention for women to be inferior, but I didn't know how to put that knowledge into action.

On my thirtieth birthday in 1978, when Paul would not *allow* me to leave the house, I stood before the bathroom mirror. To my reflection, I said, "Will you be a child forever?"

I realized I'd absorbed my parents' core principle—"Women are inferior to men"—through my *Training to be just a girl.*

My husband had complete control over me. I thought, *How did I let this happen?*

I had no identity of my own. *I've married a man like my father.*

I imagined a web of cracks crawling over the surface of the mirror and watched my reflection transform into a Picasso painting, parts of my life appearing in each fragment.

I saw the little girl, confident, happy, and free, jumping cow pies and playing in the woods, but Dad's gruesome lessons in fear distorted the reflection. I saw blissful days with each new baby, distorted by obedient despair.

What is my future?

Is it mine to choose?

My spirit was listening.

Without considering the magnitude of my decision, I changed my clothes and went downstairs. Niki and Matt were building a Lego castle while cartoons blared. I hugged each of them. "I'm going shopping; Daddy will fix your lunch," and added, "I love you." Then I went into Paul's billiard room. "There are leftovers in the fridge; I'll see ya later." He was stunned, but I was out the door before he could maneuver around his pool table. I saw him in the rearview mirror as I drove away. A look of total surprise covered his angry face. I drove sixty miles to the Florence Mall, just south of Cincinnati. I would have kept driving if not for Niki and Matt. The influence of *Training* had begun to deteriorate along with my marriage.

Perhaps, while I was away, Paul saw his own life in cubistic reflection. When I returned, powdered sugar and unidentifiable clutter covered the kitchen counter. They'd bent and ruined the electric mixer. Paul's inexperience in the kitchen was obvious, but the kids were thrilled with the birthday cake they'd made. Runny chocolate icing dripped from the Duncan Heinz two-layer chocolate cake.

Our lives had changed. I knew it and he knew it.

They sang "Happy Birthday" with one big taper in the middle of the cake, the only candle they could find.

I blew it out. No one knew my wish.

I cleaned up the mess.

One year later, I would spend the night alone for the first time in my life.

chapter seven

For the first few months of the subsequent year, just as in the preceding, I dragged myself through forgotten futile days, incapable of changing out of my blue terrycloth bathrobe until the school bus delivered my reason for living.

Alone one morning, I found Granddad's Kodak in a drawer, its brown, leather case worn soft by years of travel. Sitting on the bedroom carpet, I leaned against the inherited walnut dresser with acorn handles that once held Granddad's clothes. I opened the latch, removed the camera, and extended the bellows. Bringing the camera to my face, I saw myself reflected in the full-length mirror across the room through the viewfinder. Instead of feeling hopeless and miserable, I began to feel weightless. Humming like a despondent harmonica, I rocked the camera like a baby and allowed my mind to clear.

In a dreamy stupor, without intent, I found a beam of intermediate light between heaven and earth and traveled with Granddad. I watched the Missouri River race by and felt the prairie winds on my face. Grass swayed. Cattle grazed. I smelled the hay growing on his farm in Ohio and the bread baking in Grandma's kitchen. Early morning light suspended mist on an unfamiliar pond with cattails and waterfowl, presumably the future.

I lived in my husband's house on a hill in Kentucky, spiritually ignorant and unaware of the powers of meditation or astral projection, but my spirit was beginning to awaken.

When emotionally able, I substitute taught at the middle school. No other sub wanted the hormonal pubescent monsters, but I enjoyed their energy and the chance to escape entombment, no matter what subject I taught. I hoped to buy a 35-mm camera and zoom lens with earnings I stashed in my underwear drawer.

When I needed to use our only car, I dropped off Paul in the morning and drove five miles back, passing tobacco fields and horse farms, and then repeated the route to pick him up in the evening. Paul couldn't fathom the need for a second vehicle. His salary as a chemical engineer increased annually, but he had other priorities for *his* money.

Every day, Niki and Matt, overflowing with the energy of their elementary school adventures, spilled out of the school bus. I delighted in animated discussions of Billy Bob on the monkey bars, Miss Adams on the playground, and reports like "Billy Jo's tader cheps blowed out da winder."

"Billy Jo's potato chips blew out of the window," I said. The twang was protective coloring for my children so I didn't fuss too much. Even their teachers used phrases like "Them done it."

After a snack, the kids set the table, and I started dinner. On the days I had the car, we picked up Paul at work. Sometimes we waited for over an hour, but he insisted we arrive at five o'clock just in case he was ready.

My sister Kali announced her engagement. Tom gave her a ring on her twenty-first birthday—the day Mount St. Helens erupted. He jokingly insisted that the surprise included the "fireworks." I couldn't see the humor.

In June, Kali asked me to come to Seattle to help her plan the wedding. Universal Forces must have beguiled Paul because he agreed to let me go and gave me cash to spend while I was there. Since Paul couldn't be expected to baby-sit, Niki and Matt stayed with my parents in Ohio.

Kali and Tom lived in a big vintage house in a ritzy Seattle neighborhood. After they left for work, I wandered through the house with my coffee and settled into a huge chair on the second floor sun porch. The view of Lake Washington and Mount Rainier calmed me and gave me strength.

I imagined the house was mine and filled rooms for Niki and Matt and the master bedroom with my own imaginary furniture. While chin-deep in a hot bubble bath, I visualized the career that could make it possible. Smiling and in control, I attended meetings where men would listen to me. I wore fashionable business suits and carried an expensive leather briefcase. I drove a nice car, not prestigious but comfortable. This fantasy excluded Paul and any other man.

The manifestation, once imagined, drew breath of its own.

The next morning I gathered all my courage and rode the bus downtown. I'd never toured a big city unaccompanied. Stepping off the bus like an experienced traveler, I walked south on Western Avenue to the Kingdome then back to Belltown from Pioneer Square.

My new camera was a constant companion. Paul's Valentine's Day gift was permission to buy it with the money I'd earned as a substitute teacher. As I shot with abandon along the streets of Seattle, I knew Paul would say I was wasting film, but I also knew good images required lots of shooting. *He'll only see the good ones,* I decided.

I took a roundtrip ferry ride across Puget Sound and shot the skyline, Mt. Rainier, and sea gulls floating on the wind behind the ferry. I walked the docks and used a borrowed macro lens to photograph dark red rust under peeling cobalt paint. I used the telephoto to shoot images of bearded old men on park benches and the widest-angle setting to capture a weather-beaten brick wall that seemed to tell a sad, lonely story. I shot pilings, barnacles, salty rope coils, flowers, and unusual manhole covers with American Indian designs. My passion for photography was obvious to anyone watching, but people passed without seeing me.

Blissfully invisible, without the need to hide from judgment or consequence, I felt alive.

An epiphany of anonymity overwhelmed me.

I bought gifts for Niki and Matt at Nordstrom, rode the monorail to Seattle Center, and walked back to the bus stop on First Avenue. No one knew I was anyone's wife or somebody's mom. I felt like a whole person rather than a small part of something else.

On Kali's days off, we read *Bride's Magazine*, looking for the latest in cakes, gowns, flowers, and invitations. We visited fragrant flower shops, stuffy stationery stores, and savory bakeries. We picked out radiant colors, luscious fabrics, and tried on outrageous dresses.

Her childhood *Training* had been much different from mine. She'd developed a sense of entitlement while I felt I deserved nothing. This basic difference multiplied the unconscious conflict between us.

The day before I flew back to Kentucky, Tom invited me to come on a company-sponsored river-rafting trip on the Suiattle River in the North Cascades. Everything was first class, even the comfortable bus ride. They served sweet, ripe apricots and warm croissants from heavy wicker baskets and Starbucks coffee in souvenir pottery mugs.

The Suiattle River rushed through a lush mountain valley with snowcapped peaks all around. Moss-covered trees lined the banks. Before we pushed the raft into the current, the guide demonstrated how to hug the pontoons with our legs, like riding horseback, with one foot in the cold water and the other in the raft. We practiced maneuvering the boat with our paddles, and he explained what to do if anyone fell overboard. When we pushed into swift-moving glacial water and the current carried us downstream, I thought, *I can't believe I get to do this!* and involuntarily laughed out loud. The risk of falling overboard made me dizzy. Several people did, including the man in front of me. The guide shouted directions to everyone. We collected our lost shipmates from the icy water near the bank and pushed back into the white river. Tom had a tiny and expensive waterproof camera—this was well before digital—and caught images when the river allowed it.

On the grassy shore afterwards, my legs felt rubbery from holding on, my arms ached from paddling, and my face felt strained from the huge grin I'd sported all day.

Kali and Tom were anxious to impress his colleagues, and my Kentucky clothes sent the wrong message. Kali had urged me to wear something of hers, but I wore my own ordinary, comfortable clothes. After the ride, I noticed that these people were enormously concerned with impressing each other with the labels on the outside of their clothing. I had no interest in the represented designers.

Tom's colleagues were pleasant but not friendly. One of the more annoying women said, "Kali, it's so nice to see your sister," as if I weren't standing there. "Who's older?"

"She is," Kali snapped, more than a little irritated. I was thirty and she was twenty-one. Tom and his friends were my age.

I drifted away from the pretentious group. The oak, maple, and buckeye trees that I loved in Ohio were so different from these massive towers of fir and cedar. I sat facing the sun by a moss-covered trunk with my gourmet chili and hot cheese bread. I closed my eyes, absorbed the warm light and the bliss.

Then a shadow blocked the sun. It was the river guide, Ross, who recognized a friendly outsider. "Can I join you?" he asked.

"Of course."

Ross had dancing elf-like eyes. Wind and sun had burned his cheeks. Without a hat, his high, white forehead distorted his appearance. A long, unkempt, red beard covered the top two buttons on his blue, plaid shirt and a stringy salt and pepper ponytail slid down his back. I thought he looked like a cartoon character as he sat down next to my tree.

In the raft, he'd been engaging, insightful, and sensitive to the needs of the rafters. "I quit my corporate job to be a rafting guide during beautiful Northwest summers. I'm a ski instructor in winter. When the weather's bad, I'm a poet. Some years I'm a poet most of the time." When we finished dinner, Ross jumped up and offered his hand, "Come on, I wanna show you something." I naïvely followed him into the trees.

Soon we turned toward the river. I watched my feet with trepidation as he led me across a narrow, swaying footbridge. I tried to hide my fear. Halfway across, Ross stopped and extended his arm. "This is why I live in the Pacific Northwest! Allow me to introduce Mt. Baker." It looked close enough to touch, framed by the trees, milky blue water, and clear late-afternoon sky. I had never been so close to a snow-covered mountain. I forgot my fear of the swaying bridge as the mystical force stole my breath.

Our feet dangled over the silty, turbulent river as Ross and I watched bald eagles overhead. We talked with abandon, free in the knowledge we would never meet again. I wasn't sad, but tears freely flowed. "This visit," I said, "is only partly to plan my sister's wedding. It's been an opportunity for me to get to know myself as a separate person from Paul and my children."

He asked, "After ten days, what do you think?"

I surprised myself when I said, "I can do it!"

As the afternoon sky dissolved to dusk, my heart merged with the mountain.

Listening to the river gurgle and the wind converse with the tall trees, we watched the white snow turn to taffeta pink then to rich ripe plum. The mountain whispered to my dormant sense of independence. I felt the promise of my new life and sadness for the old one as my breath quickened and my chest pounded in anticipation. I knew I belonged to this mountain range more than I belonged to Paul and my life in Kentucky. Autonomy awoke and soaked into my bones.

I was sure someday I'd make Seattle my home.

"I'd better get back to the bus," I said.

Ross and I exchanged addresses on a small pad of paper he carried in his shirt pocket. "I carry this in case I'm inspired to write a poem," he said as he tore out the page with his address, and we headed back to camp.

The last folding table was being stowed in the cargo hold of the bus. Everyone had boarded, ready for the two-hour trip to Seattle. Kali was frantically pacing when Ross and I appeared. Ross kissed my cold, salty cheek, then disappeared back among the trees. I ignored Kali's dark stare, stepped onto the bus, and took the last available seat as we moved toward the freeway.

Reynolds, the man sharing my bench seat, talked about his job. Then he put his hand on my thigh. "Would you like to go out sometime?"

I tried not to shout. "I'm married!"

"So what? So am I!"

"I'm really not interested," I said. Embarrassed and humiliated, I had no choice but to sit next to him for the remaining hour of the trip. Reynolds' wife, three-year-old daughter, and brand new baby boy were waiting when the busload of sunburned rafters arrived at the Park-n-Ride in Seattle. He gave them all a hug and didn't look back. It was my first experience with this disgusting male attribute and helped nurture my negative opinion of men in general.

Kali and Tom said nothing as I sat in the tan, leather backseat of Tom's new BMW, feeling like a child. I assumed I was in trouble for making Kali worry and nearly missing the bus.

When we arrived at Tom's house, I went straight to my room to get ready for bed in the perfectly decorated guestroom full of turn-of-the-century American antiques. It looked as if Tom had inherited his grandmother's bedroom furniture and hadn't changed a thing, right down to the silver brush-and-comb set and crocheted doily on the oak dressing table.

Kali knocked.

"Come in."

Kali shrieked, "How could you do that to me!"

She sounded strangely like our father.

"Are you trying to ruin my life? We invite you on a rafting trip and you sneak into the woods with that mangy guide." Kali raged while I hugged my own shoulders. "Tom works with those people. What were you thinking?"

She smacked me hard across the face.

Leaving, she bumped into Tom listening at the door.

Tom looked down at me with disgust, my face crimson where Kali had left her mark. Through confused sobs, I tried to defend myself. "I'm sorry … if Kali was … worried about me … I never saw a mountain like that!"

"What mountain?" Tom said.

I couldn't stop shivering. "It was Mt. Baker, I think. The guide showed me. We couldn't see it from camp; we had to go out onto the footbridge. It was so beautiful. It was pink and blue and purple and …" I gasped for breath, trying in vain to sound calm. Tom shook his head and left the room.

We never discussed it again. Years later, I realized that Kali and Tom, and probably their friends, thought I had gone into the woods to have sex. I was too naïve at the time to think of it. In their own way, they were just as naïve, unable to imagine any other reason to spend time with a scruffy mountain man, a poet.

The next morning, I hid in the guest room until they left for work and then took the shuttle to the airport as planned. As the plane banked over snow-capped Mount Rainier, a spiritual tremble reassured me. I would be back, even if Kali and I would never be close. I was changing and finding a path different from Kali's. Kali was beginning a new life with Tom and his money.

I was determined to discover freedom and independence.

Each in our own way, we had developed survival tools to overcome our childhood.

At the airport, I bought a book, *Your Erroneous Zones: Step by Step Advice for Escaping the Trap of Negative Thinking and Taking Control of Your Life*, by Dr. Wayne Dyer. Funny what materializes when it's time. A sentence in the first chapter became my call to autonomy: "Feelings are reactions you choose to have."

So, I thought, *what you're telling me, Dr. Dyer, is that if I don't let him, Paul can't make me feel daft, powerless, or dependent?* I absorbed the message during the five-hour flight. Dr. Dyer had struck a chord, and no one could stop the vibration.

My career in Seattle would take a few more years to manifest.

Paul met me at the airport in Cincinnati, and we silently drove to Shelby to pick up Niki and Matt. Paul wasn't interested in my trip. I wasn't interested in sharing.

Although my mother wasn't surprised when I revealed my plan to file for divorce, she said, "Oh, please wait until after Kali's wedding. How would it look? No one in our family has ever been divorced." I agreed to wait and went back to Kentucky to resume my dismal days, but things were different now.

Paul worked longer hours and played golf on weekends. The kids went swimming and played with their friends while I gathered strength.

I forwarded the rafting guide a picture of the river trip that Tom sent me. The letter I enclosed glowed with the excitement of the river experience and the undertow of discontent I had revealed facing Mt. Baker. He responded to my letter, sharing adventures of the rafting season, his excitement about the upcoming ski season and winterizing his mountain cabin. He enclosed a poem he'd written:

Seasons of change excite the soul
The river impels one
Sunlit mountains hover in your thoughts
To discover beauty and newness

A feeling
A person
Something within yourself
Is reason enough
To smile
To laugh
To live

His advice and encouragement launched me back to the dairy farm and the confidence I'd felt before school started each fall. I answered his letters during the following months, exploding with frustration and dreams. When I wrote that I'd filed for divorce, he congratulated me. He offered to continue as a male sounding board, but I had no more words to write. His supportive letters had filled a niche, and I was grateful.

The time for planning had ended.

The time for action had arrived.

I'd lived in a patriarchal world, controlled first by my father and then Paul, but the crust had cracked. *Training* was collapsing. I possessed an inner strength, though barely a whisper, and I knew I could manifest my dreams.

I just didn't know how.

chapter eight

As my confidence increased, I focused on community involvement. That fall, the PTA elected me president, and I began fundraising for new playground equipment. I asked Judy, the treasurer, "Can I see the financial records?" She'd been looking after the financial records for several years.

Judy was also the drive-through teller at the only bank in town. We called it Fred's bank. She was insulted. "I bin the treasurer a this here PTA fer years and don't need no outsider a comin' in here an' demandin' stuff."

I explained, "I read in the PTA bylaws that the president of the association is legally responsible. I'd like to see where you've been as an organization so I can see what we need to do to accomplish the projects we've planned." The more she objected, the harder I pushed. Although I still acquiesced to Paul's authority at home, I was beginning to find my strength. I persisted until she agreed to give me the records.

"Here's the darn records, and y'all can find a new treasurer, 'cause I qu-it."

No wonder! She had written checks for the beauty shop, the shoe store, and other personal, non-PTA expenses. Proceeds from the bake sale, which I'd deposited at Fred's drive-through window, did not appear in the check register. I hadn't gotten a receipt because I'd trusted her to file it with the other financial records. I wondered how many previous deposits she'd dropped into her purse instead of the PTA account over the years. The total fraud I could account for came to five thousand dollars.

I met with Fred. "What should we do?"

"Uh … well, that's not a lot a money. Why don't y'all forget it? She's been workin' here for a long time. Her husband's been out a work for a while, and one a her kids is real sick."

"But Fred," I said, "she didn't deposit cash into the account at the drive-through window and used over five thousand dollars for her personal expenses."

"Ah, just let 'er be."

"Fred, I know you don't want bad publicity for your bank, but I can't ignore this. We need playground equipment and supplies for the kids."

I asked our neighbor Miles for advice. He worked for the attorney general's office. He said, "I know her father; let me give him a call." The next week her father "donated" five thousand dollars to the PTA, and the matter just went away. The teachers and kids were happy to have new playground equipment, and Judy kept her job,

Paul remained unaware of my increasing strength except to say, "Yeah, I guess they needed playground equipment."

At seven, Matt still wet the bed and often woke me with nightmares. Night after night, I found him running through the house shouting gibberish in his sleep. He opened cupboards, threw canned goods onto the floor, and kicked an imaginary soccer ball around the living room. He wouldn't respond to my efforts to calm him. All I could do was keep him safe.

Niki was much more subtle. She took money from her friend's piggy bank and from my purse, but it took me a long time to realize what she had done. She would express her anxiety and hurt years later.

One night in late August, I stood in the family room doorway. Paul's program was almost over, and the kids were asleep. With clammy palms, I said, "Paul, I think we should get a divorce." I'm sure he would say such an idea came out of the blue, but I had thought of nothing else since July.

"I don't think that's the answer," he said, "but I agree that *you* have a problem."

Tentatively I said, "Then let's go to counseling together."

"You're welcome to go; insurance will cover it. But *I* don't have a problem; *you* do. You should get a part-time job or find something to do with your time."

I saw my chance. "How can I get a job? I don't even have a car." After some discussion, he agreed to buy another car. Though not fully aware of it, I was learning how to manipulate him. How could I be free if I didn't have a vehicle?

As a family we spent the following Saturday in Louisville shopping for my new (used) car. We looked at several, drove a few. He wanted to do more research before he made the decision. I had little input but didn't care.

That Friday I took him to work so I could substitute teach. At four in the afternoon, he called from the office. "You don't need to pick me up," he said. "I have a surprise." Around five-thirty, he arrived in a dark blue, Datsun pickup truck. "It was a great deal," he said. "I bought it from a guy at work. It gets great mileage 'cause it's a stick."

He didn't allow me to drive the Datsun. He didn't think I could learn to operate the manual transmission. Presumably, the Olds belonged to me. But one morning I entered the garage, ready to run errands, and discovered he'd taken the Oldsmobile for the day.

I don't think he intentionally or maliciously left me stranded.

He just couldn't see that I was real.

When he left the truck behind, I taught myself to drive it. He never knew.

<hr />

I decided to see a psychiatrist. Although I was getting stronger, suicide was often on my mind. I knew I needed help. I thought, *Perhaps Paul's right. If I get myself straightened out, maybe I can be satisfied with the marriage.*

I called my mother, "I need professional help dealing with my Paul." I didn't tell her how often I'd considered suicide. "Do you know a counselor I could call? I don't want anyone here to know." She suggested a psychiatrist in Dayton, Ohio. It was a two-hour drive, but I could make the round trip before Matt and Niki got home from school.

The chauvinistic doctor was Dad's age. I stared at my feet during our sessions, embarrassed to expose my domestic dirty laundry. "Most of the time I feel like I want to go home, but I am home," I said during session two, trying to explain my feelings of suicide. I looked up. He was sound asleep, sitting straight in his chair. Quietly, I slipped out, not wanting to wake him.

I searched for an attorney in the tiny Flint phonebook, a quarter-inch thick with six-by-eight-inch pages. The small book listed four attorneys: Ruth, her husband, and two other men. Ruth had a reputation for being a "bitch on wheels," so I made an appointment. She had a delightful personality and a no-nonsense approach to her business. I couldn't believe such an intelligent, competent female attorney practiced in our little town. We began working out the details so I could file for divorce in October after Kali's wedding.

When I told Paul I'd filed, he looked up from the TV and said, "Oh, sure, you're gonna make a living by yourself. Geezzz," and went back to watching his program. The sheriff's deputy served papers at his office on Halloween. The method of delivery annoyed him more than the prospect of divorce. He didn't believe I'd go through with it.

"You independent bitch," he shouted. "You stupid idiot. You're too dumb to be on your own." He refused to leave and crawled into bed after I fell asleep. I changed the locks to get him out of my bed. He stayed overnight with a friend, taking nothing but the clothes he was wearing, and returned daily to collect what he needed. "She can't lock me out of my own goddamn house!" The attorney he finally hired told him I could. His attempts to badger me into submission continued, but his rage passed through me with no impact, enraging him even more. By Thanksgiving, Paul had officially moved into his own apartment, but the insults and rage continued, even in front of our children.

Ruth and I discussed alimony and child support. I was entitled to both.

"I don't want his money," I told her. "I'll be fine as soon as I get a job." Paul was more than agitated when he learned I would get half of our assets and he would be required to pay child support until the children were eighteen.

"She did nothing but sit around all day. Why should she get anything?" he told my attorney.

I bought a tablet of columnar paper and listed all of the household chores I'd managed: laundry, grocery shopping, entertaining his colleagues, cooking, cleaning, mending, sex, etc. I'd been "on call" twenty-four hours a day, seven days a week for over ten years. I charged him five dollars an hour and double-time for the years I spent pregnant, giving birth, and producing mother's milk for his children. The detailed bill was over half a million dollars.

"You can pay me for my time and trouble or you can give me half of our assets—your choice."

When we told the kids we were getting a divorce, Matt cried and Niki laughed. When Paul moved out, Matt quit wetting the bed and never had another nightmare. It was more difficult for Niki. I stood frozen at the bay window, watching as she boldly refused to go to *Dad's house*. Paul picked her up and forced her into the truck, Niki kicking and crying, Paul screaming and cursing. It broke my heart to see Niki so upset and Paul treating her so roughly, but I was barely able to breathe and incapable of intervention.

<hr />

"I'm taking the kids to my parents' for Thanksgiving," Paul said without discussion.

On Thanksgiving Day, I awoke refreshed. I'd just spent my very first night alone in thirty-one years—no brother, sister, parent, roommate, husband, or child.

I discovered the bliss of solitude, the joy in my own company.

Paul had always said, "Big fires waste logs."

I built a huge fire in the fireplace.

Paul had always said, "If you're going to mix whiskey with soda, you can drink the Cutty Sark."

In the late afternoon, I drank Glenfiddich with ice and a splash of soda.

Paul had always said, "Cooking in the fireplace causes chimney fires."

I wrapped a potato with foil, threw it in the fire, and cooked a steak over the coals.

Why had I taken so long to see it? He found the negative in every aspect of life. Without his overbearing influence, I tried to find the good in all things. Once recognized, I could no longer dismiss my own core value.

Friends called. "We're so sorry. We didn't know you were alone on Thanksgiving. You should have called us." I couldn't make them understand that it was a great start for my new life.

For no reason I could remember, I'd been afraid to drive long distances alone. Heights and water also frightened me. Crossing the Ohio River Bridge in Cincinnati traffic was a big obstacle on the way to my parents' home. Now, without hesitation, I drove to visit them for Christmas. The fear that had once stopped me collapsed with my marriage.

Their house on the hill easily accommodated our big family. Craig was home from San Francisco with his Vietnamese girlfriend, Tia, and her nine-year-old daughter, Ling. Kali and her new husband were there from Seattle. Lili and her husband came from Wisconsin with their two preschoolers. Our brother Rob, living in Alaska, couldn't be there.

Paul was also missing.

It was the first Christmas without Paul since we'd started going steady in 1965. He'd been part of our family gatherings for nearly fifteen years. During Christmas Eve dinner, Dad told stories about divorced women he knew. "They just want their husband's money," he said. My desire to be independent was unthinkable for my father. In his eyes, a woman without a man was not a free woman; she was an exposed woman, and he believed the lewd implications of that exposure.

After dinner that Christmas Day in 1980, Dad wobbled into the family room reeking of Scotch. We sprawled in front of a big fire, ready to watch the *Nutcracker* on TV. He staggered to the TV and turned it off. "We're not watchin' the idiot box on Chriztmaz."

"But Dad," Craig said, "the San Francisco Ballet is performing the *Nutcracker*. Ling's friend is in it."

"I don' care who'z in it. You're not watchin' that crap on Chriztmaz," he said.

Craig turned it on. Dad turned it off. They yelled obscenities and began hitting each other. Craig pushed Dad backwards to the floor, and they continued. My brother's suppressed rage accelerated with each blow. They broke the ping-pong table in the mayhem. Dad looked evil, and his aura had turned from red to gray, as if he were sucking all of the energy from the room.

Kali and her husband went to her bedroom. Lili's husband took all the kids and Tia upstairs to the master bedroom. As the fight escalated, Lili and Mom collected Dad's guns and hid them. It was nine at night and snowing with the temperature below zero degrees. The 160-mile drive to Kentucky was out of the question, so I packed our things and drove the slippery roads to the Holiday Inn on the edge of town. I called Paul at his parents to let him know where we were and why.

Although our individual hearts still pumped, the family was dead. We never gathered again.

The next year my mother invited Paul to Christmas dinner with Niki and Matt. I stayed in Kentucky alone. In January, I asked my mother, "Why did you invite Paul for Christmas dinner and not me?"

"Well, I wanted to see Niki and Matt, and I was afraid I wouldn't get the chance if you were here." Regardless of her intent, I felt that in my parents' eyes, I was less of a family member than Paul. My children carried his surname and I was just a girl.

chapter nine

As divorces go, it was quick and mild. Paul didn't want to spend money on attorney's fees, and he was blind to my emerging power. He insisted on including language that accommodated his expected return to work in Michigan. He wrote the parenting agreement, including how much time he would have with the children, how we'd manage holidays, who would pay for the flights, etc. He wrote for himself, of course. One sentence started "If *I* move out of state …" But Ruth pointed out that the rules applied equally to both parties, so he changed the text before we signed to "If *either party* moves out of state …" He never dreamed I would be the one to take advantage of his carefully written document.

During the heated anger of separation, Paul screamed, "You have everything a woman could want, you independent bitch. You just want to leave me so you can go fuck like a bunny!" I usually didn't listened to his insults, but as he raged, it dawned on me that the sex drive in our relationship was mine. I remembered trying to arouse him during the early years of our marriage. After getting two children to bed, I walked between Paul and the TV set wearing nothing but a negligee I'd made for the lingerie class I taught. (I didn't have the nerve to wrap myself in saran wrap as Marabel Morgan suggested.) He grumbled, "Wait 'til the game's over." By the time he came to bed, I'd been asleep for hours, the mood was gone, and the baby was waking up again.

Now, he was accusing me of finding sexual satisfaction elsewhere. It hadn't occurred to me. I longed for personal freedom, not sexual freedom. Paul was the only lover I'd ever had. Was it even possible to make love with someone else if I wanted to? Suddenly, I wanted to.

My neighbor Brenda and I watched our children board the school bus then walked back to her house for coffee. It became a routine in those days if I wasn't working. Brenda was meek and Mormon. Her long, blond hair hung in soft curls, the way her husband liked it. She made her own dowdy dresses, accented with lace. I wouldn't have spent much time with her in normal circumstances, but she was friendly and available when I faced a day of aching loneliness. Her spirituality was just dogma in my opinion, devoid of any kind of knowing or awareness. She was a literal believer, and it was difficult to have a conversation about anything but our children. One morning she began talking about God. I think she was trying to convert me.

"Maybe you and Paul would have done better if you were more … well …" she searched for the right word, "… obedient."

I bit my lip.

"The Bible says that God made woman from Adam's rib, and men should have power over us, so I try to do what my husband wants," she said.

"His rib, my ass!" Anger eclipsed etiquette and spilled over our fragile friendship. "Brigham Young was just a twisted man, a pervert who made up rules to fit his desires."

"What do you mean?" she gasped, unable to understand the slightest objection to her *Training*.

We stopped having coffee together, and Matt no longer played with her son after school. I'm sure she thought I was going to hell.

I was angry.

I was angry with Paul for not being the husband I'd dreamed I'd marry.

I was angry with my mother for not supporting her children.

I was angry with Dad for not loving us.

I was angry with teachers who had expected me to become no more than someone's wife.

I was angry at the church and anything spiritual.

Since first grade, they'd bullied me into submission: father, mother, siblings, husband, teachers, and ministers. No more.

Independence emerged as my anger subsided.

chapter ten

Anthony, the school maintenance supervisor, became a good friend when I led the planning and implementation of the playground restoration project. He was four years younger than I with a strong, stocky build. His black, wavy hair and neatly trimmed, blue-black beard attracted women like breeding plumage, but that handsome exterior was not what I noticed most. He seemed interested in everything, read ravenously, and enjoyed intelligent conversation on any topic.

One balmy summer night, Anthony called. "What're ya doin'?" he asked in his Kentucky accent.

"Not much," I responded. "It's nice just to have the house to myself."

"How 'bout a glass a wine? I got a bottle a red I can bring over. *Cosmos* is on tonight."

"Sure, come on out," I said. "I'll scrounge up some crackers and cheese."

I considered Anthony a "friend of the family." The three of us, Paul, Anthony, and I, had watched the early TV episodes of Carl Sagan's *Cosmos, A Personal Voyage.* We were enthralled, had lively discussions, and delighted in spitting out the "B" in "billions" the way Carl Sagan did. For a few hours a week, I had felt alive and intelligent.

We on Earth have just awakened to the great oceans of
space and time from which we have emerged. We are the
legacy of fifteen billion years of cosmic evolution …

Carl Sagan
Cosmos, A Personal Voyage
"Episode 1: The Shores of the Cosmic Ocean"

After the program, Anthony and I finished our wine on the deck
above the Kentucky River valley, framed by a vast wooded state park. I
sat on a bench leaning against the railing, and he sat on the chaise longue.
The Milky Way staged a brilliant show with no moon or city lights to
interfere. Over the cacophony of frogs, crickets, and night creatures,
Anthony and I discussed the *Cosmos* episode and then photography,
another common passion. He loved his new 28-to-200 zoom lens. "I
can go for long hikes and not worry about carrying a lot of lenses and
changing all the time," he said.

Close-up photography was my current obsession. He had loaned
me his old macro lens for the Seattle trip. "I'm really having fun with
that old lens," I said. "I think I got a great back-lit shot of dewdrops on
a spider web this morning."

We sat in the starlight, drank too much red wine, and discussed
opinions and feelings on an assortment of issues. Suddenly, as if a
conductor had lowered his baton, the frogs' croaking subsided, and a
mist rolled up from the woods below like a soft blanket to hide us. In
the stillness, Anthony said, "Did you ever have sex with anyone but
Paul?" I was naïve, not even slightly aware of his objective.

"No, he was my first and only," I said, my flushed cheeks hidden
in the darkness.

"How old were you the first time?"

"A freshman at Ohio State, eighteen, I guess." I took another sip
of wine and began to feel something besides fog in the air.

"Didn't you want to do it in high school?" he said, staring into
the night.

"Oh, I came close with my boyfriend, but I jumped out of the
car when he unzipped his pants. Then Paul tried, but I thought I had
to wait until we were married. When we got pinned, sort of engaged

to be engaged, and once we did it, I felt like we were married. I never considered dating anyone else after that."

"Do you ever think about what it would be like … with someone else?" His tone exposed his motive.

"Sure, I think about it." I said, looking at him in the darkness. I knew only married sex, in my case, the opportunity to evaluate the accumulated dust on the etched-glass ceiling fixture—but I didn't say so.

"Can I come sit by you?"

"Sure," I said too quickly.

He bent to kiss my hair, my cheek, my eyes. I held my breath, hoping he wouldn't stop. It was a warm night, but I shivered, afraid, curious, starved. He bent further to kiss my neck just below the collar of my pale blue blouse. His beard tickled my skin. Then he put his hands under my arms to lift me to my feet. His forearms pressed against my breasts. My blouse and bra soon dropped to the deck to wait for his shirt.

What am I doing? I don't love this man, and the divorce isn't final. I was a pool of emotion, fearful but curious, as he kissed and caressed the parts of me no other man had touched. Curiosity melted anxiety, and bare desire surpassed curiosity. I reached for his belt buckle, and his jeans were on the deck. Like a naked creature with four legs, we descended the stairs to the lawn. I rolled backward, sandwiched between hot man and cold grass. In the space between abandon and amazement, I experienced my first electrically charged orgasm. I didn't know this was possible.

A week or so later, Anthony called. "Can I come over? I've got somethin' for ya."

He handed me a brown paper bag.

"A back massager?" I said as I opened the box it came in.

"It's a vibrator," he said. "Every single woman should own one. If you can take care of yourself—that way—men won't be able to manipulate you."

He offered to show me how to use it but my shyness seemed more acute since our night in the grass. "That's OK," I said. "I'd rather experiment by myself." The electric appliance looked like it should be used to relieve back tension, and that's how I used it at first.

It hummed when it was turned on, and so did I.

I'd never touched my own genital area except for sanitary reasons (nice girls didn't), but alone that weekend, I ceremoniously introduced my new companion. I filled the living room with candlelight, spread a soft blanket on the carpet in front of a hot fire, and positioned the sex toy next to me. In my private tantric ritual, universal energy flowed into me. I abandoned my blue terrycloth bathrobe along with all inhibitions. Naked in the heat, I surrendered to the pulsating accessory. I was extraordinarily conscious and simultaneously free of any thought that could inhibit this powerful autonomous pleasure. Afterward, I fell asleep by the fire and rolled into the blanket when the embers cooled.

At the time, I didn't see the symbolism. This tantric toy represented my surge toward total independence.

Anthony gradually spent more and more time at our house. He stayed with Matt and Niki when I got a job. One night I came home, troubled that I'd spent so little time with them, knowing they would be asleep. I walked into the family room, dark except for the blue flickering light. I expected to find Anthony asleep on the sofa in front of the TV. Instead, they were all watching *Porky's*, an R-rated movie. "You guys should have been asleep an hour ago; tomorrow's a school day. Come on, I'll tuck you in," I said in a voice that fooled no one.

When they were settled, I turned on the light in the family room "What the hell do you think you're doing?"

"Oh, it's not that bad. You're overreacting," he said.

"The hell I am. You think lines like 'Give me pussy or give me death' are what I want my nine-year-old telling his friends at school? They're my kids, and I decide what is and is not appropriate. You knew bedtime was nine o'clock, and you knew I wouldn't approve of that movie. How could you be so disrespectful?"

"Oh, relax. Get into y'r robe 'n snuggle with me."

"I'm in no mood to snuggle. Just get out! If you can't have respect for my decisions and my children, then you can get out of our house and never come back." Anthony was stunned. Reluctantly, he left but soon called to apologize and begged to come back. Later that week, I let him.

We shared intense passions, good and bad, but I felt out of control during a time when I was struggling to find personal power. After another disagreement about the kids, I collected all of his belongings and pitched them off the deck. I tossed his beer out of my cooler. The cans rolled down the hill into the trees. For weeks, Anthony called and dropped by, but I stood firm.

Anthony knew more about a woman's body and emotions than most women. He'd read erotic books and sex manuals and become an expert. Giving a woman pleasure was his domain. When most men his age were practicing vulgar pickup lines, Anthony was getting laid by older women, practicing for his life's work. His first *project* was a teacher who caught her husband in bed with her best friend. Anthony became her confidant and counseled her through emotional pain and separation anxiety. He read the books she should have read and translated them into a language that became his own.

No emotional dungeon held his project captive. Inevitably, she moved on, or if she was reluctant, he used his finely tuned manipulative skills to make her feel healed and ready to face the world without him. She never felt jilted. He was brilliant.

I was his first *project* including children, and he'd failed to research the "single mother" category. He thought he knew about raising children, just because he was once a child himself. Niki and Matt impeded his strategy and led to his demise as my sorcerer. I still didn't know exactly who my Self was, but I knew what kind of mom I wanted to be. He was caught off guard when I tossed his counsel out of my life, his beer out of my cooler, and became the sorceress.

He probably loved each of his projects, including me. That night under the stars when we began our love affair, my naïveté prevented me from seeing his sorcerer-istic plans for me—a link in a chain of divorced women he would *fix*. As our love-doctor, he offered a prescription that healed broken hearts and eliminated toxic emotional debris. It took many years for me to admit that I'd been an emotionally emaciated experiment in his love laboratory. He brought me back to life with sexual touch and intellectual inspiration. I remain nonjudgmental about his life's path and have no regrets. The black-bearded sorcerer counseled me through a difficult developmental phase and introduced me to orgasm. I am grateful.

chapter eleven

Tobacco, chemicals, and foundries built the Flint County financial system, and the small-town attitude made outsiders unwelcome. Finding a job wasn't easy. I had no experience except for summer jobs and the day care. I applied at the foundry where no skills were required and wore a suit to the interview. "You'd have to get dirty in this job," said the interviewer. I would have looked more employable with rollers in my hair.

A series of serendipitous events resulted in my first real job. A friend's husband, Dan, worked at Flint Chemicals. "Dan says they're looking for two entry-level lab techs," she said. "Didn't you graduate from Ohio State? Almost no one around here went to college. You'll have a pretty good chance."

"I took two chemistry courses," I told her, "and some microbiology and biology, but my degree's in home economics!"

"Perfect!" she said. "Dan always says it's cookbook chemistry!"

I gathered my courage and phoned the Personnel Department at Flint Chemicals. I was surprised that I knew the man who answered. His wife had been Matt's kindergarten teacher, and I'd recruited him to be the new PTA treasurer when I'd discovered Judy's deception. I had no idea he was handling all of Flint Chemicals' new hires while his boss, Phillip, recovered from cancer. The interview seemed like a social visit.

My salary was two dollars an hour less than the new male lab technician they hired the same week. The other tech was a fresh Kentucky University graduate with a BA in psychology who lived with his parents. In the eyes of corporate America, men supported families, women did not—as if that made a difference in an employee's value to the company. Men had a business advantage based purely on anatomy.

So skilled at mirroring the demeanor required to survive, I began to morph to man-like behavior, like many working women in the early 1980s. I dressed like the male lab techs—long pants, long-sleeved shirts, and tennis shoes. I wore no makeup and pulled my hair into a ponytail.

Still, when I walked the alley from the parking lot to the lab, men hung from the windows to catcall and whistle. The union workers began using the lab as a corridor to the next building because they wanted to see the "divorcée lab tech." They considered all divorcées "hot to trot," and a few asked me out for "a roll in the hay." I was humiliated but needed the job. After thirty years of making every effort to be more attractive, I practiced the opposite inconvenience. I walked the alley each morning and afternoon, wearing my black rimmed safety glasses with the plastic side panels and a hard hat. If that didn't turn them off, *nothing* would.

❦

Paul insisted on selling our house. I would need a place to live. I contacted a real estate agent to inquire about renting a house that had been empty for six months. Its contemporary architecture was unusual in the little southern town. People called it the butterfly house because the gable was inverted, making the roof low in the middle and high on the sides. An architect had designed it to suit the hilly wooded lot. The front deck was bigger than the house and floated over the sloping lawn. The owners wanted to sell, not rent, so I made an outrageously low offer to buy it. The appalled agent sent the offer to the owners in Connecticut, who were so happy to have a buyer they didn't even counter-offer.

I went to Fred's bank for a mortgage. The employees, who considered me a meddling outsider, slid aside like the Red Sea when I asked to see Fred. He knew he could trust me, and he had the power to make the lending decision. Because I was a first-time female buyer, no down payment was required. My small income qualified, and I signed the papers. Now I was a home-owning adult with responsibility for a mortgage and two children.

I parked in my new driveway and wandered through the empty house, ignoring the six-month accumulation of cobwebs and dust. The downward-sloping roof seemed to collect universal forces and charged the house with positive energy.

Sliding glass doors led to the huge deck. I sat on the boards and smelled the woodsy air, hidden from the street by a row of maples. A red-bellied woodpecker landed on the dogwood growing through a hole in the deck.

The unusual little house had a small galley kitchen, three bedrooms, and two bathrooms. After hours of cleaning and painting, we moved in. I put houseplants in the living room, mayonnaise in the refrigerator, and crunchy Skippy on peanut butter and jelly sandwiches. Only a year before, without getting dressed, I'd stood in the yard of Paul's house, wondering if I would survive.

As a waste water lab technician, I tested water from the waste treatment facility. It was mundane and repetitive. I tested for solids, BODs (biological oxygen demand), and CODs (chemical oxygen demand). Every day, same tests. One morning, even before testing, I noticed a foggy sample that should have been clear. Before starting my daily routine, I took the sample to the engineer in charge. He discovered that chemicals were leaking from the plant into the final clean-water pond that would go directly to the Ohio River. The chemicals would have flowed into the river all day if I hadn't taken action. In addition to the pollution, the company would have lost thousands of dollars in product.

The next day it was business as usual. No one said thank you. The men working in the plant should have noticed the leak when they collected the samples, long before I arrived in the lab. The female-outsider-divorcée had made them look bad in front of the "bosses." The parade of men past my lab bench subsided.

Although being a lab tech was not my chosen career, I hoped it would continue until I was ready for a move to Seattle. There was a national recession in the early 1980s, however, and the job ended in the fall. Men who had worked for Flint Chemicals for twenty years also lost their jobs.

My manager scheduled my exit interview with Phillip, the VP of personnel. John had introduced me to Phillip a few weeks after I started in the lab. He had been recovering from cancer surgery when John hired me. Phillip was ten years older than I was, about five foot eight with a slight build and very thin hair. Cancer treatment had ravaged his body, but the day we first met, his kind brown eyes and playful smile captivated me.

At the exit interview, he said, "I wouldn't have hired you because of your recent divorcée status. Most women in this town, or anywhere, need time to adjust to being single and finding day care, so they're employment risks. You're different and you've done a great job in the lab." Then he said, "As your employer, I couldn't ask you out, but since you no longer work for the company, would you like to go boating on Saturday?" I accepted. I found out much later that the VP usually didn't interview exiting employees at my level.

He picked me up in a 1966 British racing green Alfa Romero. I would have been thrilled to ride anywhere in that car.

"It's a great little car, but the back tires are more worn than the front," he joked. "It spends a lot time behind a tow truck."

He drove to a nearby lake, and we had a delightful time picnicking and laughing on his friend's powerboat. In the weeks that followed, we began seeing a lot of each other when my children were with their father.

Phillip had always wanted to build a sailboat and ordered a kit from a company in New York. A freight transporter truck deposited the hull, mast, and boxes filled with sails and hardware on the front lawn of Flint Chemicals. Phillip borrowed a pickup to haul the parts home. When we were together on Saturdays or Sundays, I used sandpaper and varnish to finish the galley table and other woodwork while he installed hardware in the fiberglass hull.

By May, we'd finished the *Mandala One*. We began the maiden voyage on the Kentucky River and floated about a hundred yards into the Ohio River. I held my breath as he maneuvered the boat into the wind and cleated the mainsail and jib. It worked! We were sailing! We realized that we'd installed spreaders improperly and forgotten to put the battens in the mainsail, but it was great fun. After a short sail, we cleaned the boat for an hour. We knew, better than most, the quantity of pollution in the Ohio River. His fussiness surprised me. He hadn't cleaned his apartment since we'd met.

We often shared dinner either at Phillip's or in Cincinnati with his boating friends. After one beautiful meal, Phillip ordered brandy, my first. The waiter slowly poured a small amount of dark amber liquid into four large snifters. Phillip was absorbed, as if he and the liquid had a special understanding. I awkwardly rotated my glass between my palms flowing Phillip's lead. The first whiff held a hint of vanilla, then fruit and nuts emerged. He rolled the brandy around the sides and allowed droplets and streams to return to center, leaving a pale, viscous crown in the snifter's bowl. He closed his eyes, inhaled the sensuous bouquet, and sipped the velvety flavor. Our eyes met and tenderness swirled. Heat rushed up my spine.

I hadn't known that Phillip's cancer had caused serious damage "down there." He wasn't sure if his intimate equipment would ever perform again. That's why we'd spent months working on the boat with no pressure for intimacy.

Phillip treated me like a person, not *just a girl*, and I loved it. After the warm brandy, it was natural to kiss, touch, and discover. I was patient, and gradually his vigor returned.

At first, he tried to be part of my life. One hot Sunday, we decided to take Niki (eleven) and Matt (nine) sailing. We loaded his big van with life jackets, snacks, and picnic provisions, but my children didn't want any part of it.

"Why do we have to go?" they grumbled.

"It's too hot."

"I wanna play with my friends."

Then Matt proudly announced from the back seat, "Mom farts." I was not amused.

Phillip and I slid the boat off the trailer while my usually well-behaved children fussed and whined and refused to enjoy the cool water on that hot summer day. They were uncomfortable with my dating. Phillip was a stranger to them. They thought Anthony was "cool" and couldn't see why I'd rejected him.

So *certain* he never wanted children, Phillip had had a vasectomy when at twenty-two. After their performance, he *really didn't want* mine. That was the last time Phillip took the kids on the boat and the last time we were together when the kids were home.

Our relationship became independent of anything else in my life.

When Flint Chemicals cut back, I combed the want ads. I put together a résumé, simple as it was, and applied for a backroom desk job at an insurance company. During the interview, the managing director asked me to stand up and turn around. At first, I stared at him but finally did as he asked. I needed a job. He didn't hire me, of course; I had no experience, which he knew without ogling.

Finally, I found a retail position at the Casual Corner Store in Louisville, sixty miles away. The cost of baby-sitting, transportation, and wardrobe outweighed my paycheck, and bills piled up. Some nights, after the kids were in bed, I cried myself to sleep thinking, *I can't do this!* In the morning as I dressed, I remembered the days I hadn't gotten dressed at all. I couldn't go back. I *could* do this. I *had* to do this.

The night before Thanksgiving, I had responsibility for closing the store at 9 p.m. The kids were in Ohio with Paul. I'd promised Phillip I'd fix lamb for Thanksgiving dinner, so around nine-fifteen, I stopped at the Kroger store on the way out of Louisville. The parking lot was full, and I drove around until I found an empty spot in a far corner. I heard a loud pop and discovered a Coke bottle protruding from my right front tire. Being the independent woman that I was, it never occurred to me to ask for help or call AAA. As it started to rain, I confidently pulled the jack and little spare from the trunk. I knew how, but the lug nuts were stubborn. I cut both hands on the glass. My hair and suit jacket were soon drenched. "I give up," I said aloud. I found a payphone and called AAA, then waited in the car fuming until they arrived and changed the tire in an instant. By then, the parking lot was nearly deserted.

I reentered the store, but it looked as if piranhas had ravaged every aisle. I headed straight for the meat department. Trance-like, I stared into the cold, empty space where steaks and roasts once waited. There I stood—assistant store manager, mom, girlfriend—so disappointed by the lack of lamb that I began to cry. Mud and blood stained my face and hands. The husky, bald butcher took pity on me—alone, miserable, dripping rainwater in a puddle around my high-heeled shoes. He approached with a wad of paper towels and asked, "What happened?"

He helped wipe the mud, blood, and tears from my hands and face while I tried to explain. "I ... I ... I had a flat tire ... and it started raining ... and I couldn't get the lug nuts off ... and I promised my boyfriend I'd fix lamb tomorrow ... and it's all gone and I don't know what I'll fix and there's nothing left in the store and ... what will I do for Thanksgiving dinner?" Crying was not my style, but clearly, I was not myself.

I became the butcher's holiday project. He said, "Wait here." He walked into a giant cooler and retrieved a small lamb roast. Putting it into my basket he said, "I saved this for myself, but you need it more than I do." He led me to the produce department where he selected a clove of garlic. "Slice this into small slivers, poke holes in the lamb with the point of a sharp knife, and put the slivers inside. Do as much as you like. Set your oven temperature at about three hundred degrees and cover the roast with a small tent of foil; don't seal it up. Let it cook all day. Your house will smell great, and your boyfriend will think you're a great cook." He must have thought I was twenty years old. Then he gathered green beans, carrots, and celery. Next, we went to the bakery where a plump woman in a strawberry-stained apron put two dinner rolls in a paper bag and two chocolate cupcakes into a Styrofoam container. There were no pumpkin pies. I didn't care.

"Thank you" seemed inadequate, but I told the butcher how much I appreciated his help, then paid for my precious groceries, and began the hour-and-a-half drive home.

I called Phillip when I got there. He was dozing on his sofa but offered to bring over some brandy when I told my story. I met him at the door, freshly showered, with wet hair and no make-up, in my blue bathrobe and fuzzy pink slippers. He half-filled two small brandy snifters and placed them over glasses of hot water. As I sipped, he gently taped Band Aids over my cut palms. I'd never experienced such natural kindness, and quickly forgot the childish flat-tire trauma. I was transported back to contented days on the farm and realized I had happy times ahead of me. I fell asleep in his arms.

In the morning, Phillip carried in extra logs while I started a fire. In our bathrobes, we drank hot coffee, ate the cinnamon rolls he had brought, and sat on the floor by the fire. Just before noon, we began to prepare our Thanksgiving feast. Together we snapped the beans for steaming, cleaned and peeled the carrots and celery for dipping, and wrapped the rolls in foil. He sliced the garlic while I poked holes in the meat. With our heads together, as if performing delicate surgery, we carefully inserted garlic slivers into the roast.

As the butcher predicted, the house soon filled with the smell of contentment. We spent the afternoon reading novels, listening to classical music, and cuddling by the fire.

I didn't even ponder those Thanksgiving dinners I'd prepared alone in the kitchen when I was married. Those difficult times when I held a child on one hip and entertained the other in a highchair while I basted turkey, mashed potatoes, and listened to football blast on the TV in the family room. This was far more civilized.

Fulfilled as a woman, I banished all real-life challenges.

Ruth, my attorney, phoned in January 1984. "You've talked about moving to Seattle. Are you serious enough to sell your house? I have some new clients that might be interested."

"I'll sell it if the offer's right," I said.

In that moment, my life changed—again.

I met with the buyers, agreed on a price 100 percent more than I'd paid, and Ruth did the paperwork.

Paul went ballistic. "You can't take my kids out of state!" he shouted over the phone. "I'll put a stop to this!"

"I already discussed it with Ruth," I told him. "Remember that section of the parenting agreement you wrote so you could go back to Michigan? You did a great job, and it applies to me too."

The kids and I traded Kentucky's brown winter landscape for the emerald promise of Seattle. He had no choice.

I gave two weeks notice at Casual Corner. "I've sold my house, and we're moving to Seattle," I told the twenty-something store manager.

She'd lived with her parents all of her life and behaved like a spoiled child. "Where will you stay until you go?"

I didn't try to explain. I was SO glad to be leaving.

I had no idea what I would do for a living in Seattle, but I continued to visualize the suit and briefcase and prepared to dress for success. I bought three suits, three blouses, and a two-piece red silk dress using my discount before I left Casual Corner. All the pieces were interchangeable.

I had made the decision to move to Seattle but still had questions to answer.

Should the kids stay with Paul and fly out after I found a house?

I was concerned that he would never send them.

Should I ship the car with the furniture and fly out with the kids?

If we flew, the kids wouldn't understand how far away they were or the magnitude of the adventure.

I decided on a road trip. Four weeks later, the Bekins moving van backed up the driveway. Two men loaded my furniture and boxes. A new sense of adventure softened my terror.

The night before we left, the kids stayed with Paul, and I spent the night with Phillip. He took me for a lobster dinner in Louisville, and I wore my new red dress. The soft touch of silk on my skin and the heat of his body next to me in the little green Alfa made the trip erotic. After dinner, we couldn't wait to get back to his apartment.

The next morning, I waved from the open window at the end of his street.

He watched me drive away. I didn't cry. Too young, naïve, and probably too emotionally impaired to fully appreciate his patience and love, I was inadvertently callous. So focused on my independence, I sublimated emotions that might have hindered my escape from Kentucky.

Matt, Niki, Cylon—Niki's dog—and I headed for Seattle on Interstate 80. I'd traded in the Oldsmobile for a Subaru sedan with a stick shift shortly after I got the job at Flink Chemicals. I think I did it just because Paul said I couldn't.

"It's got a standard shift, you idiot, you can't drive that!"

"Oh, yes, I can." And I did.

The trip would have made a great Subaru commercial. The overloaded little blue car drove easily through twenty inches of snow in Nebraska, passing jack-knifed semi-trucks with their goods strewn on the median. The exits remained unplowed so I kept driving through the deep snow.

As we loaded our overnight bags to leave a motel near Salt Lake City, Utah, one morning, Cylon escaped into the shrubbery.

"Here, Cy! Here, Cy!" Niki called frantically. "Cy, come back!" Big tears formed in her eyes and trickled down her cheeks. This move was traumatic enough without losing her beloved best friend. Cy was a forty-five-pound, grey-and-black keyshound. Paul would not allow neutering, so the dog was adventurous. After two hours of calling and searching, I was considering another night in the motel when Cy came bounding out of a small ravine. He was dirty, wet, smelly, and very happy with his little runabout. Niki hugged him hard, put his leash back on, and pulled him into the back seat. We headed for Idaho with the windows open to clear the wet-dog smell.

Soon, storm clouds obscured the mountains. A strong wind whipped a floury dust over the road, obscuring all but taillights. The driver ahead touched his brakes and spun into the ditch but the road looked clear. I'd never heard of black ice. After driving only two hours that day, my shoulders were stiff and my fingers numb from clutching the steering wheel. During lunch in a steamy dark diner, I heard a man say he'd been driving south when he watched several cars follow each other off the side of the mountain. I was glad to be eating a stale sandwich and drinking watery Maxwell House. We checked into the small motel next door.

In the Blue Mountains of Oregon, I braved another snowstorm. Signs by the road said "chains required," but I had no idea what that meant and drove on. The sun came out, and the peaks glowed. If Niki hadn't taken photos out the window, however, I would have totally missed those gorgeous mountains. I was focused on driving.

Before we'd left Kentucky, Kali had offered to find us a rental house. I called several times from the road but never talked to her. When we drove into Bellevue, I still didn't know if she had followed through. I called her from a pay phone at a gas station. She gave me directions to a real estate office in Bellevue, just east of Seattle. "Ask for Sheila," she said. "You can sign the paperwork, and Sheila will give you the key."

"Thanks for helping us," I said. Then I thought, *I hope finding a job will be as painless.*

"I'll pick up something for dinner and stop by," she said. "I have the address. I'll be there at five."

I followed Shelia's directions and found the house at the end of a cul-de-sac. Driving into the carport, I noticed that the flowering cherry tree in the front yard was about to bloom.

I'd endured harsh winter and arrived at spring.

We entered the ranch-style, fifteen-hundred-square-foot house. A see-through fireplace divided the living room and kitchen. An unusual shade of violet covered the walls of Niki's room. She thought it was great, even though it would clash terribly with her old bedspread. Matt's room was so small his twin bed would touch the walls at the head and foot, but there was room for his dresser and a box of toys. Inspecting what would be my room, I realized that my queen-size bed would just fit. I planned to put my dresser in the hall by the bathroom, which was smelly and dark.

I found an old vacuum in the hall closet, and Niki began vacuuming while Matt carried in our luggage. Then I drove to a nearby Red Apple grocery store for cleaning supplies. I cleaned the bathroom, and Matt cleaned the empty refrigerator. We spread our sleeping bags on the carpet in our rooms and prepared to spend our first night in the Seattle suburbs.

At six-fifteen, Kali knocked on the door. I was so busy cleaning I didn't notice how late she was. She held her two-year-old son on her hip, and her pregnancy was obviously near term. In the other hand, she balanced a bake-at-home pizza box. In those days, you needed a cookie sheet for bake-at-home pizza, but mine was on a truck somewhere between Bellevue and Kentucky. I went back to the store for paper plates and plastic forks while smoke billowed from the oven.

That Monday Niki enrolled at Tillicum Middle School, within walking distance of our rental home, and began to make friends, but it wasn't easy for her. In Kentucky, she'd been a beautiful princess, shining like a star among the other girls her age. In Bellevue, she was just another pretty girl.

Matt's school experience in Kentucky had been the opposite. He always seemed sad. "Did you have a bad day at school?" I'd ask.

"I wish there was someone here like me," he'd say. I knew what he meant. Emotionally, he was at grade level, but his advanced cognitive capabilities far exceeded those of his schoolmates.

I'd inquired about an enrichment program, but the principal in Flint had said, "The smart kids will do fine in the world, but the handicapped kids need help." He funded remedial classrooms with a one-to-one student-teacher ratio.

His attitude was so annoying I pushed back. "But some of the handicapped kids will never learn to read or even learn their colors. Kids like Matt will become the breadwinners who pay taxes to support them. Don't they deserve funding?" My politically incorrect opinions got me nowhere, even if I was PTA president.

I bought books and games to enrich Matt's elementary studies as much as I could and waited for my chance to escape.

In Bellevue, I asked a school official to test my son before I enrolled him in the neighborhood elementary school. "Just enroll him. We'll test later. Every mother thinks her child is gifted." His eyes rolled up, and my determination strengthened.

"He belongs in a special class," I argued. "I moved clear across the country to get this kid an education, and I'm not going to enroll him until you test him." I didn't until they did. As I suspected, he was in the ninety-ninth percentile of kids his age in math, science, and social studies even after four years in the Kentucky school system. He took a bus to Stevens Elementary and enjoyed the genius of Betty Skibo. She had an uncanny sense for each of her sixth grade students and gave them an abundance of intellectual stimulation. During an astronomy project, Matt's class arranged to name a star Skibo after their teacher. No longer an anomaly, he flourished.

That spring, when school was out, I put Matt and Niki on a plane to Kentucky to spend the summer with Paul. He called to let me know they'd arrived safely and that he would not be sending a child-support check while they were with him for the summer. I didn't get angry. I asked, "Should I rent their rooms or move for the summer? I don't need the space for myself. What do you suggest?" He had no answers.

I called Ruth, and she called Paul. "We can divide the annual child support into nine or ten payments if you like," she told him, "but the annual amount can not be reduced."

The checks arrived on time.

When they came back in August, my children had a new appreciation for their mother and a deeper understanding of their father's idiosyncrasies.

"Wow, fruit!" Matt said when he saw a bowl of bananas and apples on the table.

"Didn't you eat fruit at Dad's?" I asked.

"No, Dad says fresh fruit is too expensive," Niki said as she peeled a banana. "He bought canned fruit cocktail instead."

That night, when I tucked her into bed, Niki asked, "Why did you marry Dad? You don't seem anything alike."

"It's so complicated," I told my thirteen-year-old daughter. "I'm not sure I know myself. Maybe someday when you're older I can explain."

I went to bed and tried to read a book, but the book dropped to my lap. *What about this life* isn't *complicated?* I thought. While the kids had been at Paul's, I'd started a job, attended Chamber of Commerce after-hours events, read a book every week, and dated a little. Now that the kids were home, I would help with homework assignments and arrange for afterschool transportation to soccer practice. They'd be latchkey kids with three hours of unsupervised time, and I'd be distracted at work. Weekends would be filled with sleepovers and soccer games in the rain. I smiled. I was *so* glad they were *home.*

While they were away, I'd interviewed with every employment agency I could find, and took a job with a small placement firm, commission only. It would allow me to meet new people and learn about business in the community, but commissions were sparse. Representing the agency, I responded to a start-up telecommunications company's ad in the newspaper for a "Dynamic Customer Support Rep." I tried to get the listing, but they offered me a job instead. The same week, I heard from another company I'd applied to, Microsoft, but when their personnel office called, I'd already accepted the offer at McCaw Cellular Communications.

I started in January 1985, almost a year after we arrived in Seattle, and just in time. We'd been living on child support and equity from selling the house. I had ten dollars left in my account and five dollars in my wallet. It's odd that I wasn't more concerned, but I knew a job would materialize.

As a sales assistant, I delivered marketing collateral to stores in the greater Seattle area. Within four months, I was a sales manager and achieved 130 percent of my goal for the year. For the next three years, quotas increasing, I continued to overachieve.

My new friends were powerful women, mostly in sales. Jane, a commercial real estate agent, made over $200,000 a year when I happily brought home $20,000. Kara worked her way to sales VP for a telecom company and a $150,000 comp package. They both drove a Mercedes and wore Armani suits in dark colors, accented with bright silk blouses and Hermes scarves. I was in awe of them.

Lynda, the most interesting of my new friends, had a unique strategy. She used *Training* to compete in a male dominated world. A deceptively ditzy housewife, she'd caught her bank-executive husband in their bed with another woman. After the divorce, she began her job search. One of her husband's friends was a senior VP of a big bank and knew what a scoundrel her husband had been. She persuaded him to hire her as a sales rep. "I'll bring new business to the bank, I promise," she cooed, taking coy to a new level. Her base compensation was $10,000 a year, with 3 percent commission. If she brought in a million dollars of business, it would be worth it, he assumed.

Lynda could have doubled for Stephanie Powers, with brown, doe eyes, wavy, brown hair resting on her shoulders, and an impish smile that duped even the most experienced. She knew how to get what she wanted and deliberately became a lure for powerful businessmen. She never made a *cold* call. As a former bank executive's wife, she had known the movers and shakers. She'd call them to chat and then make an appointment. They warmly received her. She wore her skirts short, and when she sat down, men forgot the purpose of her visit. Her just-a-little-too-tight blouses stretched over her double Ds, making men become foolish. Business executives followed her to the bank just as the children of Hamelin followed the Pied Piper to the German cave. She made over $300,000 the first year. The bank had never had a sales-MAN; they *really* didn't know what to do with a successful sales*woman*. They tried to renegotiate her commission structure the second year, but she'd developed a reputation for getting business. If they lost her, she'd go to a competitor. Eventually, she met a man and moved out of town.

Meanwhile I was selling cellular phones and service. It wasn't easy. The phones weighed twenty-five pounds and cost fifteen hundred dollars. Most people in 1985 couldn't imagine why they would need a car phone. I didn't have the contacts Lynda had, and I was a lot more conservative. "I will not become a sales slut," I solemnly vowed. I wore fashionable dark suits with straight skirts and high heels. My long legs got me in doors that male colleagues couldn't penetrate, but my blouses fit properly. To camouflage my bust line, I wore scarves that looked dangerously similar to a man's tie.

I developed a passion for individual achievement, unnatural for a woman, some people thought. I needed the paycheck. A sales position paid me for what I sold, regardless of my gender, and provided a scoreboard to measure my success.

During one appointment, a man named Frank kept staring at my chest, trying to see around my scarf. Finally, he said, "Are you wearing a plaid bra?" Not sure what he really wanted, I kept the price high and closed the deal without compromise.

I called on a pair of commercial real estate tycoons, Saul and Elias, in their top floor office in a Bellevue high-rise. I stood by the huge walnut conference table, opened my leather briefcase, and the men listened to my presentation. I tried not to stare at Mt. Rainier in the distance. They expected me to drop the price of the equipment, and I refused. "I'm sorry, this is as low as we can go," I said.

"What's your problem? You wearin' a jock strap?" said Saul, a short bald man with a small chin, beady eyes, and potbelly. While hoping my internal anger didn't interfere with getting their business, I proceeded with the sales call as though men regularly asked me this question. Pleasantly smiling down at the little man, I closed the deal for four phones.

chapter twelve

*T*hat first summer in Seattle, I took a break from job hunting when Phillip visited and the kids were in Kentucky. He rented a forty-foot powerboat to explore the San Juan Islands. His old friends, Steve and Linda, joined us. We started each foggy morning with a Bloody Mary, then lounged and fished during cloudy afternoons. The Northwest fish were as elusive as the sun, but I barely noticed. One afternoon we watched Orcas breach and crash back into Puget Sound. I wondered if the whales were escaping the confines of their environment or jumping for joy. I could identify with both.

The next summer, Phillip transferred to New Jersey, and I visited him there. We sailed his twenty-seven-foot Jeanneau, the *Mandala II*, in New York Harbor to participate in the 1986 Liberty Celebration. He invited another couple to join us, Jacques and Adele. Jacques worked in Phillip's office in France, and English was difficult for him. Adele spoke almost no English.

We were among the six million mesmerized spectators as the parade of ships and yachts passed by, including thirty-three massive naval vessels from fourteen countries. Phillip was awestruck as twenty-two Tall Ships with square white sails passed in review. As the sunset faded, a thirty-minute, two-million-dollar fireworks display erupted from thirty barges and building tops to overwhelm the New York skyline. The Statue of Liberty shone in the glare of exploding rockets while the Boston Pops Orchestra inspired spectators with the "Star Spangled Banner." Conversation was unnecessary.

With a smell of sulfur thick in the air, we waited for three hours among thousands of other boats and yachts to follow the tide out of the harbor. We drank red wine, compliments of Jacques and Adele, and enjoyed an assortment of meats, cheeses, bread, and fruit that Phillip had bought at a City Island deli.

Dim light tinted the still water as we slid toward Phillip's moorage in City Island Harbor. In spite of Jacques watching for anchor lights from the bow, our prop tangled on the anchor line of a wooden ketch. Until my eyes adjusted, I could see only white underwear bouncing about a pristine deck. The African captain was literally hopping mad. When he jumped, his knees nearly touched ears. The man shouted in an accent that sounded English to me. "You imbecile! I sailed from Africa without incident and kept away from the goddamn Liberty Celebration to avoid such incompetence." Phillip was very apologetic. We had breached a sailor's code. In the galley, Phillip found a pair of pliers attached to a cord. He tied the cord to his wrist and jumped into the inky saltwater. He came up for air several times and eventually untangled the line. Once the African was certain that his anchor was in its proper position, we continued a few more yards to Phillip's moorage. Without changing into dry clothes, Phillip took Jacques and Adele to the dock in the dinghy, and I fell asleep in the captain's quarters. He returned just as sun broke the horizon.

Phillip and I enjoyed each other on trips but continued our separate lives. I was busy with teenaged children and building my career while he sailed progressively bigger boats and counted the years until retirement.

"Will you meet me in London?" I asked on the phone.

Sarcastically he replied, "Sure, Marcia, I'll meet you in London!" waiting for the rest of the joke.

"No, I mean it! I won Circle of Excellence and a trip for two to London. If you can join me, I'll send the tickets." We planned to extend the trip in Europe with a train tour through Holland and France, his treat.

I waited for Phillip in the lobby of the Grosvenor Hotel across from Hyde Park in London, idly admiring a display of historic teapots. A very handsome American man with a full head of wavy brown hair sidled up. "Hi," he said in a captivating voice. "The English do like their tea." We chatted for a few minutes. He mesmerized me with his charisma, hypnotized me with his charm.

Who is this guy? When I looked straight into his eyes, I realized it was Gary Hart, the Colorado senator. He had just withdrawn as a Democratic candidate in the 1988 campaign for president of the United States after lying about an extramarital affair with Donna Rice. He could have triumphed over George H. W. Bush, and his liberal politics would have led the world in a much different direction, but he was forced to resign because he'd lied.

Charisma gives men power to move people. It also gives them a special dynamic in their relationships with women. After our short conversation, I understood how such men can easily abuse that power and make women their toys. Donna Rice's modeling career soared after the scandal, but she was still his toy, *just a girl*. She became well known for screwing a powerful politician and married man. He was intelligent, handsome, but way too smooth and overly polished for my taste.

I didn't let on that I knew who he was and excused myself when I saw Phillip standing with his luggage by the big revolving door. I didn't know how long he'd been standing there. Phillip gave me a big hug, "Well, I'm about as welcome as a root canal," he said. "When I saw you talking to Gary Hart, I didn't wanna interrupt. He likes blondes, ya know." I led Phillip to our room and provided reassurance before dinner.

McCaw Cellular Communications paid all expenses while we explored London: Westminster Abbey, Tower of London, Harrods, Buckingham Palace, St. Paul's Cathedral, Soho, the stage production of *Chess*, and many double-decker bus rides. The morning before our flight to Amsterdam, we ate an early lunch at a street café near Chiswick Pier.

"We should sit down for a while," Phillip said.

"Why? If we eat quickly, we can see the boats before we catch a cab to the airport."

"Marcia, if you don't rest, you're likely to faint before departure time. You look exhausted."

"Now that you mention it, I am a little dizzy."

After lunch, we hailed a taxi to the airport.

British Air was having a special promotion, so our round-trip tickets to Amsterdam were free. Phillip had reserved a quiet room with clean, cot-like twin beds. Most of the old hotels in Europe didn't have private baths, but our room had a huge, freestanding, footed tub. He was right; I was exhausted from our attempt to absorb London in four days. Phillip left me, submerged in hot water and bubbles up to my chin while I tried to seal the memories.

He returned thirty minutes later with a basket of huge, ripe strawberries, cold champagne, and paper cups. I added hot water as he climbed into the tub with me. We lingered with entwined legs, sharing the bubbly champagne and fruit. The sweet treat that followed was even more delicious, and I slept soundly, completely content.

From Amsterdam, we traveled by train through the brilliant tulip fields of Holland and rolling French countryside to Paris. April in Paris. Every morning, we walked for hours through blossom-scented spring air then stopped for croissants and cheese at a street café. Our boutique hotel on la Rue Bonaparte had a tall, double window that we left ajar. Before I opened my eyes one morning, I felt a cool, coffee-scented breeze on my face and smelled pastry baking. Then a child's voice:

> *Frère Jacques, Frère Jacques,*
> *Dormez-vous? Dormez-vous?*
> *Sonnez les matines, Sonnez les matines.*
> *Ding, daing, dong. Ding, daing, dong.*

A familiar song I'd sung as a child in Ohio. I giggled when I realized the child was singing in his native tongue, and I had no idea what the words meant.

We were first in queue at the Musée du Louvre with a plan to beat the crowd to da Vinci's *Mona Lisa*. The surrounding canvases dwarfed the small painting, but its enormous power drew me closer. Clearly, da Vinci had applied more than paint to that canvas. I lost track of time as its energy fed my inner Self. I could feel the heat of my spiritual embers ready to ignite, but too soon, reality summoned.

Within a few months, I was promoted to regional training manager. Before taking on the new challenge, I discussed it with Niki and Matt. "I'll need to travel a week or so every month. Can you help a little more around here when I'm on the road?" They were supportive and promised to help with household chores. Niki was sixteen and driving. She ran errands and brought Matt, fourteen, home from football practice. It went well for the next year. They seemed to thrive on the responsibility and trust. They didn't know that the neighbors kept a close eye on them.

I taught a two-and-a-half-day Professional Sales Skills seminar for twelve, eager new-hires in Oklahoma. Randy, the regional president, came into the conference room late on the second day to see how we were doing. I smiled as the participants reported their excitement. When my students left the room, Randy said, "We're having dinner tonight at the Hyatt across the street where you're staying. Would you like to join us?"

I had no idea who "we" were but said, "Sure. What time should I meet you?"

"I have a few things to finish up here. How's six-thirty?" he said.

When I stepped off the elevator at 6:25, Randy was waiting. The server led us to a table for four. "Who's joining us?" I said.

"No one; I wanted to be alone with you," he responded in what *could* be considered a professional tone.

I didn't want to assume the worst. Gray highlights streaked the tall, handsome man's dark hair. He was married and about ten years older than I. "Well, the classes have gone very well. Jennifer seems to be catching on quickly, and her experience in retail is helpful. Chuck will need a little more help, but I think he'll be a pretty good sales guy." I wanted to keep talking until we finished dinner.

"Great, great," he interrupted. "How about you? Do you like teaching the classes?"

"Oh, yes," I gushed, nervous now, his inappropriate thoughts clearly reflected in his eyes. "The sales guys are always so eager to learn, and my background as a sales rep is really helpful … blah, blah, blah …" Passionately, I chattered about teaching sales skills as if I could eliminate world hunger.

His legs came around mine under the table, and he reached across to take my hands. I quickly scooped up my napkin and used both hands to hold it in my lap. Then he slid around the table to the chair next to me and leaned in close.

"You are the most beautiful woman I've ever met," he whispered. *Yeah, right!* I thought.

"I wanted you the first time I saw you." He leaned back. "That's why I requested a sales training class. Let's finish our wine and go up to your room. Maybe you can teach me a few new skills."

Ick, ick, ick. I wanted to make a scene and not show up for class in the morning, but he was an RP (regional president) with power to ruin my career. In a milky voice that didn't sound like me, I said, "Randy, you are a very attractive man, but I'm involved in a serious relationship and would feel just terrible if I compromised his trust," batting my eyelashes more than necessary. "I hope you understand."

Bullshit! I didn't have a boyfriend, and it galled me that I had to lie to this creep. He was surprised. Apparently, he normally got what he wanted. I stood. "Now, if you'll excuse me, I need to call my children." I slid behind him and tried not to break into a run before I made it to the elevator.

I called my manager on his cell phone. "Hi, John, it's Marcia. I just had a weird experience I want to report to you. It's sort of embarrassing, but I think you should hear about it in case there are repercussions."

"One of those Okies give ya a hard time?" he said, assuming that a student had been difficult in class.

"Well, sort of." I explained the entire evening from the invitation in the conference room to my hasty retreat from the dining room. John was silent. I went on. "It sounds like Randy usually gets his way down here," I said. "I'm not trying to get him in trouble, and I won't press charges or sue or anything. I just don't want him reporting that I was insubordinate. Oh, and John, I'd rather not do any more training in Oklahoma—if ya don't mind."

"Of course, I understand," he said in a flat tone. I couldn't tell what he was thinking. I held my breath. Then he said, "That bastard." He believed me. I could breathe again.

"I have to agree," I said. "I'll finish the class in the morning. My flight leaves around three. I'll see you Monday."

John and I discussed it briefly the next week. I doubt that anyone spoke to Randy, but I never went back to the Oklahoma market. I was sure I wasn't the only woman he harassed, and I was sure that women slept with him to keep their jobs. Years later, I felt guilty that I hadn't stood up for the women in his control, but at the time, I still lacked the strength and knowledge to support my business sisters. I'd avoided anything that reeked of womanhood to keep a well-paying job in a male-dominated industry. Although I didn't realize it at the time, I'd rejected femininity along with *Training* in order to gain financial security.

My career blossomed. I was promoted to marketing manager then corporate marketing director. At the corporate office, we dressed more casually. I carried a leather briefcase and drove a new Honda. Men at the conference table listened to me while I fought flashbacks of the original vision of this career during my first trip to Seattle.

We sat around the conference table, the men and I, discussing issues *de jour*. The men had their own vocabulary. "That's mice nuts" meant something was trivial. "A cold douche" meant something was shocking. "Hung up in your underwear" was one of my favorites. I guess it meant overly concerned with details, but the metaphor was vulgar if I thought about it—so I didn't.

I'd earned the right to sit at their table in spite of my girl-ness. Voicing displeasure with their euphemisms would have emphasized gender differences. Maintaining a male-like "disguise" protected my career, if only by my tolerance of their behavior. I valued my job more than I detested their treatment of women.

Occasionally I made business trips to the East Coast and met Phillip, at least for a drink, sometimes overnight. On one occasion I called to tell him I'd be in New York, but he said, "Can't talk now; call ya right back." About an hour later, as I drove the I-90 bridge across Lake Washington, my cell phone rang.

"Hello," I said.

"I'm getting married!" he said, without preamble.

I managed to keep the car on the bridge while my vision blurred.

During phone conversations over the years, he'd often recounted a ballet performance or an opera he'd enjoyed, and I was sure he wasn't going out alone. The confirmed bachelor was getting married!

"What will she say when we go on trips together?" I said.

He laughed. I knew this was difficult for him.

"Congratulations. When's the wedding?" I said, trying to convince myself I was happy for him.

"Next month." I could barely hear him.

"Can I see you one last time?" I said. "Just for a drink?" We arranged to meet the following week at a bistro near my hotel in New York. After ordering a glass of Pinot Grigio, I handed him a blue Tiffany's box tied with white ribbon. Blue velvet fabric lining secured two crystal brandy snifters. I wondered if he remembered the night our relationship transformed from friends to lovers after my first taste of brandy.

I'd hoped our relationship would endure until the kids were grown and I'd quenched my thirst for independence. He had no way of knowing how I felt. Did she love him as much as I did? Until then, I was unaware how much I did love him.

We stayed in touch through Christmas cards and an occasional phone call. A few years later, planning a trip to the East Coast, I called him. He suggested that I have dinner at their new home in Philadelphia so I could meet his wife, Susan. I asked, "How will Susan feel about that?"

"We're over fifty! Susan had a life before me, and I had a life before her. Our past wasn't erased when we got married. You two have a lot in common. Anyway," he teased, "she'll be happy to meet the 'London woman.'" Apparently, they'd been dating before our trip to Europe.

Phillip met me at the train station in mid-afternoon on Friday, before Susan got home from work. We had time to catch up without feeling self-conscious. The energy between us was undeniable, but he loved his wife. When Susan joined us, Phillip was nervous, which I found comforting. She was as tall as Phillip, very thin, with dark-blond, curly hair, and an air of confidence that comes with "family money."

Susan insisted I stay in their guest room, so I canceled my hotel reservation. Early Saturday morning, Phillip left to play golf while Susan and I ate breakfast together. She'd also been a corporate training manager, and we shared stories. I knew it would take a special woman to charm Phillip out of bachelorhood. She was perfect for him.

She asked me to join them overnight on their new sailboat. "We'll sail across to Baltimore on Sunday morning," she said. "You'll have plenty of time to catch a taxi and your flight back to Seattle."

I accepted.

She had errands to run so I spent the day sightseeing, alone. I made a plan to see as much as I could before we left for the boat. I started at the Historic Waterfront District and enjoyed the juxtaposition of diverse architecture, from ornate Victorian homes to sleek steel-and-glass skyscrapers. I walked past the Liberty Bell and wandered through Independence Hall, where our forefathers signed the Declaration of Independence and wrote the Constitution. I could feel the energetic vibration of history as I sat on a bench under ancient oak trees in Independence National Historical Park, watching tourists while I ate my hoagie.

I walked to the house where Betsy Ross made the first American flag and thought how Grandma would have enjoyed this part of our country.

During the long drive to their moorage on Chesapeake Bay, we ate a picnic dinner in the car. We arrived late, said good night, and I settled into the aft cabin, knowing that Susan and Phillip slept in the captain's quarters. I pushed the what-ifs from my mind, let the lapping water became a lullaby, and slept like an infant.

With Bloody Marys in hand, we set sail on Sunday morning. The cold wind whipped my hair, bit my cheeks, and smelled like the ocean. The clouds were low and dark, and I felt occasional raindrops. I couldn't have enjoyed it more on a sunny, warm day.

Susan had never sailed until she met Phillip. She soon realized, as I had years ago, that if she loved the man, she also had to love sailing. I watched as Phillip stood back and Susan took the wheel of the magnificent thirty-three-foot Pierson, named the *Great Mandala*.

We docked the boat and had hot soup and sandwiches in a small café by the marina in Baltimore. While Susan drank coffee and read the paper, Phillip walked me to the taxi station near the dock. We didn't speak. His hug was long and firm. He opened the taxi door, and I got in. I waved to him through the back window, then choked on heavy sobs all the way to the airport.

Monday morning, with swollen eyes and a latte, I stared at Lake Washington from my desk. It was surreal; less than twenty-four hours before, I'd been sailing the Chesapeake. Memories swirled like the cold Chesapeake wind.

Through Phillip, I discovered a woman could be respected and loved by a man. Phillip understood, enjoyed, and loved the soft, subservient, feminine side of me, so well trained to please him; but he also recognized and respected my hunger for knowledge, adventure, and independence. *What if we'd met after my kids were grown up, my career was established, and I'd recovered my Self? What if?*

chapter thirteen

I traveled a lot during Niki's high school years. We usually talked on the phone after dinner when I returned to my room. One night during her senior year, the phone rang at eleven o'clock in my Portland hotel room. I answered, "Hello?"

"Mom, we broke up," she sobbed. Then for an hour, she told me what a jerk her boyfriend, Rex, was. "He says I'm his girlfriend, and then he goes out with other girls!" Within days, they were "back together."

After their high school graduation, Rex followed a football scholarship to Central Washington, and Niki went to a small college in Kentucky, not far from Paul. It was a financial decision and had nothing to do with what was best for Niki's education. She qualified for in-state tuition because her dad lived there. Since he paid the bill, it was his choice.

With no career goal for motivation and her boyfriend in Ellensburg, Washington, she was soon back home. It was a difficult time for us. At nineteen, she struggled to grow up and find herself, separate from me, while I wrestled with encouraging her independence and keeping her close.

~ ~

My friend, Mary, hired Niki in her beauty shop. As the receptionist, Niki greeted clients, answered the phone, and swept the floors after each haircut. I came home from work early one afternoon to find Niki baking chocolate chip cookies. "You're home early. How was work?"

"I didn't feel like going today," she said.

"Why not? What did you tell Mary?"

"Oh, I didn't call. Tomorrow I'll tell her I was sick."

"Niki, she counts on you. You can't just not go to work. You can be sure tomorrow you won't have a job."

"You can call and tell her I was sick," she said.

"No, even if you call Mary yourself and apologize, she won't hire you back."

"Why won't you call her?"

"Niki, I don't work for Mary, you do—call her," I said.

She refused to make the call, stomped to her room, and slammed the door.

I called Mary and fell on my sword. "I'm so sorry. I don't know what to say. I guess my daughter has more growing up to do than I thought."

Niki blamed me for losing her job.

One evening Niki said, "I'm going to baby-sit for that weird woman from the gym so I'll probably spend the night." I was surprised. The "weird woman," Judy, was single and often didn't come home until morning. Sometimes men came home with Judy after a date, and one had made Niki uneasy. Niki and I had agreed that she wouldn't baby-sit for Judy again.

At noon the next day, I called home from the office, but Niki didn't answer. I got a strange feeling and tried repeatedly to call Judy's number but couldn't get an answer there either. I grew more and more concerned and finally left the office in Seattle around two in the after-noon. I knew vaguely where Judy lived in Kirkland so I drove down her street, thinking I might see Niki's car. Around four, I called again from my cell phone. "Hi, Judy, this is Marcia. Could I speak to Niki, please?" I asked.

"I haven't seen Niki in months," she told me.

"Oh, I'm sorry. I thought it was you she was baby-sitting for. Sorry to bother you."

I hung up then called several of Niki's friends and her boyfriend, Rex, "Is Niki with you?"

"She isn't here," Rex lied. "I haven't seen her."

"Well, if she calls, will you have her call me, please?"

"Sure," he said.

My imagination was an inferno of TV shows and news reports—with visions of Niki locked in Judy's basement or worse. I was considering calling the police when my phone rang.

"Hi, Mom, it's me," said my twenty-year-old daughter. "I'm with Rex in Ellensburg."

"I'm glad to know you're OK. I got worried when Judy said she hadn't seen you."

"You called her?" she said.

"Yes. We'll discuss this when you get home," I said, my irritation no secret.

A blizzard at Snoqualmie Pass on I-90 prevented her return the first day. Then her car broke down. Rex borrowed his coach's vehicle to go get her and arranged for a tow truck to deliver her car to a mechanic, at my expense. When we were finally together, Niki was spiteful.

"I didn't do anything wrong. I knew you wouldn't let me drive to Ellensburg, so I lied."

"You're right. That old Scirocco is unreliable, and who do you think has to pay the towing bill? On top of that, the tires are shot. You could have been killed!"

She rolled her eyes

"Niki, I love you, but this behavior has got to stop. You wouldn't treat a roommate your own age with this much disrespect." My daughter's beautiful blue eyes were defiant, but I maintained my resolve. "You can stay here until March first; then you'll have to go back to school or find your own place." That gave her six weeks to get her act together. Inadvertently, I'd been enabling her lack of responsibility. It was time for her to grow up.

As the deadline approached, Paul jumped at the opportunity to take control and save his daughter from "the independent bitch," as he not so fondly referred to me. No doubt, she told him I was evicting her for no reason. He paid for her apartment and gave her expense money, but her irresponsibility continued. She had a heart tattooed on her ankle with money I gave her for groceries and pawned my engagement ring. Later she told me, "You would have given it to me someday anyway."

At twenty-one years old, Niki decided to go back to college in Kentucky. Paul probably insisted. I didn't mention the missing engagement ring or the tattoo. What was done, was done. She was unhappy and floundering. I wanted to see her eyes sparkle again.

Two months after spring break, Niki and Rex announced they were getting married. At first, I thought it was another dodge of responsibility, but Niki told Kali about her pregnancy. Kali delighted in telling me.

Love, disappointment, frustration, fury, and joy swirled inside me. Soon I'd be a grandmother. I took two weeks of vacation to organize her June wedding and hoped that supporting Niki's decision would improve our relationship.

Niki and Rex had been friends since eighth grade. They'd hung out with a group of four boys and four girls then paired off junior year after prom. Niki confided in me only when Rex was being a teen-aged, hormonal jerk, so my understanding of their relationship was incomplete. I didn't know then how much they loved each other, but it was clear what had happened during spring break.

I called Paul. "We'll need to have a wedding. Are you willing to help pay for it?"

"Yeah, I guess so," he said. "I can't talk her out of it."

"I need a budget. What are you willing to spend?"

"Just do the best ya can."

I knew him too well. "No, really, tell me what you're willing to do. I'll pay the other half. I need a budget to work with." He refused. When he got nasty, I quit pushing.

Once Niki realized I would support her decision to marry Rex, the air between us seemed a little softer. My sister Lili was not so supportive, and neither was Paul. They both tried to dissuade Niki, suggesting she wait or consider adoption. What did they know about the love between Niki and Rex?

We spent days looking for a wedding dress and wandered into a bridal shop in Kirkland to look through a sale rack.

"Can I help you?" asked the round, middle-aged clerk.

"We're looking for a wedding dress," I said.

"Wonderful! When's the wedding?" she asked too sweetly.

"This month," I said as I sorted through the rack of dresses intended for mothers, aunts, and grandmothers.

"Ah-ha." She looked at Niki with disdain, and her voice grew sore. I wanted to turn my back and slam the door, but I saw a dress on the rack that might work. Niki tried it on while we endured the rudeness. A layer of ivory Alençon lace draped over a mid-calf, ivory, satin slip while the flowing dolman sleeves provided camouflage. It required alterations to fit properly, but it was in our price range. It took me three days to finish the alterations.

I reserved my condo community's clubhouse and mailed fifty inexpensive invitations. To decorate, I bought yards of cheap tulle and found two dozen bud vases for ten cents each at a discount store. The fresh flowers came from the wholesale market where Kali worked. A friend in the wine business offered a deal on wine and champagne. Niki and I made hors d'oeuvres and stored them in my small freezer. On the day of the wedding, Paul paid for three trays of food he told Niki to pick up at Larry's Market.

Rex was in place at the "altar" of our makeshift chapel. It was time to take my seat. I grasped Matt's bicep, trying not to cry. He looked so handsome and grownup in his rented suit. Suddenly the doors opened, and Kali and Mom hurried in. I was glad I hadn't known of their tardiness. My other siblings didn't attend. Matt quickly seated each of them, came back for me, and then took his place as a groomsman.

Walking down the aisle on Paul's arm, Niki's face glowed as she made eye contact with Rex. He looked surprisingly adult, but the muscular linebacker was a bucket of tears throughout the ceremony.

A week after the wedding, I sent Paul a detailed expense report, using an Excel spreadsheet attached to copies of receipts, and a short note asking for the half he had promised. A month went by so I called him.

"Did you get the report I sent?" I tried to sound emotionless.

"Yeah, I got it. You paid too goddamned much for that dress, and you went crazy on the goddamned decorations and flowers. I paid for the food; that's enough."

Some things never change.

Niki had to find her Self, and I had to let her. I'd tried so hard to avoid *Training* her the way I'd been trained. I'd bought both trucks and dolls when she was small, but she preferred the dolls. I'd tried to give her space to just *be*, but she saw that space as abandonment. I'd hoped she would follow in my footsteps and enjoy the doors that I'd fought so hard to open in the workplace, but ironically, she wanted to be a housewife.

chapter fourteen

On an unusually sunny Christmas Eve morning, I volunteered at the 1991 Forgotten Children's annual charity event. Hundreds convened at a warehouse in south Seattle to deliver toys, bicycles, and boxes of food to disadvantaged children. Some of us were dressed as elves with bright red lipstick dots on each cheek and red-and-white stripped knee socks. Others were dressed as Santa. A bank of helpers applied elf makeup, assisted with Santa costumes, assigned routes, and loaded toys and food onto the "sleighs" (a.k.a. trucks). From experience, the organizers knew that the contents and even the truck would be stolen if left unattended, so one team member never left the truck. Elf Stuart, leader of my group, was six-foot-two with reddish hair and a happy round face, with or without the red dots.

Stuart had belonged to the Forgotten Children organization for many years and had done this innumerable times, but I had no idea what the day would bring. I'd spent the last forty-plus years isolated from abject poverty, only vaguely aware that it existed in our country. I'd sold my *nice* house with a *nice* view and bought a *nice* condo when Matt had left for college that fall. My career allowed *nice* clothes, a *nice* car, *nice* furniture, *nice* friends. My life was *nice:* colorless, plain, and predictable.

On the first stop of our philanthropic adventure, a man urinated from a third floor window, and we walked into the street to avoid the splash. There was mud where grass should have grown. Residents had strewn trash, the paint was pealing, and the wood was rotting where a downspout should have been. While Santa and two other elves kept each family's children busy with toys from Santa's big bag, Stuart and I put food in the kitchens. We found cans of beer more often than cartons of milk or eggs.

Afterward, isolated in my Honda, I allowed feelings of gratitude. I knew how lucky I was. There'd been days in the not-so-distant past when I had only enough money to buy pasta, vegetables, and milk, but I never had to live like those unfortunate people. I said, "Thank you," to whatever guided me.

Our team of elves met at Anthony's Home Port for a quick lunch. We needed to create distance between the experience and our relatively luxurious Eastside homes and well-fed, happy families. Strangers when the day began, we elves had become friends. We exchanged business cards.

Stuart called after Christmas to ask me out for New Year's Eve. He picked me up in his restored 1966 silver Jaguar convertible. He was so proud of it I was put-off rather than impressed. The twang of country music filled the tiny interior. I preferred jazz or classical, but of course, I said nothing. He parked on the street in front of a Bellevue restaurant so he could keep an eye on the car throughout our seafood dinner. We watched the fireworks from top of Somerset Hill, and he left me with a peck on the cheek in my condo.

That first date with Stuart wasn't great, but dating in general was difficult for me. Switching to feminine behavior was complex and annoying. In my business life, I was becoming more and more man-like, and I functioned as both father and mother for my children. I felt like I needed to give Stuart another chance, so when he called a few days later and asked me to go skiing. I agreed. We drove to Stevens Pass in his SUV (the Jag never left the garage in bad weather). He'd been a ski instructor and on Ski Patrol for many years. I watched him float down the mountain while I struggled on the bunny slope on my rented skies. He was a patient teacher, and by evening, I was able to follow him down the steeper slopes.

One of our more glamorous dates was the Commodores' Ball, a black tie event held at the Museum of Flight. I didn't understand why he called himself a commodore. He didn't own a boat and had never served in the Navy, but it sounded like fun. I bought a floor-length, gold-and-black sequined gown at a consignment shop. It had a V-neck and a slit up the side—very sexy—but I felt like a child impersonating a lounge singer. After the event, I had the dress dry-cleaned and resold it at the consignment shop. I knew I would NEVER wear it again.

Steam rose into the cool air as we sipped chardonnay in the hot tub early one evening that summer while Niki and Matt were in Kentucky. We watched a hot-air balloon sweep the treetops. He said, "Let's go for a hot-air balloon ride some time."

"No thanks. I'm afraid of heights," I said. "I'd sit in the bottom of the basket with my eyes closed for the entire ride."

"Nonsense," he said.

A month later, he gave me tickets for a hot-air balloon ride. I felt ungrateful. We never used the tickets.

Once he noticed, "You never wear jewelry."

"I don't like to wear jewelry," I said. "Necklaces tickle my skin, gold makes me itch, and my neck is too short to look good in a necklace."

"Nonsense," he said. "Every woman loves jewelry."

He gave me a gold necklace for my birthday. A Chinese gold coin hung from a short chain. As he helped me do the clasp, he said, "See the panda? I know how you love 'em."

"Thank you, it's lovely." I hesitated. "Would you mind if I exchanged the chain for a longer one? I have such a short neck I'd wear it more often if the chain were longer." But I knew, even with a longer chain, I would wear it only when I was with him.

"Nonsense," he said. "It looks great." Again, I felt ungrateful.

For Christmas, he gave me an exquisite strand of pearls. The necklace was short enough to ride just above a crew-neck sweater. "You know how cute Dick's wife, Mary Ella, looks in her pearls. She wears 'em with everything. They look great, especially when she wears a sweatshirt." Then he added, "You wear sweatshirts all the time."

"Thank you." Again, I felt ungrateful. The pearls were expensive, and he had meant well.

In January, I tried to gather the nerve to end the relationship. I liked him, and we had fun together, but I knew it would never go any further—not that I was looking for a serious relationship. I just felt guilty. At the time I couldn't see that I'd escaped *Training* in my career but still let *Training* control my dating life.

When he came to the door that night, he carried a set of women's golf clubs and airline tickets to Hawaii. "Hey, pretty lady, we need to get away from this awful Seattle rain and play some golf," he said. "I made reservations at the Halekulani Hotel on Waikiki Beach."

What could I do? Golf wasn't my favorite, but I enjoyed being outdoors, and who wouldn't want to go to Hawaii for a weekend in January?

The following weekend, I sat on my deck drinking coffee and had a long discussion with myself. "He might be the best that ever comes along. What's your problem?" I asked.

"Yes, but, he doesn't listen to me," I replied.

"He loves to take care of you and give you expensive gifts," I said.

"Yes, but, he doesn't know who I really am," I replied.

"He loves you," I said.

"He loves who he wants me to be," I replied.

There never was a resolution. I kept having an almost wonderful time with hopes that my feelings would catch up.

chapter fifteen

My job managing the new national accounts team was as unsatisfying as the relationship with Stuart. "I miss the start-up stuff," I told a colleague in the employee lunchroom. "I get bored when everything's running smoothly."

"Did you see the Hong Kong posting?" she said.

"What Hong Kong posting?"

"We're part of a joint venture starting up a cellular network in Hong Kong. They're looking for cell site technicians, a customer service manager, marketing staff—everything," she said. "I can't go, but your experience would be perfect." Serendipity. My life would change again.

I contacted the Human Resources Department, interviewed with the project director, and within a month, I left for Hong Kong. Matt was a freshman at Colorado State, and Niki was married and living in Ellensburg. Except for Niki's pregnancy, the timing was perfect.

Stuart was surprisingly supportive. "It's only temporary, and I'll visit when I can."

As the airplane banked out of SeaTac, boats cut white wedges in the cobalt waters of Puget Sound, and the matching sky contrasted with snow-capped Mt. Olympus. I remembered the flight back to married life in Kentucky after my first visit to Seattle. It seemed like someone else's memory.

Sixteen hours after take-off, Hong Kong's brown polluted harbor, reflecting skyscraper lights, appeared in my little business-class porthole. I followed an Indian family from the plane through customs. The woman wore a yellow and blue sari, and her husband wore a blue turban. The couple behind me spoke German, and behind them, I heard Italian, Chinese, and other languages I couldn't identify. Military guards in khaki uniforms scrutinized the diverse crowd with Uzis held in both hands. I was glad to see my new boss, Brad, waiting on the other side of the customs counter, looking tall and American. He knew I'd be overwhelmed. A blast of humid, sour air assaulted us as Brad helped with my luggage and hailed a taxi.

He handed the driver a card with "New World Harbour View Hotel" written in English and Chinese. As the driver pulled away from the curb, Brad gave me a stack of cards. "Keep these in your purse; it's the best way to communicate with taxi drivers. They usually don't speak English. Even when they do, they act as if they don't understand and take you for a ride." I saw the driver glance at Brad in the rearview mirror. The cards included vendors and businesses I was likely to visit and shopping areas. "You can ask Janis to make cards for any place you want to go."

"Who's Janis?"

"Janis is your secretary. Don't call her an 'admin' or 'executive assistant'; 'secretary' is a better title," Brad told me. I looked out the window and noticed we'd moved only a few feet. In this traffic, it would take ninety minutes or more to navigate twenty-five miles through the tunnel and over the maze of freeways to the hotel on the opposite side of the harbor.

The New World Harbour View Hotel shared restaurants and a swimming pool with the Grand Hyatt in Wan Chi. When I checked in, the TV was on, and the screen welcomed me—Marcia Breece—to the New World Harbour View. I took a photo of the TV screen.

The next morning, I realized I could see the entire harbor from my room. A fisherman in a sampan held a long pole over a nuclear-looking green slick, and I decided I wouldn't eat fish during my stay. The *Star Ferry* carried commuters from Hong Kong Island to Kowloon where a huge modern cruise ship docked. It was difficult to get dressed and leave the view from the room, but adventures awaited.

I stopped in the lobby for coffee and a scone, then walked across the sky bridge to take the elevator to the forty-eighth floor of the Sun Hung Kai Center, as Brad had directed. I was happy to avoid taxi drivers, busy streets, and humid, acrid air. My first day of work in a foreign country would be challenging enough. I soon discovered that my new office also had a view of the harbor. I rearranged the desk so that the view was on the side rather than at my back.

I was concerned that members of the expatriate team as well as the local staff might not want a woman on the team. As it turned out, I was not the only American woman. Janet would be in charge of billing. She'd been living and working with her husband in Karachi, Pakistan. One morning their driver was gunned down while he stood in their driveway. She quit her job and came to live in Hong Kong, where her son attended the American School. Her husband joined them on weekends until he finished his contract.

We were all "gui-lo"—white-devil, foreigner—including George, an African American sales manager from Kansas. We became an expat family, eating most meals together and working from nine in the morning to eight at night weekdays and nine to one on Saturday. Our staff of locals didn't leave the office until we did. One afternoon, we left around four for an off-site meeting. Brad waved to the receptionist, "See ya later." She waited until nine that night, thinking we would be back *later* that day.

Communication continued to be an issue. When I asked, "Is the report finished?"

Wu responded, "Yes."

But when I asked to see the report, Wu replied, "It not finish." I discovered "yes" meant "I heard you."

After a Saturday morning in the office, Brad and I took the MTR (under the harbor) to Mong Kok to find computer parts. During our search, we discovered the famous Mong Kok Bird Market. Thousands of exquisite cages held talking mynas, finches of every color, bright green parrots, multicolored macaws, lovebirds, and colorful species I couldn't identify. We watched leathery, bent Chinese men interlace dark, aged bamboo into the intricate birdcages and then attach tiny blue-and-white porcelain bowls, just like the human-sized ones in my flat. I thought of Gramps in the woods near Columbus, Ohio, where he'd watched familiar red cardinals, goldfinches, and great horned owls, uncaged and free.

To return, we boarded the *Star Ferry* at Tsim Sha Tusi and crossed Victoria Harbour to the Central District, then walked toward Wan Chi. We were hungry for familiar food and found a restaurant on Spring Garden Lane. We stared at the menu of discolored greasy photos posted on the wall and decided the bowl of steamed rice and roasted chicken looked normal. I watched the Hong Kongese patrons take bites with chopsticks, chew with open mouths, and spit the debris directly onto the table, although the restaurant provided a big spoon for this purpose. I attempted to capture a bite of rice with chopsticks but dropped every grain on the way to my mouth. I awkwardly seized a bite of chicken only to discover the need to liberate meat from the bone. Lips tightly closed, I wheedled each bite then discretely spit the remains onto the big spoon and tried to find a way to conceal the debris. I must have looked as strange to the Hong Kongese as they did to me.

On my birthday, the local staff brought a special treat to me—chicken feet cooked in soy sauce. While Brad ran the video camera, I tried to eat them. Nothing I had ever tasted compared to the claws, gristle, and soy sauce. As the camera rolled, I kept smiling and nodding as though chicken feet were delicious.

Our favorite restaurant was La Traverna on Icehouse in the Central District. The air smelled of tomatoes and garlic, and stained Italian prints in wide gold-leafed frames covered the walls. Hundreds of dusty Chianti bottles hung overhead. A diminutive Thai singer with a guitar that hid half of his body strolled among tightly placed tables. He sang Elvis, Neil Diamond, and John Denver songs in perfect English. Brad bet Jamie $500 in Hong Kong currency (about $65 USD) that the singer wouldn't know any Patsy Klein songs. When Brad made the request, we realized the singer didn't speak English, but he understood "Patsy Kline" and belted out "Crazy" with so much emotion tears welled in my eyes. Brad paid Jamie, and he gave the surprised singer his winnings.

Frank the Swede—that's what we called him—was a six-foot-two technician from Stockholm with huge shoulders, black hair, and egotistical but stunning ladies-love-me brown eyes. He looked more Italian than Swedish and never went back to his flat alone after dinner. He met plenty of women willing to entertain him. I didn't see the attraction except for his enchanting Swedish accent.

One morning, Frank the Swede and Jamie, the tech from Portland, Oregon, offered to take me to a cell site they were building in Sheckou. They were building the cellular network all over Hong Kong, but they knew this site would be the most interesting to me. I jumped at the chance to get out of the office and see more of Hong Kong Island, even if it meant working until ten at night. The cell site was on the roof of a family's home, a concrete structure unlike any house I'd ever seen. The bare overhead fluorescent tube cast an eerie green light in the tiny space where the women cooked. Frank could reach from wall to wall. The rough concrete counter held a blue plastic bucket full of dirty water, a green plastic tub stacked with dirty rice bowls and chopsticks, and a hot plate attached to a gas canister under the counter. There was no faucet and no sink. I peeked into the doorless bathroom where a water closet hung over a ceramic hole in the floor. No doubt it drained directly into the sea. Frank had trouble navigating the narrow, winding concrete stairs to the roof; he was too tall and his shoulders too wide. The sun was bright, but a salty breeze off the South China Sea cooled the air, very different from the bitter-smelling side of the island where we lived.

For lunch, we walked through deep, dry sand to a Thai restaurant on a beach near Sheckou. It had a roof to shelter its customers but no walls except for the one blocking the view of the kitchen. Jamie peeked behind the wall and suggested that I stay on my stool if I didn't want to lose my appetite. There were no sanitation standards, but I never got sick eating at places like that one.

With my feet buried in the sand, I thought, *Is this really me, the girl from Ohio, eating spicy Thai food with two male colleagues I barely know, and my eyes squinting from the reflection off the South China Sea?* I felt independent and grown-up. *It's about time,* I thought.

To burn restaurant calories and relieve stress, I worked out in the hotel gym almost every morning. MTV blasted Annie Lennox, "Walking on Broken Glass," and Sinead O'Connor's "Nothing Compares 2 U."

Foreigners like me occupied the new Precor equipment, making me feel at home for an hour. Even the sweat smelled familiar.

On weekends, I explored the streets and alleys of Hong Kong with my camera—Wan Chi, Mong Kok, Causeway Bay, Aberdeen, Stanley, Central, streets lined with herbal medicines, dishes, clothes, cheap trinkets, and two-hundred-year-old antiques.

In November, Stuart's carry-on luggage was a picnic cooler full of vacuum-sealed roasted turkey, stuffing, mashed potatoes, and gravy. Our expat kitchens were extremely small with miniature appliances, including a microwave but no oven. Stuart carefully orchestrated the meal. George took the mashed potatoes to warm in his microwave. Brad warmed the gravy. Sweet potatoes were assigned to Jamie. Don and his wife, Julie, warmed the stuffing. I warmed the turkey. Everyone brought a plate and glass from his or her own flat. All fourteen members of our expat family, including the Swedes and Brits, sat shoulder to shoulder on the floor of my tiny apartment, grateful for a rare taste of familiar food and an unexpected Thanksgiving feast.

Stuart visited again on Valentine's Day. Together we spent three cold, rainy days in Beijing. We hired a guide—he told us to call him Bob—for the three days. When he took us to the Great Wall, I was amazed to see new cell sites popping up like noxious weeds. The lives of Chinese people would change once communications became available in remote areas near the wall.

We climbed the stone steps, worn smooth and concave by two thousand years of visitors. I could feel the energy of those travelers, their hopes, dreams, and fears. But I wasn't ready to acknowledge their presence.

Bob sat in front with the driver as we rode back to the hotel that night. We passed a man sitting high on a cart piled with sticks, pulled by a donkey.

I asked Bob, "What are the sticks for?"

"Cooking, of course," he replied. Then he twisted in his seat to ask, "What do you use for cooking?"

I knew "natural gas" would mean nothing to him, so I said, "I have an electric stove in my kitchen." Puzzled, he turned to face forward again. How could I explain?

At the Forbidden City, a group of farmers from western China gathered around us. Bob said they had never seen white people. Stuart was a red-headed giant, towering a foot above them, while my blond hair and fair skin fascinated them more than the emperors' history.

Tiananmen Square was bustling. Students and children spoke to us, seizing the opportunity to practice English. I flashed back to the TV screen just a few years before, when I watched a student stop a row of army tanks in the square. I asked Bob about the fate of that student, but he wouldn't say what had happened. From the look in his eyes, I knew it wasn't pleasant.

On Monday morning, Stuart flew home and I returned to work.

We frequently talked on the phone at 10 p.m. my time and 7 a.m. his time. The conversation helped ease my homesickness before I slept. He understood the business issues I dealt with and, because he'd been a bachelor all his life, he also understood my loneliness.

We talked about going to Tibet, but I couldn't get away from work.

I often photographed Wan Chi's street market with clucking chickens, quacking ducks, tubs of swimming fish, and an occasional cage of yipping puppies. I shot a series of photos of a man pulling a fat, six-foot snake out of basket. He cut off its head with scissors and squeezed the blood into cups. The customers drank the blood and ate the meat his wife made into soup. I didn't try it.

I was an alien in a place where my blond head stood four inches above most people on the street. Their staring made me uneasy and very aware that I represented our country with every move I made. Still I felt safe. When I smiled at a child on the street, he or she would say, "Hell-o, hell-o."

Using both Cantonese and English, I'd say, "*Jo Sun*, how are you today?"

The child would try to repeat the syllables. "Hu yu to de." Then we'd laugh and start again.

One Saturday afternoon, my colleagues and I took a ferry to Lan Tao Island in the New Territories to visit the giant bronze Tian Ta Buddha at the Po Lin Monastery. The seated Buddha, 250 meters tall, raised its right hand, representing the removal of affliction. Its left hand rested in its lap, signifying human happiness. The fragrance and smoke from thousands of joss sticks encircled the Buddha. Joss sticks look like long, narrow, Popsicle sticks made of incense. Worshipers burn them during religious ceremonies and daily prayers all over Asia. The smoke represents prayers going to heaven.

I felt a new awareness. I knew nothing of Buddhism, but now I wanted to learn. I didn't believe in the God that Reverend Swinehart ranted about, but I was aware of a presence or spiritual energy I called "guardian angels" or "guides." I often thanked whatever it was.

chapter sixteen

My granddaughter Paige tried to arrive on my forty-fourth birthday, December 9, 1992. Niki's water broke on the seventh. She was in hard labor for three days. Her doctor finally performed a cesarean at six in the morning on December 10, after Niki's blood pressure had dropped dangerously low. Rex called to tell me, then quickly returned to his wife and baby. I sat at my desk in a swirl of Chinese office mates who didn't understand the tears of joy and fear that moistened my cheeks. I worried about Niki. It seemed odd that the doctors let her go so long after her water broke. Although Rex was happy to be a new father, his voice was full of concern.

The next day I called from my desk to talk to Niki. The nurse was rude, and after scolding me for calling at such a late hour (in my excitement, I'd miscalculated the time difference), she told me Niki had been rushed to Yakima, a bigger town not far away, but refused to give me the details and hung up. I was frantic and called Paul in Kentucky. His new wife said, "He's on a plane to Washington."

"Why? What's happened?" I asked.

"I don' know," she replied.

"Is Niki OK? Is the baby OK?"

"I don' know."

I don' know, I don' know, I don' know—I wanted to choke her! Paul had never bought a full-fare ticket in his life. I knew something serious had happened.

I called Stuart and asked for his help. Coincidently, his cousin worked in the same hospital, and he quickly got information. Niki had lost a lot of blood, her temperature was high, her blood pressure was weak. She received a transfusion in Yakima, and when the doctors determined she was stable, they returned her to the hospital in Ellensburg. I tried to change my ticket home, but the Christmas holidays made a change impossible. I was forced to wait until December 20, Niki's original due date.

Waiting and worrying made concentration at work difficult. While I stared out the office window, a man on a rope suddenly appeared on the outside of the glass. He was installing Christmas lights. As he descended out of sight, I noticed an army of Chinese men rappelling down all the skyscrapers. They installed light displays thirty stories tall with Santas, reindeer, and holiday greetings. In January, they returned to cover the skyscrapers with Lunar New Year's dragons, firecrackers, and Chinese characters—Kung Hei Fat Choi (Happy New Year).

Stuart and I arrived in Ellensburg ten days after Paige was born, the same day they came home. Niki's skin was the color of ashes, her face warped with pain. Her normally bright aura had receded to a gray haze. This should have been a happy day, but she was indifferent and despondent. I wondered if she was suffering from postpartum depression but couldn't be sure until I spent more time with her.

Rex told us about the nasty night nurse. "I was standing by Niki's bed holding Paige when that night nurse said, 'Your wife probably won't make it through the night.' I sat down, thinking what a short time Niki and I had together," he said.

His openness moved me. The body-building football-player loved my daughter and wasn't shy about it. I thought of the love my Granddad had felt for my Grandma when he had rushed her to the hospital in 1923. I thanked the guides for ambulances and modern medicine.

I wanted to destroy that nasty night nurse.

Stuart and I spent a few days in Ellensburg with Rex, Niki, and Paige. Rex went to work, Stuart did their laundry, and I gave Paige her first bath at home while Niki dozed on the sofa. As I gently dipped

Paige into her little tub filled with warm water, I finally got a good look at her. Like many newborns, she had spiky dark hair that she had already rubbed off in the back. Her skin was smooth and pale, almost transparent. "You'll be a blonde, too," I told her.

The smell of baby soap filled the kitchen. Walking gingerly, Niki came to watch. After the bath, I diapered and dressed Paige. She looked so cute in the pink Gymboree pajamas I'd brought from Hong Kong.

"Thanks, Mom. I don't know what we'd do if you weren't here." Niki's voice was weary and didn't sound like her.

Niki wasn't able to lift her new baby and didn't seem to care. I arranged pillows so she could nurse football-style with Paige under her armpit instead of cradled in front.

Rex came home from work and held his daughter while we ate supper. He cradled her on his shoulder with confidence then changed her tiny diaper as if he were a nimble piccolo player. I realized she was just two weeks old, and her father had held her more than mine had held me during my entire life.

On Christmas Eve, we drove to Seattle. I'd rented my condo to a colleague, so we stayed at Stuart's big house in Bellevue. Matt was spending part of Christmas break with Paul in Kentucky and arrived in Seattle in time to accompany me back to Hong Kong after briefly meeting his new niece. Fortunately, Niki's pain and depression had subsided, and her skin had regained its peachy glow. The decision to return to Hong Kong would have been impossible if she had remained so ill.

Over the Pacific, Matt slept soundly next to me in business class while I sipped complimentary champagne and reflected on my life. I wondered if I would always carry the undertow of self-effacement, the feeling that men deserve more than women—more admiration, more money, more rights, more freedom, more gratitude, more respect. Vaguely, I remembered pre-*Training*, when my cell memory still knew that no divine intention required female depreciation, but forty years of brawny messages had seeped into my flesh as if I were an unwilling sponge.

Had the messages leaked into Niki as well? By her tenth birthday, the circumstances of my life had annihilated my self-esteem; only a whisper of cell memory remained, leaving me unable to guard Niki from the onslaught. She must have needed more than I had been able to give.

Had our patriarchal planet stunted her self-esteem as well?

Would her new daughter fight the same battle, or would Paige triumph with her daddy's love and encouragement? I fell asleep and dreamed of my new granddaughter growing into a woman, confident and in control of her balanced life.

I went back to work while Matt explored the streets of Hong Kong. He knew how to find a taxi back to the hotel, and I knew he'd be safe. From his six-foot-tall perspective, his photos of temples and markets looked as if an undulating sea of black filled the streets. His blond head must have looked strange, bobbing above the crowds.

On New Year's Eve, we joined my colleagues on a pub-crawl in Stanley. We walked the streets with hundreds of drinking revelers, mostly expats, and watched fireworks over the South China Sea. Matt drank a lot of beer, and during dinner, the men on the team encouraged him to taste foul-smelling spirits.

Around two in the morning, I couldn't find Matt. Some of my team-mates helped me search the bars and bathrooms. I was getting frantic when I noticed his blond head on a park bench, sound asleep—passed out more likely. They helped me pour him into a taxi. At the hotel, he wobbled from the elevator to the room, where he fell asleep on the sofa. I took off his shoes and covered him with a blanket. Next morning, I had a terrible headache, but he was as chipper as ever.

"What's for breakfast? What're we doin' today?"

"Please don't shout," I said, annoyed that *I* was the one with a hangover.

Three days later, he flew back to Colorado.

⚬ ⚬

I completed the assignment in April. Before returning to Seattle, I met Stuart in Hawaii. He'd been born there and wanted to show me where he grew up. I stepped off the plane into the sweet Hawaiian air and realized I'd become accustomed to the stench of Hong Kong.

"Let's go snorkeling," he suggested.

"I'm embarrassed to say I don't swim," I said.

"Nonsense. Didn't you learn as a child?"

"I learned to tread water, and I can stay on top, but I don't have the confidence to swim in the ocean with big fish all around," I said. "You can go. I'll stay on the boat and watch."

He arranged for a tour of Molokini. The catamaran anchored in the crescent of the small island, and I watched families with children as young as two or three jump overboard with fins, masks, and snorkels. When all the others were in the water, Stuart gave me a nudge. "Just wear the mask and put your face in the water; you can stand on the ladder."

With gear in place, Stuart jumped in. I stepped onto the ladder, my back toward the boat. Inching into the salt water, I bent to submerge the mask while keeping a death grip on the ladder behind me.

Stuart said, "Look at that big fish."

I was on the deck in one leap.

Stuart and the tour guides were incredibly patient with me. Eventually, I got into the water and paddled around on a float board like the children. We watched schools of yellow tang, orange-and-black clown fish, striped angelfish, and many other tropical varieties I had seen only in aquariums.

That night Stuart hugged me and said, "I'm glad you got up the nerve to go into the water."

"Me too! It was amazing; the fish were gorgeous! Thanks for helping."

"Maybe someday you'll gather the nerve for a hot-air balloon ride." Then, with a tighter grip, he said, "What have they done to you?" He didn't mean the fish, and he didn't expect an answer.

He knew me better than I knew myself.

Stuart expected me to move in with him, but I needed my own space after living in over-populated Hong Kong. Still, I spent a lot of time at his place. His hunter-green leather sofa and chairs, framed prints of rainbow trout, stuffed pheasant on the coffee table, and moose antlers over the fireplace revealed his bachelor status. One evening, relaxing by the giant TV in his family room, he was folding his laundry and watching sports while I read a book. He idly commented, "If I ever get married, I'll never fold another sock."

I sucked in a lung full of air but decided not to speak.

At home one evening, the phone rang.

"Hi, Marcia. This is David. Do you remember me?" said a young man's voice.

"Of course I remember you, David! You were like my own child. Wow, you must be in college." It was Cindy's son, the baby I'd cared for while she taught at Western Michigan. "How's your mom? I haven't seen her in ages."

"Well, that's why I called." He paused for a long time and my heart sank. "She died a few months ago."

"Oh, David, I'm so sorry. What happened?"

"Heart attack." I could hear him crying. "I tried to call you, but the lady that answered your phone said you were in Hong Kong. I wanted to tell you myself so I didn't leave a message."

"David, I am so sorry. I wish I'd been here. You guys were so important to me. Is there anything I can do? How's Tina?" His sister was two years younger than he.

"She's fine; she's a senior in high school."

"How old is your baby brother?" I talked just to be talking. I didn't know what to say.

"He's in first grade. It's really hard on him, so I spend a lot of time there."

The rest of the conversation blurred.

Cindy's "perfect" marriage had ended shortly after Paul and I had moved to Kentucky. They'd shared household chores, and Cindy had made as much money as Dale, but he was as domineering and opinionated as Paul. It was taking years for me to develop my independence, but Cindy had been independent from the beginning. It didn't take as long for their marriage to flounder.

Cindy had remarried, moved to Florida, and had another baby.

We'd been so busy with our careers and families, we rarely took time to call, but we exchanged Christmas cards every year.

I'd visited Tampa on business a few times and stayed with her family. Every visit felt as if we'd seen each other yesterday.

She was only forty-four.

A heart attack. Too young.

Late in 1993, Stuart and I enjoyed toast and scrambled eggs for breakfast in his dining room. The sun warmed the back of my neck, and the coffee tasted hot and satisfying. I felt content, happy to be alive. The Hong Kong separation made me appreciate him more, and we seemed to be doing well in our relationship.

Then he blurted, "I've been offered a five-year assignment in China."

"Wow, that's great! What will you be doing?" Stuart was currently the regional director of real estate for a fast food chain in the Northwest.

"Pretty much what I do now, except in Chinese." He laughed. "I'll be in charge of real estate for new stores all over China … I was hoping you could go with me."

I studied my coffee as if the mug knew what was coming next.

"If we were married, the company would pay for you to fly home to see the kids, and we could travel all over Asia together."

There it was, the m-word, exposed to the morning light.

My hesitation surprised him.

After a long, uncomfortable silence, I told him, "Stuart, I'm not ready to give up my career and my life in Seattle and go to China with you." I couldn't say what I was thinking, *I'm not in love with you.* Our relationship was never the same, of course. He wanted more than I had to give.

A few months later, he left for China.

We stayed in touch. His beautifully written letters brought China home to me. He told stories of ancient Chinese cities that seemed lost in time. He recounted tales of the people he met, the duck tongue and other odd dishes he ate, and strange customs that slowed his business efforts.

He called occasionally, but we avoided discussing our dying relationship, as if it might rematerialize in five years.

chapter seventeen

Kali called. "Let's have coffee at Sweet Addition on Saturday morning."

Except for my stint in Hong Kong, I'd been in the Seattle area the past ten years, but we rarely visited. I hadn't seen Kali since Niki's wedding. We weren't close. I was never quite sure *what* she wanted me to be, but she made it clear I wasn't. She was married to the rich, banal, jerk Tom, who stayed busy impressing his friends and colleagues. He had done well selling commercial real estate in the late 1970s when the Seattle market was on fire, but the real money came from his family. Tom's father had made millions in real estate development, first in residential, then commercial.

When the commercial real estate market cooled in the 1980s, about the time I moved to Seattle, Tom's high-income career also dwindled. Someone talked Tom and Kali into Amway, a pyramid scheme for selling soap products. Kali struggled to manage a three-year-old, a nursing baby, and Amway deliveries, so before I started working full time, I drove her through the ritzy neighborhoods to deliver Amway products to Tom's besieged relatives, friends, and colleagues.

One weekend in 1984, a few months after we'd arrived in Seattle, Niki, Matt, and I had breakfast at their brand new, architecturally impressive home and enjoyed playing with three-year-old Jason and the new baby, Annie.

I sat at the kitchen table finishing my coffee. Kali stood at the sink, washing up. Niki, Matt, and Jason were playing with big red-and-blue Legos on the floor between us, and the baby was asleep in her bassinette. To any observer, it would appear as a convivial family gathering. Suddenly, Kali reeled around, spewing dishwater on the imported terra cotta tile floor. Her face was twisted and her voice shrill. "You're too damned important to support our business," she said.

"Kali, I buy the soap and help you deliver product. Do you expect me to be an agent?" I looked at Matt and Niki. They were wide-eyed. I said, "Maybe it's time for us to go home; it's been a long morning." I began edging Niki and Matt toward the car. Kali threw the dripping dishcloth into the sink, splashing dishwater onto the window. She swept her son from the floor and kicked toys from her path as she followed us out.

"I should love you like a sister, but I don't. I don't even like you. I only spend time with you because I have to," she shrieked.

"I'm sorry, Kali, I'm sorry." While Kali shouted insults, I kept apologizing—for what, I didn't know. I got behind the wheel. She stood by my car window with Jason on her hip. As I rolled it down, I said, "Kali, I'm sorry you think I'm not supportive. I care about you and your family, but I can't get all that excited about Amway." Through the open window, she punched me in the mouth with her fist.

I put the car in gear and backed out of the driveway. My split lip began to swell and throb. Eleven-year-old Matt gave me a tissue for the blood. Niki, almost thirteen, cried in the back seat. Matt's face glowed red with anger. We drove home in silence. I fought tears and wondered how I could help my children understand their aunt's outburst when I couldn't understand it myself.

Kali and I didn't speak for over a year. Then, the following summer, our parents came to Seattle for a visit, and we all gathered as if nothing had happened. We never discussed it, but like the rafting trip, the emotions lingered.

It wouldn't be the last time she reminded me how much she didn't like me.

Despite having the same *Training*, we reacted to it differently. Kali developed a sense of entitlement, absorbed Dad's anger, and rejected *Training*, while I grew up fearful, with a sense of unworthiness, and absorbed *Training* to my bones. Did she escape due to the temperament she was born with, or was it a result of our parents' maturity? Probably a combination of both.

"Hi, Kal." I waved as she walked toward my table by the window at Sweet Addition. She looked tense and stiff. I stood to give her a hug. She didn't acknowledge that she was an hour late, and I didn't mention it. I'd brought a book to read while I drank a latte. Her tardiness was notorious. Kali was always late and controlled the beginning of every get-together.

"Hi, how was Hong Kong?" she said, but she didn't really want to know. Her voice had a thick timbre. On guard, I didn't say much. The truth began to emerge. "Tom and I are getting a divorce," she blurted.

"Oh, Kal, I'm so sorry," I felt sadness but no surprise. They never seemed to enjoy each other very much. We spent an hour at the café, discussing her children and their reactions to the news. I tried to be supportive but gave no advice. I withheld comments like "I understand, I've been there" or "I know what you mean." She was angry that I carried the experience of our nine-year age difference. She could never catch up, and it galled her.

Mom left Dad shortly after Kali's divorce became final. My parents' marriage had lasted fifty years and two weeks. Mom stayed with a friend, and when she went back a week later to get more of her things, Dad's girlfriend wouldn't let her take anything but clothing.

Mom told me, "That woman wouldn't let me have my electric mixer."

"Why didn't you just take it?" I asked on the phone. "It's yours."

"Oh, I couldn't. She wouldn't let me." I went no further.

Lili, Dad's favorite, persuaded him to allow Mom access to her things and helped Mom move to an apartment in Columbus. The electric mixer was gone. I'm sure there were things left behind that I would love to have had, but I inherited my treasures when Granddad and Grandma died: the Kodak, the wooden tripod, and the walnut dresser with acorn handles.

When Dad sold the house, Mom invested her half of fifty years of equity. Dad was sporadic with spousal support payments, so the court garnished his social security. Dividends, spousal support, and social security covered Mom's small apartment and living expenses.

Dad moved in with his girlfriend and used her garage to store the remaining household goods that had once belonged to his children, Gramps and Grandma B, and Granddad and Grandma. Within months, he abandoned the girlfriend and the legacy in her garage, telling my brother, Rob, "I don't need any of that crap."

He abandoned a hundred years of family mementoes, photo albums, and keepsakes in a stranger's garage. "That crap" included a relationship with his children.

The metaphorical finale.

chapter eighteen

Ray asked me to meet him at the "North Office." Actually, it was the Yarrow Bay Café, next to our offices at Carillon Point in Kirkland. When I was on his staff, before Hong Kong, we often discussed departmental issues while having lunch, so we called it the "North Office." I had no idea what he wanted. Maybe a new project? I ordered a diet coke and watched a sailboat come about on Lake Washington.

Before I'd left for Hong Kong, I reported to Ray. Together we'd traveled the United States, meeting with corporate account sales teams. He treated me with respect, and I enjoyed working and traveling with him.

When he walked by the windows and into the café, I noticed his lean frame. *How handsome he is,* I thought. A neatly trimmed black mustache occupied his upper lip but didn't interfere with his perfect, wide smile. I knew from previous conversations that his father was Lebanese and his mother Italian. Her heritage softened his features. His black hair thinned on top and I thought, *What a striking child he must have been when thick, black hair covered his whole head. How different from my tow-headed, transparent-skinned family.*

He climbed mountains and ran marathons, but his macho persona didn't camouflage his tender heart. I could see it in his dark eyes.

"Have you been waiting long?" He pulled his chair to the table.

"No, I just got here," I said. The waiter arrived, and I ordered my favorite salad on the familiar menu, with chicken, gorgonzola, pecans, and cran-raisins.

"That sounds good. I'll have the same." Ray seemed nervous as he added iced tea to his order. When the waiter walked away, Ray was quiet and then suddenly blurted, "If you're at all interested in going out with me, I'd be interested, too." He fell back in his chair.

Rather than answer one way or the other, I said, "I have tickets to *Phantom of the Opera* at the 5th Avenue Theater on Saturday night. Would you like to go?"

I saw relief in his face. I'd known him for so long; it didn't feel like a date.

Ray picked me up in his freshly washed, hunter-green Jeep with the bike rack on top. He looked handsome in pressed trousers, a starched blue shirt, and dark tie.

We had an early dinner at Palomino's with its tasty food and noisy atmosphere. It was not the least bit romantic, but this was clearly a date.

After *Phantom*, we slipped into a quiet piano bar and hid together in the smoky cobalt shadows. We rolled brandy snifters in our palms and felt the romantic rotation of our previously professional relationship. At home, he kissed me goodnight.

We went bike riding on Sunday. I rode his old mountain bike because I didn't have a bike of my own. Then he cooked dinner. Tuesday we went for a run along Lake Washington after work. As the weeks passed, we ran, biked, or hiked together every weekend.

I saw him occasionally at the office, passing in the corridors or eating in the lunchroom. "How are you?" he'd say.

"Fine, did you have a nice weekend?" I'd say, even though we'd spent the nights exploring each other in bed.

"Wonderful!" he'd say with a grin as he passed, lightly brushing my arm with his.

Harmless deception was part of the intrigue. No one at the office knew we had a romantic relationship.

Low clouds over Lake Washington made the view from the employee cafeteria a consistent shade of gray. I found Ray eating alone. "May I join you?"

Over our turkey sandwiches, he said, "My friend Wade and I are planning a trip to Patagonia in March."

"I see you wearing a lot of Patagonia labels around here. Isn't it a little extreme to camp out at the store?" I joked.

He rolled his eyes in mock disgust, "We're not going to the clothing store. We're going to South America, where the clothing store got its name," he said.

"I saw an article about it. Are you going to Chile or Argentina?"

"Both!" He was excited about the trip. "You're one of the few people I've talked to who knows where it is."

"I'd love to photograph the area, but my women friends wouldn't even consider a trip like that."

His piercing dark eyes looked up, turkey sandwich suspended in midair. "You want to join us?" he said before he took a bite.

"You're not serious!" I said, hoping he was. "Are you sure Wade wouldn't mind having a girl on the trip?"

He shook his head as he finished chewing. "I'll ask him, but he usually doesn't mind sleeping in tents with pretty ladies."

We discussed the trip several more times. I made plans to join them.

Ray gave me a detailed list of gear I'd need for the trip. I filled a borrowed backpack with twenty pounds of essentials, including Capilene pants and tops that would dry quickly and waterproof jacket and pants for the inevitable sheeting rain. We could expect temperatures below freezing, so I packed a windproof polar fleece jacket, hat, gloves, and pants. Matt shipped his Therm-a-Rest mat and down sleeping bag to me from Colorado.

We each agreed to bring a paperback book we could trade. I brought Ken Follett's *Lie Down with Lions*. Ray and I had traded books when we'd traveled on business, so I knew he would like it. I'd heard it had some great sex scenes, so I figured Wade would like it too.

Packing light was important. I cut most of the handle off my toothbrush, bought a small tube of toothpaste, a tiny handleless hairbrush, a sample-size sun block, and deodorant. The lipstick was standard size—I couldn't go without lipstick. Face cream was the only thing that smelled like a girl. I packed a plastic mug and bowl appropriate for dehydrated lasagna, oatmeal, or soup. We each packed two poly-bottles for water. Ray would carry the stove, cooking gear, and a first aid kit. Wade would carry our three-man tent and the water filter pump.

For me, the most important gear was my camera and film. Counting on my photography, they left their cameras at home. I attached a waterproof pouch to the waist strap of the pack so the 35-mm Canon would be safe and accessible. A new Tamron 28-to-200 zoom lens and a tiny tripod with a Velcro strap replaced standard gear. I had room to carry only fifty rolls of professional film, fewer than two per day. I'd need to shoot frugally.

Ray and I flew out of SeaTac. Wade flew out of Colorado and met us at an outdoor café in Santiago, Chile, before we checked into the Grand Hyatt, the most extravagant hotel I'd ever stayed in. Ray and I had a king-size bed and a view of Santiago. We used frequent flyer miles and split the remaining cost of the room.

It was the only comfortable bed for the duration of the trip and the only night I felt like his girlfriend.

From then on, I felt like one of the boys. Ray and Wade had been roommates at Colorado State in the 1960s. Wade was about five-foot-nine, a little on the round side, with receding blond hair. Once we started hiking, I discovered he was more athletic than he appeared.

Before we finished dinner that first evening, I said, "We should discuss our expectations for the trip." I thought the men would want to visit a specific glacier or peak. Instead, they started laughing.

Ray said, "Don't be appalled if I fart in the tent. It'll smell pretty bad."

Wade added, "I'll need plenty of time in the woods alone for … well … you know."

Ray laughed. "Yeah, that's why we called you TP LaRose in school!" They went on like potty-mouthed elementary school boys.

"I got some great Australia underwear for this trip," Ray said. "They're called down-undies." I felt as if I were at the Underground Comedy Club with Henny Youngman. This was going to be fun!

More serious than my hiking partners, I said, "I'll need a little privacy. I'd like to be first into the tent each night. I'll cover my head while you guys crawl in." They thought this was a reasonable concession for my girl-ness.

In Los Glaciares National Park, we stepped from the bus and leaned into a sixty-five-mph wind. A gust blew me over onto my backpack like a helpless turtle. Ray and Wade helped me to my feet, and we walked in single file. Wade blocked the wind as we walked about a quarter mile to a rustic campsite near a slow, glacial stream. The site would be home base for three nights. With difficulty, we pitched the tent among some weathered trees then crawled inside to eat salami and bread. The REI WhisperLite backpacking stove would have blown away. That also meant no hot water for washing. We were asleep by eight-thirty, crumbs and all.

At five in the morning, I got up to go into the bushes. The clouds were gone, the wind had subsided, and the sky was bright. Just three hundred yards above us, snow glowed in the early morning sun. I stuck my head into the tent and said softly, "Hey, you guys, it's beautiful out here." Then a little louder, "Let's go hiking!"

They came out of the tent in their boxers to see if I was joking. I couldn't help noticing Ray's lean muscular body. He was hairier than any man I'd ever known. *How can his head be so smooth and his body be so furry?* I thought.

We'd set up camp among the trees in a bowl between the base of the mountains and the river, and our view of the mountains was blocked. We were eager to see them.

We quickly dressed in layers, packed water, food, and essentials in our daypacks. TP LaRose spent a few minutes in the trees while Ray and I brushed our teeth. We were on the trail by six.

Within fifteen minutes, we came around a knoll and discovered Fitzroy's granite face reflecting the morning sun. After four hours of hiking toward it, through meadows and up steep trails, we came to a sort of village built with tree branches and discarded mountaineering equipment. It served as base camp for the technical climbers who scaled the eight-thousand-foot granite spires. From that point, the mountain got steeper, and the ground soft and rocky. Wind had removed the snow, but my feet slid, and I landed on my belly already close to the steep incline. I froze, terrified I'd slide all the way back to base camp.

Face down on the steep slope in the dirt, I tried to ignore my fear. "I can do this. I can do this," I said aloud.

"It's called 'scree,'" I heard a voice say. "The loose gravel, I mean." I looked at his boots and twisted my neck to find Wade's understanding face. "It feels like ball bearings if you're not careful. You'll be fine; just take it slow." I pushed to my hands and toes, a downward-facing-dog yoga position, the best my fear could manage on the steep slope. Inch by inch I made it through the steepest part like a child imitating an elephant. Wade carried my pack. He scrambled through the dirt and rocks like a mountain goat. "It just takes experience," he said. When the trail flattened on solid rock, I stood. Dirt smudged my face.

Wade handed me my pack and camera. "Thanks," I said. "I think I'd still be lying there if you hadn't come back for me."

"No worries" he said. "This is a pretty steep hike for a newbie." My fear of heights remained secret. "Ray's so far ahead he doesn't know I came back for you."

Deep patches of snow remained in the shadows, and a shallow, clear lake reflected the three granite towers and cloudless sky, an intense color of blue not seen at lower altitudes. Soon I stopped trembling. I lay on my belly in the rocks near the lake with my camera on the six-inch-tall tripod. I used the slowest possible shutter speed to capture the depth and the widest possible angle on my new multipurpose lens.

To the east, over the crest of solid rock, a silty, turquoise, glacier-fed lake reflected an opaque glow. I could see only a small hint of the glacier behind it.

"What's that noise?" I asked. "The sky's clear, but it sounds like a storm." My fear of the steep mountain was strong enough without lightning adding to it.

"Glaciers are always moving," Wade said. "It's too slow to see, but the ice is cracking as it moves; the sound is called 'glacial thunder.'" We were in a bowl framed by towering granite peaks in all directions. The thunder echoed all around us.

I walked along solid rock, closer to the silty lake, and sat where I could photograph the layers of intense colors: white glacier, opaque turquoise water, and brown granite. The sky was intense cyan, unobstructed by atmosphere. Ray sat close to the edge and made a red dot in the photograph. Again, I had to wait until I stopped trembling to shoot.

Coming off the mountain was just as frightening, I felt as if I would fall forward and overcompensated by scooting down on my bum while Wade carried my pack. Ray wasn't as patient and soon hiked far ahead of us. Wade and I silently passed the weather-ravaged trees, occasionally catching blurry glimpses of Ray's red coat in the distance. A pair of pileated woodpeckers fed a downy chick poking its head from an oblong hole in a dead tree. "Why don't you catch up with Ray? I'd like to photograph these birds."

"Are you sure?" He was glad I'd offered. "You OK alone?"

"I'll be fine. I have a map in my pack. Anyway, there's no way to get lost if I stay on the trail." My right knee was aching, and I needed to rest. Photography gave me an alibi. Wade's yellow jacket disappeared over the hillside as I sat on a patch of grass, grateful for time alone among the gnarled trees.

I absorbed the serenity of a solitary moment. I felt clear, alive, sure that my everyday life blocked this kind of deep self-awareness. Perhaps it was my first meditative experience. "Thank you," I said as I got to my feet some time later and began the trek back to camp.

I arrived around six o'clock, well over an hour behind Wade and Ray, tired but exhilarated. I hadn't seen another hiker since Wade had left me on the dusty trail. They'd devoured the leftover salami and bread and opened the "box-o-wine," as they called it, that Ray had bought in El Calafate. We drank from our plastic coffee/tea/water/wine mugs. The box of Chilean wine tasted OK after such a long day. A few days later, we opened another box and decided it would be an excellent substitute if we ran out of fuel.

It was my turn to cook that night. Ray had gotten off easy the night before because of the wind. Wade selected dehydrated lasagna. "Let's do the lasagna while we've got access to fuel," he said.

Ray agreed. "The stew cooks pretty fast. We can eat it when we're further out in the sticks."

I stood by the old wooden picnic table on exhausted, rubbery legs. Ray and Wade continued reading while I tried to start the WhisperLite backpacking stove, not wanting to admit my inexperience. Suddenly the picnic table was on fire—or at least the fuel I spilled was burning. "Hey, I need some help over here." Just twenty feet away, they ignored me. In a louder but normal voice, I said, "You guys, the table's on fire."

Still they ignored me. "Well, I'm not going to scream like a girl," I said under my breath. I found a water bottle, doused the flames, and tried again. Finally, I persuaded the little monster to burn properly and began to boil the remaining water. When the aroma of rehydrated lasagna filled the campsite, Wade looked up from the Ken Follett novel. "What smells so good? Hey, what happed to all the water I pumped through the filter?"

"I doused a burning picnic table," I said. "Will you fetch more?"

Wade shook his head. "That stove can be a stinker to light," he said. Gathering the empty poly-bottles and his filter pump, he headed for the lethargic glacial river not far from camp.

After dinner, we sat on our sleeping mats to protect us from the cold ground. Campfires were forbidden. While the guys told college stories, I went into the woods with a smashed roll of toilet paper and a zip-lock sandwich bag for collecting whatever happened. Like dogs in a city park, we quite literally carried out *everything* we carried in. We deposited the bags in a designated garbage container at the edge of the woods. When I came back to camp, I washed my hands and face with the warm water left in a pot on the picnic table. My little towel and washcloth hung in the tree branches nearby. The guys were gone. Then I heard them giggling in the tent. "We couldn't find you so we went to bed," a male voice came through the tent wall.

I looked inside. "Yeah, right! Cover your appalling furry faces." Kindly, they had put the mat back under my sleeping bag. I don't think I ever slept more soundly.

We camped and day-hiked for three days, then found a rustic *hosteria* and got rooms so we could take hot showers, eat real food, and get away from each other for a few hours. Then we caught a rickety bus to Pehoe. The plan was vague: Torres del Paine, Pehoe, Fitzroy, Grey Glacier, and Moreno Glacier. We could change our plans based on the weather. The rain, however, cooperated, coming mostly at night or while we were on a bus traveling with the locals and their chickens.

If a picture is worth a thousand words, the ones I shot in Patagonia are worth millions. It was that breathtakingly beautiful. I couldn't do justice: the majestic spires of Torres del Paine, condors and albatross soaring overhead, huge ice chunks calving off one-hundred-foot Moreno Glacier with no landmark to measure the magnitude of the huge waves it created, and icebergs that looked like backlit cyan glass. I stalked llama-like guanaco herds, silhouetted against the granite walls, as they teased my lens to come closer.

I had no idea that one day I'd own a herd of their domestic cousins.

Back in Seattle, when I told my women friends animated stories about the trip, they made me feel like an over-stimulated longshoreman. "What were you thinking? Are you crazy? You should have demanded special treatment. If men know we *can* do all that stuff, we'll *have* to do it."

I told my friend Rochelle, "The day it rained, we hiked for four hours through the woods just to see Grey Glacier, then hiked back out."

"Couldn't you just take a taxi?" she said, almost serious.

It never occurred to Ray that I would not keep up or that I would need girl-like pampering. He knew me from the office, and as he expected, I held my own. I got dirty when the men did, hiked as far as they did, and wore grimy clothes. We didn't shower or wash our hair for days at a time, which had little impact on their balding heads but left me a greasy mess under my baseball cap. The trip took my man-like behavior to the extreme.

I didn't know how to be capable, strong, *and* feminine. I completely disclaimed womanhood.

I thought I might stand up to pee.

chapter nineteen

"Hi, Mom, my water broke," Niki said on the phone. I was playing with Paige while Matt and Niki went Christmas shopping. "I called Rex. He'll meet me at your condo. Can you keep Paige?"

"Of course!" I said. "How's Matt taking this?"

"Oh, I think he can drive safely." She laughed at her brother. I heard her say, "Matt, it's OK, I can walk."

Rex arrived with a small duffel for Paige—including the all-important blankie. They sat on the floor and played with her blocks. "You're going to have a sleepover with Grandma Marsh and Matt tonight," he said. "We'll see you tomorrow."

Niki and Matt came in. Niki sat in the rocking chair.

"Shouldn't you be going?" Matt said.

"Relax, Matt. I feel fine," Niki said.

When they were sure Paige had settled in, Rex and Niki left for the hospital.

Paige and I curled up on my bed and I read to her while she stroked the satin on her tattered, multicolored blanket. She fell asleep, and Matt stayed with her while I went to the grocery store.

My cell phone rang. "Mom, you better come home; Paige's really upset," said Matt. I abandoned the milk, bread, and peanut butter in my cart.

I lifted Paige from Matt's arms and sat in the bentwood rocking chair by the bay window. The evening sun formed a halo around her blond head while her three-year-old body shuddered and sobbed. Matt retrieved her blankie and covered us. I rocked and hugged her until she recovered.

"What shall we have for dinner?" I said.

Without hesitation she said, "Steak, potatoes, and Caesar salad."

"She's her daddy's girl," I told Matt.

I roasted new potatoes with olive oil and kosher salt the way she liked them. Matt grilled the steaks while Paige stood on a stool and tore the lettuce into the big salad bowl. Then she helped me set the table.

She devoured a whole T-bone steak, several small potatoes, and a huge salad.

That night Paige and I snuggled in my queen-size bed. I read, *Wind in the Willows* while her long blond hair floated on her pillow.

I remembered snuggling in Granddad's feather bed right after Lili was born. He had stroked my hair and read Zane Grey until I fell asleep.

Around six in the morning, Rex called to announce the birth of his second daughter. Taylor weighed nine pounds six ounces. I hugged her before she was an hour old.

Upon my return from Hong Kong, I'd worked on various projects, reporting to Rod, the VP of corporate marketing. His admin stuck her head in my office. "Brian wants to see you in his office." Brian was Rod's boss. At sixty, he had no idea how to use a mouse, and he was the only executive with a secretary who typed his reports and memos. He ran five miles a day, but he looked frail, with white hair and melting jowls.

I stepped into his office. "You wanted to see me?"

"Sit down. I understand you've applied for a position in India."

"Yes," I said, "Rod and I discussed it."

"You're poised to take on a lot of responsibility when the reorg happens in a few months. The India assignment could ruin you career." This was "corporate-speak" for "If you go you won't have a job to come home to," but I ignored it. I knew the reorganization would be like musical chairs, and I knew I wouldn't have a seat when the music stopped.

"I realize it's a risk, but India needs communications, and I'd like to be part of the team that builds it," I said.

"I won't stand in your way, but I hope you know what you're doing," he said.

There'd been a time not so long past when I wouldn't have considered such a career risk. My identity and my job entwined, but I began to capture a flicker of my Self beyond my career.

I accepted the position in February. It felt like the right thing to do. My salary would be double for the duration of the "hardship" assignment.

Meanwhile, Ray applied for project director. I would report directly to him. My decision to go had nothing to do with his, other than shared wanderlust.

I'd miss Taylor's babyhood just as I'd missed Paige's. It wasn't easy to leave them.

chapter twenty

In Pune (POO-na), Maharashtra, India, I began to live and work among women covered from head to toe in brightly colored saris while they carried water, bricks, and laundry on their heads. I'm sure a blond woman wearing American business clothes and carrying a briefcase appeared just as strange to them.

I opened the corrugated boxes I'd shipped to myself, eager to find the canned tuna and other normal food. I heard unfamiliar noises coming from one of the boxes. I pushed it onto the terrace and stood safely behind the sliding glass door, staring at my reflection while contemplating my next move. "I'll have the maid unpack for me," an executive decision.

She found nothing alive in the boxes. The unwelcome creature must have escaped in the meantime.

On Saturday afternoon, my driver took me to Laxmi Road where I wandered the street market looking for vegetables and fruits that were safe for foreigners. I didn't feel the need for a bodyguard, but the driver was never far behind. After preventing an inferior selection, he helped me choose mangos so fresh they tasted nothing like the imported mangos at the market in Seattle.

Bread from the open-air bakery wasn't safe, so I walked to Derabjay's General Store. I bought packaged bread, tea bags, honey, cheese, Ritz crackers, soap for washing vegetables or dishes, and a can of bug spray, all expensive items by Indian standards.

Six-inch lizards shared my flat, but I didn't mind. They ate bugs. The three-inch roaches were too big for the lizards, and the spray had no impact. Tiny spiders lived in the bathroom and hopped a foot at a time to avoid the lizards. The spiders survived the bug spray, but it incapacitated them long enough for me to find a newspaper.

Even when monsoon rains cooled the night air, I slept with the windows closed and the air conditioner on, except when there was no electricity, a frequent occurrence. The hum helped drown the wandering night-watchman's whistle. He blew it all night long to notify residents that he was awake.

I usually ate meals at restaurants with colleagues rather than cooking in my small kitchen, but when I did, I soaked my food for an hour in a solution of bottled water, bleach, salt, and turmeric. I washed the exterior of fruit with soap and bottled water before peeling. Hindus are vegetations, so the store sold no meat. I longed for a big steak and green salad.

I tried to work out at the nearby hotel's sparsely equipped, non-air-conditioned gym. They allowed women only at midday. A sign next to the treadmill read "15 minute maximum," which the attendant enforced though I was the only person in the gym.

I began to run with Ray every morning while it was still relatively cool; otherwise, the heat was unbearable and traffic unsafe. If we tried to run after work, in addition to the heat, we had to deal with cars, trucks, auto-rickshaws, bicycles, oxcarts, cows, pigs, hawkers, beggars, and an occasional camel or elephant. It was also good to run before too many people saw me wearing shorts and a T-shirt. With temperatures over ninety degrees, even at five-thirty in the morning, I refused to run in long pants or a skirt.

Ray, Guy, a teammate, and I bought bikes to add variety to our exercise program—the first bicycle I'd ever owned. It had fat tires, front suspension, front and rear brakes, eighteen gears, weighed about forty pounds, and cost a whopping 2300 rupees. That was a small fortune for most of the locals, but worth the $80 USD for Ray, Guy, and me. To put it into perspective, the frame on Ray's new Klein at home weighed about three pounds and cost about $2000 USD, enough to feed several families in Pune for many years.

On our first ride, we saw thatch-and-mud-hut villages where the women cooked over burning dung patties. We passed a dairy farm with a herd of water buffalo. The huge, skinny black creatures with their long horns stared at us as we rode by, just like the black and white Holsteins on Granddad's dairy farm in Ohio. As we pedaled on, the farmers got excited, pointing and chattering in Marathi, trying to direct us back to the main road. The concept of exercise was as foreign as we three aliens in bike shorts.

At six a.m. on a Saturday in late June, we headed out of Pune on Koregoan Park Road. The monsoon rains made the flat countryside lush and green with relatively fresh, humid, 80-degree air, a sharp contrast to the harsh 120-degree dry heat and ubiquitous dust of previous rides. Beyond the pavement, we road the narrow, packed-dirt roads through little villages until we reached the muddy trails formed by foot travelers with ox and water buffalo. Mud and manure from monsoon puddles splattered our legs. Occasional squalls and light winds refreshed us as we rode for two and a half hours to a footbridge over the swollen and polluted Mutha River. Without hesitation, Guy and Ray rode over the narrow bridge. The filthy water rushed an inch below. I dismounted. Balancing on a tightrope at the circus would have been less terrifying. On this narrow bridge, my feet scarcely fit between the bike and the water's edge, but I did it!

A few miles downriver, we arrived at the next footbridge. The surface was at least twelve inches under filthy moving water. We had to make a decision: use the makeshift ferry system—an enterprising local with a small boat—or go back the way we'd come. If the little rowboat capsized, there was no chance of survival. We would be swept away by the current and surely die from ingesting the filth. There was no waste treatment for millions of inhabitants living near the river's shores. All waste ran untreated into the river.

We'd been riding for over three hours. "Let's take the boat," Guy said. "It's been raining hard. The other bridge is probably flooded by now." The heavy load of Ray, Guy, and me, our three bikes, and the "skipper" brought the filthy water dangerously close to the gunnels, leaving no room to rock. I closed my eyes and held my breath. I focused on a mental image of the pristine Missouri River in 1919 when Granddad had been a skipper.

It took about twenty minutes to cross, and fortunately, the current was calm close to the grassy shore where we easily beached the boat. Ray paid the "ferry-walla" a hundred rupees, knowing that it should have been less than ten. The walla was quite pleased. Using the miniature Olympus camera I carried in my bum-bag I took pictures of the dark-skinned walla with his big, white grin.

In a village at the top of the riverbank, Guy yelled from behind me, "Your tire's going flat." There were no cars in this village. Everyone here rode bicycles, so finding a repair walla was easy. I just pointed to the tire, and a young man pointed in the direction of the tire walla. As always, Ray was far ahead, so Guy rode to retrieve him while I waited for the repair. When Guy and Ray returned, they easily identified my baseball cap among the mob of a hundred men and boys that surrounded me. The women hid in their huts and concrete buildings. Without a doubt, I was the only blond woman in bike shorts these villagers would ever see. I could have been from Mars.

By the time we rode into the apartment complex where Ray and Guy stayed, it was raining so hard that finding the driveway was difficult. We were soaked to the skin, and greasy mud encrusted our bikes. The torrential rain had no impact on the clay-like muck caked to our legs and shoes.

The driver was waiting. When we turned the corner, riding single file in the heavy rain, he stood on the porch with a curious look. The entire scene must have seemed like something from a movie, but I doubt he'd ever seen a movie. The brim of my baseball cap dripped water in front of my eyes; my heavy white T-shirt clung to my skin, and dirt splattered my legs. Guy and Ray were also wet, but the driver glued his eyes on me. He drove me home, two blocks away, hardly moving his eyes from the rearview mirror.

My wet T-shirt and bare legs may have been titillating or erotic, but that wasn't the only cause of his fascination. As an unmarried female, I'd cycled muddy trails in monsoon rain with two unrelated males—strange enough in his world. I lived alone. I had a job. Women in India were *Trained* to be obedient, modest, and docile, with no freedom compared to me. My life was beyond his comprehension.

Avoiding eye contact in the rearview mirror, I reflected on my own *Training*. I was thankful that my country now allowed—even encouraged—independent women like me.

When I got out of his car, my gawking neighbors watched me climb the outdoor concrete stairs to my fourth floor flat. I'm sure they discussed my condition with the puzzled driver, but I couldn't understand a word of it. Anyway, I was intent on a hot shower. A thorough, soapy scrub with lots of hot water dislodged the greasy mud. I felt invigorated. Few days in my India experience matched this one! "Thank you," I said.

Jaideep, the Pune Customer Care manager, Nahid, the Ahmadabad Customer Care Manager, and I spent two days instructing six new-hires in Ahmadabad. Afterwards, Nahid took Jaideep and me to her favorite restaurant. Because it was Thursday, Jaideep needed to stop at the temple for Puja (prayers). He always worshiped Ganish, the Elephant God, before his Thursday evening meal. Jaideep stayed in the temple five minutes, and then Nahid drove us through the muddy streets to the restaurant. The monsoon rains were heavy enough to make a muddy mess but not heavy enough to lower the 120 degree temperatures.

The interior of the restaurant, called "Tomatoes," looked like Billy McHales in Seattle. Faux American antiques covered the walls, and the menu looked deliciously familiar. Mouth watering, I ordered chicken ranchero. I lost my enthusiasm when the not-so-pleasant waiter delivered curry chicken and rice, like every other Indian dish, except it contained chicken. I feigned delight so as not to dash Nahid's satisfaction in bringing us to this *American* restaurant.

I wondered what she would think of my favorite Indian restaurant in Seattle.

Intense heat assaulted our return to the muddy street. A bent old man waited near the door with a cane and dented metal cup, calling, "Bah, Bah" (bread, bread) as he tapped his toothless mouth with bent, arthritic fingers. He wore a dirty once-white *dhoti*. The long piece of unstitched fabric wrapped like a diaper between his frail, deformed legs. The end hung over his emaciated chest and bony shoulder. A tangerine-colored turban overwhelmed his gaunt dark face.

A dirty little boy in sienna-stained rags stood next to him while an ear-ringed pet monkey vulgarly humped the boy's head. The dirty beggars were an emotional shock after the American atmosphere of Tomatoes. Hunger more than satiated, we hurried past. My eyes stung with gratitude.-

A severe stomachache had bothered Jaideep for several days, and the hotel doctor prescribed medicine. We stopped at a chemist for the prescription. While Nahid and I waited in the car, a skeletal toothless woman with a skinny baby on her hip begged at the open window. Nahid gave her a coin. Soon a parade of beggars shouted insults when Nahid and I ran out of coins. Even in the heat, we rolled up the windows until Jaideep returned a few minutes later.

The next morning, Jaideep and I were lucky to get a seat on an eight o'clock flight to Pune. Otherwise, we would have had to wait for the train leaving at four in the afternoon. Back at my flat, I called Ray to let him know I'd arrived safely and I wouldn't be coming to the office. I was feeling queasy. By Saturday morning, even in the Pune heat, I had chills and my fever was 103 degrees. My body ached for four days, and I slept most of the time if I wasn't reeling to the bathroom. Ray phoned to check on me, but I couldn't talk.

On Sunday, he came to my flat and insisted I go to the hospital. I refused. I'd seen the hospital. The windows had no screens and the rooms no air conditioning. I'd read in the newspaper that, to save money, they reused "disposable" syringes and other equipment. My chances of survival were better alone in my flat.

By Tuesday, I kept down a cup of canned broth that Aruna, the maid, heated for me, but it was weeks before my strength returned to running or biking capacity.

In early August, Ray, Guy, and I planned a trip to Manali, a picturesque hill station in the Himalaya foothills. We flew to Delhi on Thursday after work and checked into the Grand Hyatt. The company's travel agent booked three rooms for us, but I canceled mine and shared with Ray. That night we ate pizza with real pepperoni, drank wine, and slept with clean, fresh sheets on a real mattress and box springs.

Friday morning we blissfully ate bacon and eggs, toast with butter, and fresh coffee with real cream, then headed to the airport only to find that the single-engine plane had crashed. I tried to get more information, but the agent at the counter spoke little English and didn't seem too concerned. Hindus believe in reincarnation, which I think lessons their sense of loss when human lives are lost. The incident also heightened my awareness of safety issues.

Back at the Hyatt, we drank coffee, again with "real" cream in the Regency Club and developed plan B. A pilgrimage to Agra and the Taj Mahal was our unanimous decision. Using the concierge, we booked train tickets for Saturday morning and then walked to the Red Fort or Lal Quila. The fort was very large, made of very red clay, and housed very aggressive pickpockets.

Lal Quila, once a magnificent fort, had become a crowded market called the "Meena Bazaar." Shah Jahan, the medieval Muslim emperor, had the fort constructed in the mid fifteenth century.

High humidity, 110-degree temperatures, heavily polluted air, and the assertive shopkeepers overshadowed the historical significance of the fort. Vendors hawked antiques, paintings, fake ivory jewelry, and woven carpets. Tourist traps are alive and well even in Delhi, India. We each bought a brass singing bowl and walked back to the hotel's oasis.

At the Hyatt, I took a sturdy, hot shower, dried with plush, white towels, and coiled into a soft hotel bathrobe. Ray and I read, took a nap, and relaxed in air-conditioned luxury. At seven that evening, we met Guy for wine in the Regency Club. We had dinner at the hotel's Italian restaurant, avoiding exposure to the hot, dusty streets. We drank red wine and ate pasta with meat sauce.

I promised myself I would never take such luxury for granted.

Overnight, I vomited several times, but Ray never stirred. I didn't know if my body had rejected the rich food or if I'd eaten something tainted. I vomited regularly during the India assignment, so I thought nothing of it. I brushed my teeth and went back to bed.

At six in the morning, we found beggars, hawkers, and families sleeping in the dirt at the train station. People stared as we waited. Ray could pass for a local with his black hair and suntanned skin, but Guy was six-foot-two and overweight, a giant compared to local men. I looked like a pale space invader. A group of teenage girls congregated near us. One tentatively touched my blond hair and recoiled as if it were hot. I doubt they'd ever touched or even seen blond hair.

The Agra train station was the worst I saw in India. Deformed and dismembered beggars mingled among the multitude of travelers. One boy's foot was bigger than an elephant's. I learned later that this condition was treatable if the proper drugs were available. With difficulty, we conquered our shock, assumed a confident posture, and moved rapidly among the hawkers and deformed beggars tugging at our sleeves until we reached our prearranged hired car.

From a distance, the Taj Mahal's white marble glowed in the poor, muddy city of Agra, a sharp contrast to the squalor beyond its gates, underscoring the disparity among the classes in India, then and now.

Starting in 1632, twenty thousand workers toiled for twenty-two years on the banks of the Yamuna River to build the memorial to Mumtaz Mahal, the wife of emperor, Shah Jahan. He built the Taj Mahal as a tribute to their love when she died giving birth to their fourteenth child.

Gems adorn the Taj Mahal: lapis, carnelian, turquoise, agate, coral, garnets, onyx, amethyst, and jade. Its diamonds, rubies, and sapphires had been pilfered years ago. To me, the spirituality had been pilfered as well. I tried to imagine what it must have been like in the 1600s and suspected little had changed, especially for the women.

⚬ ⚬

At our office construction site, three-and four-year-olds cared for their smaller siblings. Children older than five had jobs. A little girl with baby teeth collected recyclable ceiling material in a big white bag. I watched the foreman scold her in a tone and body language anyone could understand. When I asked Jaideep about this cruelty, he said, "Marcia, she will be having a rupee for eating." Without her wages, the five-year-old would go hungry. I thought of the pot roast and potatoes my grandmother fixed for me when I was five. My farm chores were entertainment not sustenance. I thanked the guides for my good fortune.

Our offices were smelly and dusty with no air conditioning. Both genders used one bathroom where Western-style toilets had been installed. They were unusual. The locals were accustomed to the porcelain, floor-level style used for squatting. The women we'd hired stood on the seat, leaving mud and scratches. I used the bathroom only when utterly necessary.

One day I left to have lunch and to use the bathroom in my flat. It was clean and the hum of the air-conditioner masked the cacophonous clatter in the street below. I decided to work at home for the rest of the day.

As I booted up my laptop, Birdie, the toothless caretaker, rang the bell. When I opened the door, five tiny, dark-skinned, shirtless men burst into the room, chattering in Hindi. They were the air conditioner maintenance crew. One man dragged an upholstered chair from the dining area to use as a stepstool. I didn't want to think where his bare feet had been. They removed the filters and used a hair dryer to blast out the dirt. Dust filled the room. I began coughing. *It will take Aruna longer than usual to clean this afternoon,* I thought. A barefooted fellow came through the room with dripping wet filters he'd washed in the shower. *The bathroom will need Aruna's extra attention as well.* Finally, they turned the air conditioner back on, I stopped choking, and Aruna arrived at three-thirty. I was ready for a Scotch!

The woman across the hall, Mrs. Pradundh, had a reputation for being rude and demanding to anyone she considered less than she, which was most of India. Her husband was an engineer for my company. The woman revered my title—general manager of customer service—a but found it odd that I didn't have a husband. She treated me like a carnival sideshow attraction. As I put the key in my door after grocery shopping one Saturday, my dark-skinned neighbor opened her door. Bright sunlight backlit her green-and-gold sari and filled the small hallway between our two flats. "You will be having tea with me?" she said with her head rocking from side to side, ear to shoulder.

Unable to think of an excuse, I said, "Thank you. I'll be over in a minute." Groceries stashed in the little fridge, I crossed the narrow hall. Mrs. Pradundh filled a pan with tap water. I asked, "Would you mind using bottled water? I have plenty," pointing in the direction of my flat. "Oh, that is not being necessary," she said, rocking her head while adding water-buffalo milk to the pan. The milk was worse than tap water. When the mixture began steaming, she added slices of fresh ginger root and ground black pepper and let it steep while she sliced what looked like pound cake. She put the cake on two small wooden plates and poured the tea into handless mugs. I carried mine and followed her into the living room. I sat across from her on an uncomfortable chair exactly like the ones in my flat. Like a *well-trained girl* from Ohio, I sampled the ginger-pepper tea and ate a small piece of cake. Both were surprisingly tasty. She asked me a lot of questions but ignored my answers. I couldn't wait for the obligatory summit to end.

Diarrhea plagued me for the following four days. Mrs. Pradundh tried several times to invite me to dinner, but I managed to avoid all invitations.

A few weeks later, Jaideep and I met in his third floor office to discuss the PBX (phone system). Through the window behind him, I watched a small, reedy woman dressed in a bright-green Maharashtra-style sari. The front looked like a normal sari, but the back looked like baggy pants. She climbed four flights of rough concrete stairs with no shoes and used one thin arm to balance a board with six large, rough, bricks on her head. Her other arm secured a gaunt, dirty child. Eight hollow-faced women followed her on the open concrete stairs, all balancing boards piled with big red bricks. I lost my concentration. Ludicrous, ridiculous, absurd, pointless. We were discussing electronic telephone technology while these women carried bricks to the fourth floor of a construction site because it was cheaper than using a mechanical hoist. "What am I doing here?" I accidentally said aloud. Jaideep turned to find my distraction. "Will our cellular system have an impact on these people? Will their children benefit?" I asked. I didn't really expect an answer.

Jaideep was confused; the scene looked normal to him. I thought, *We're building the Golden Gate Bridge over Kelsey Creek.*

"India is being very different. You must be having a shock." Then he asked, "What is living like in America?"

Where could I begin? Women's rights, human rights, basic sanitation? It would be difficult to explain in a place where untouchables collected cow dung in the streets, dried the patties in the hot sun, and sold them for cooking fires, a place where cows freely roamed the city streets. "Very different, Jaideep," I said, "very different."

"I am watching *Melrose Place* on cable TV. Is that like America?" he asked.

"Well, uh, more or less, I guess ... uh ..."

Ray came in. "How are plans coming for the call center?" I was thankful for the reprieve. I knew that Jaideep and his wife were Brahmans, the highest social caste in Hindu culture. The women I watched on the stairs were Sudra, the laborer caste. Though customs were changing, I was sure Jaideep's father or grandfather would consider these people no higher than most animals and much lower than cattle or rats. "Yes, life in America is *sort of* like *Melrose Place*. Now, about the PBX ..."

<hr>

Before I'd left Bellevue, I'd bought two video cameras, one for Niki and one for me, so we could exchange videos of our disparate lives. I sent videos of these women wearing saris, carrying bricks and babies. I sent shots of oxcarts lumbering through the mud streets. Niki sent videos of my granddaughters getting a bath in clear water, Paige playing in the green park, and Taylor on the carpet rolling over for the first time. I watched them repeatedly but the videos made me even more homesick.

I wondered if these women had guides like mine. I always achieved what I wanted. The difficulty was figuring out *what* I wanted. These women never considered asking; they knew their fate by the caste they were born into. It would not change until their next life; no sense asking. I was sure that if they believed more was available to them in this life, they could have it, but I was helpless to change their situation.

Aruna was different from most Sudra. She and her sister cleaned house for Guy, Ray, and me. Aruna wanted more in life and successfully did her Hindu *puja* (prayers) for what she achieved, including a tin roof for her home. She was too embarrassed to take me there, but I'm sure it was built with sticks and rags.

"What does your husband do?" I asked.

"Do?" She looked at me curiously. "Nothing."

"Has he tried to find a job?' I said.

"Why?" she said.

"No reason." I switched away from a conversation we couldn't have. "Tomorrow, would you teach me to make nan?"

She'd taught herself English so she could work for foreigners, who paid more and treated her with respect.

When Aruna found a quarter on the floor, she asked, "What is this?"

"That's a quarter, one fourth of a US dollar."

In an instant Aruna replied, "Oh, about eight rupees?" She would have done well with an education.

The night before I left India, Jaideep and Roma, his wife, hosted a farewell party at their apartment. Aruna helped me wrap my blue-and-gold sari for the party. I found my exposed midriff embarrassing, then realized how silly that was. Indian women cover all parts of their bodies, except for the midriff. I was accustomed to exposing my legs, not my middle.

Ray looked like a local in the long, beige pajama *kurta* he wore to the party.

In the office, the men wore jeans and polo shirts, while the local women and I (sometimes) dressed in *salwar kameez*, a mid-calf cotton dress worn over baggy pants that narrowed at the ankle. A long scarf, a *dupatta*, completed each *salwar* set.

That night, however, the women wore their more formal saris, and the men wore very American-looking shirts and trousers, emphasizing the changing Indian society and the position of women along the continuum.

Even before Jaideep opened the door, a bouquet of enticing aromas filled the hallway: cardamom, cinnamon, peppers, onions, and garlic. Roma prepared vegetarian dishes common in India, including *nan* (flat bread), *daal* (lentils), *paneer* (cheese), potatoes, green beans, and yogurt sauces. There were fruits and vegetables I'd never seen, spices I'd never tasted, and a coconut sauce I'd love to make at home.

The drive to my flat after dinner was my first and only traverse through Pune at midnight. Hoards of people slept by the streets. Occasionally we saw a blanket bouncing, customary nighttime behavior in any country, but more likely on a bed, not a crowded sidewalk. There'd be another street child in about nine months.

I knew I'd miss spending time with Ray until his return to Seattle in a few months, but I was ready to go home. As the small plane left the ground in Pune, I held my breath. I knew the meaning of quality and didn't want to think about the safety of the plane. They'd overbooked the plane, so the flight attendant stood while a customer sat in her rear-facing seat during the two-hour flight.

The six-hour flight from Delhi to Hong Kong departed at midnight, but I couldn't get comfortable enough to sleep, even in business class.

Then United Airlines delayed the Hong Kong departure to San Francisco for two hours because the plane was too heavy. They offered passengers $400 to take a later flight. I whispered to the stranger next to me, "United doesn't *have* enough money to get me off this plane."

During the fourteen-hour flight, I vomited several times, probably Roma's unintentional oversight. While vomiting had become commonplace during my stay in India, I was ready for it to be over. The flight attendant gave me Pepto-Bismol, but I couldn't sleep, I couldn't read, I couldn't think or feel. I felt numb and strangely unattached.

Going back to life in Seattle would be difficult. Some stateside friends had seen photos and chapters of my journal I'd sent. Some had commented on the disagreeable smell of my stationery. Still, to my family, friends and colleagues, this assignment had been an exotic foreign holiday. They had no idea what immersion in the Indian culture meant on a daily basis—they liked Indian food, but eating it never made them vomit.

We landed in San Francisco at the connecting flight's departure time. Because this was my first port of entry, I had to claim my luggage and recheck it after customs. The flight attendant said I had a chance to make my connection because the Seattle flight was also late. Then the security guard stopped me. "Please turn on this portable printer," she said. As perspiration dripped from my greasy hair, I focused my energy on being calm and polite. "It's impossible to turn on the printer without setting up the computer. Why don't you just keep this little old printer?" I said with tears in my eyes. "I really don't need it any more … I'm going home!"

With amazing compassion, the guard smiled at me. "No problem," she said. "Run along and catch your flight."

"Thank you," I said, not just to the security guard. I closed my briefcase and made an impressive eight-minute sprint to the domestic gate.

My plane was still there. I ran down the gangway and hurried past the gate attendant into the cabin, but a tall, smiling man occupied my first class seat.

"I'm sorry, miss; you'll need to take the next flight," said the attendant, preparing to close the door from the outside.

"No, *I'm* sorry! I'm booked on *this* flight," I said, surprising myself.

"But, ma'am..."

"Look," I checked my watch. "I left my apartment in India thirty-four hours ago. I just want to go home. There must be one empty seat on this flight."

"Yes, ma'am, there's a seat in coach." He was shocked that I would fly coach instead of waiting an hour for first class. I got a middle seat in the back of the plane, but I drank free Bloody Marys and used the first class toilet, important to someone who'd been living in India.

Niki, Paige, and Taylor met me at the gate. Four-year-old Paige hopped with excitement, and Taylor, in a stroller, stretched her chubby, dimpled hands toward me. *What more could Grandma want?* I thought. My tears flowed freely. We hugged.

Paige said, "Grandma, you don't smell very good."

"I'm sorry, sweetheart. I've been traveling for a long time." Niki and I laughed.

At home, after a long hot shower, I reflected on my life in India and my journey to freedom. I wrote in my journal:

HOME AT LAST!!! I'm as sensitive as a skinless blister to the subtle things I never noticed or thought important. It feels peculiar to brush my teeth with tap water, rather than bottled water. The water pressure is sufficient to rinse shampoo from my hair, and I can open my mouth when I wash my face without fear of diarrhea. It isn't necessary to tap on cupboard doors to notify uninvited occupants of my approach. My bed is comfortable and clean. I have no concern for huge crawling roaches, lizards, or black, hopping spiders. I can't smell moth balls, rancid trash, or human feces. No leper sits on my street corner, begging for help. There is no whistle-tooting night-watchman or AC fan blended with the rickshaw horns, dancer's drums, and other Indian night noises. It is absolutely still. The air is fresh and clean. I treasure Seattle, especially on warm, sunny, clear days like today, but I will never treasure it more than I do on this day!

I remembered the tender childhood days on the farm when Grandma served homemade ice cream on hot summer days. I remembered Gramps' woods when my brothers and I played in cool, clean, creek water that flowed through the ravine. I remembered the miserable days when I thought I'd never escape the house on the hill in Kentucky, when my identity was so submerged I thought my Self would drown. I remembered my fear of the Ohio River Bridge and the long drive through deep snow to spring and independence.

I'd based my decision to go to India on a vague, involuntary sense of destiny. Nothing in my life could have forecast the impact. Most Indian women are valued less than rats or cows and have no hope of changing until their next lives according to Hindu indoctrination. I compared my *Training* to theirs and felt strengthened. As an American woman in the 1990s, I had the *freedom* to struggle toward my own path. Although my career remained the end rather than a means to an end, I began to realize that my corporate life didn't honor my true spirit. Appreciating the significance would require additional effort. I remained focused on making a living in a male-dominated environment.

chapter twenty-one

Once Ray returned from India, we often hiked alpine trails. We mountain biked in the Okanogan. We ran our daily five miles together, even when we'd planned long bike rides. Whether biking, running, or hiking, he always stayed several yards ahead of me—too far to hear me shout. Occasionally, he'd wait for me to catch up, then he'd leave before I had time to drink water and catch my breath. I tried to be OK with this part of our routine.

He usually zipped our sleeping bags together even when we hadn't showered. I tried to convince myself the mingled sweaty odor of exhausted bodies was natural and intimate, but I never felt sexy. I refused to acknowledge the longing for more feminine-ness and blindly maintained my sporty façade. I'd packaged myself in a tom-boyish wrapper, just as I had tried to be "fancy" for Stuart. *Training* had taught me to please the man. Predictably, the rhythm of a loving relationship eluded us.

One afternoon, he stayed uncharacteristically close while we hiked in the Cascades. Without skipping a step, he blurted, "Let's go to the next level." I was breathless and not from the elevation gain. Warblers sang their spring mating song, a musical mountain stream trickled its tune, and a gentle breeze moved the sweet alpine air around us, alone on the trail. He hadn't held me in his arms and said, "I love you, I want to spend my life with you." He'd said, "Let's go to the next level," without even looking at me.

My brain raced. *"If this means he wants to marry me, it wouldn't work if he can't say so. If he wants me to move in with him ... well, that won't work either."* I made a vague remark like, "Wouldn't that be something," pulled a long draw on my water bottle, and rummaged for a Cliff Bar in my bum-bag. "Here, you want half-a this?"

I loved him, but I'd been play-acting. He loved me, too, in his stifled, cryptic way. He was unable to share the warm heart hidden deep inside. I stopped pretending I didn't need it. For ten years, Ray and I had been colleagues with an off-and-on romantic relationship. It was over.

chapter twenty-two

*S*tuart and I continued to communicate after he moved to China. My relationship with Ray ended just months before Stuart planned to return home. Stuart arranged to meet me in Guangzhou. We planned to spend time with our friends, Harvey and Xiaobao, and finally visit Tibet.

I checked into a hotel in Guangzhou at midnight. In the morning, Xiaobao answered the phone when I called. "Glad you made it OK, but there's a problem: Americans bombed the Chinese Embassy in Belgrade. There are anti-American protests all over China. It's not safe for you to leave the hotel." I had planned to spend the day exploring Guangzhou. Stuart would fly from Beijing, meet me at the hotel, and we'd have dinner with Harvey and Xiaobao. Plans had changed.

I closed the curtains and turned on the TV. The Chinese stations were running film, but I couldn't understand the language. BBC reported that NATO planners mistakenly believed the embassy was the headquarters of a Yugoslav military organization. The report showed the burning embassy in Belgrade and picketers in China.

The NATO secretary general said it was a mistake.

Bill Clinton offered "profound condolences."

Russia's U.N. ambassador called it "a barbaric action."

BBC ran film of Clinton justifying NATO's mission in Yugoslavia, "Someone, sometime, has got to stand up against this sort of ethnic cleansing and killing people wholesale ... solely because of their religion and ethnicity."

I turned off the TV. I knew I'd never learn the truth, no matter what the pundits said.

I made hotel coffee in the bathroom, ate a granola bar, and settled on the bed with a book.

A few hours later, Xiaobao called. She and Harvey would come to the hotel to help me check out and take me to their compound.

Stuart would meet me there. We planned to have dinner with Harvey and Xiaobao to celebrate Stuart's retirement and pending return to the US, then fly to Chengdu to get our travel visas for Tibet.

Picketers couldn't see me through the darkened van window. Harvey explained, "There are strict rules governing this sort of public display. The government buses the protesters to the American Embassy and Consulate and distributes signs to carry. Then they bus the protesters home." Still, I was uneasy.

My apprehension faded once safely inside the gates of their walled city block.

Harvey and Xiaobao's business was restoring antique furniture. Their kitchen, bedroom, and bathroom were in the same building as their showroom. Xiaobao's mother and father lived in another house while the artisans lived in still another.

While Xiaobao arranged for tea, Harvey took me on a tour of their compound. First, we passed the lush garden with green beans, yellow squash, peas, corn, long, purple eggplant, and other vegetables I couldn't identify. A dark-skinned Chinese man in a conical straw hat bent over a hoe, chopping at small weeds between the rows of vegetables. I felt as if I were in a movie.

Room after room was filled to high ceilings with dirty old furniture that looked beyond repair—all shapes and sizes of cabinets, chairs, tables, wooden buckets, and items I'd never seen before. One room contained tall stacks of old lumber and beams from dilapidated barns and homes. Harvey explained, "The artists use the old lumber to carve replacement parts so that every inch of the restored piece retains the patina of aged wood."

Next, we toured the artisan's quarters. Twenty men lived in immaculate barracks. "These talented artists come from all over China. They leave their families and live like college students because we pay so much more than they could make in their villages," Harvey explained as we walked to the studio where the men performed their magic.

Small-framed Chinese men, young and old, hovered over unrecognizable parts of furniture, using ancient tools to restore each piece to museum quality. They were so intent on their work they hardly noticed me.

One man carved a face the size of a thumbnail to restore a Xian cabinet defaced during the Cultural Revolution. Another man worked on a table leg once gnawed by rodents; others used soft cloths to remove years of filth from a cabinet. Before we left the studio, I picked out the cabinet I wanted. At home, it would be worth more than $5,000 but I paid the much cheaper local price, less than the cost of shipping.

We crossed a small courtyard to the showroom and their living quarters. Brilliant, red bougainvillea and other tropical flowers glowed in the midday sun. The gallery resembled an America furniture store with groupings of restored ancient pieces, accented with silk rugs, primitive pottery, original paintings, and glassware. When we reached the area where restored bedroom furniture and cabinets were displayed, Harvey said, "Do you mind sleeping here tonight? Xiaobao and I will be in the next room. We bolted the doors and gates. You're quite safe here."

"I'm grateful for the invitation," I said.

I settled into the studio's display museum, remarkably relaxed in the large space and unusual surroundings. I slept in a restored, eighteenth-century, Qing Dynasty canopy bed, worth about $300,000 in the foreign market. The carved wood panels depicted *chi* dragons among scrolls and clouds. Exotic birds and flowers embellished the apron, while phoenixes and peonies, symbolizing longevity and abundance, decorated the base. The mattress was seven feet square.

I slept soundly in the historic bed and awoke tucked inside the mosquito netting. I wore a heavy silk nightgown and left the matching purple bathrobe on the bed. Oblivious to the bolted door and unsettled world beyond, I wandered barefoot through the treasures in the dim early-morning light. The cold stone floor and rough brick walls contrasted with the smooth warm woods and luxurious silk rugs.

I touched delicate carvings and felt the presence of the original artisans. The air was thick with their gratitude. Harvey had recognized artistic significance beneath years of neglect and granted each piece the opportunity to endure, lucky to be chosen for restoration but not as lucky as I felt to move freely among these treasures and spend time with Harvey and Xiaobao, their liberators.

Harvey found me roaming in the filtered amber light. I quickly put on the heavy, raw silk robe and joined him in the dining room for coffee.

An ancestral painting, fifteen feet wide and ten feet tall, hung on the wall by the finely carved dining table. Harvey explained: "The painting is a historical record. Family members are shown wearing their finest silk garments, which proclaim their rank or status." The people in the painting sat on elaborate chairs one row above the other, as if on risers. Each person looked straight ahead, solemn. "These commemorative portraits were painted posthumously, so several generations are represented here, even though they look close in age." The images were nearly life-size.

The women in the painting hid their erotic bound feet behind their robes and long sleeves concealed feminine hands; otherwise it was difficult to distinguish females from males. "The painting depicts a family from the Qing Dynasty," he said. "Paintings like this began to disappear with the advent of photography."

"How old is it?" I asked.

"This one was probably painted around 1850."

"I feel as if they're watching us," I told Harvey.

"They are," he said.

He poured hot coffee into beautiful blue and white mugs. We discussed life, art, and business. Harvey had a unique gift for coaxing passion from his art and from the people around him.

A loud clank of the brass knocker on the five-inch-thick wooden door broke the spell. The door nearly reached the top of the fifteen-foot ceiling. The locking bolt made a screeching sound as Harvey moved it aside, and the huge rusty hinges creaked. Xiaobao's elderly parents entered. Mother wore a square-fitting, flowered blouse and baggy, straight-legged, plaid pants. Father's navy-blue, Mao suit was well-worn. They both wore black *bu xei*, cloth slip-on shoes with thin plastic soles. They would be joining us for breakfast. They spoke no English.

Xiaobao's father, Xikun Yao, was a veteran of China's epic Long March, and her mother, Fengying Gao, had been an active revolutionary during the Sino-Japanese War. They hated the American government. I was Harvey and Xiaobao's friend, however, and the old people welcomed me regardless of my nationality. Xiaobao joined us and translated for her father.

"How can American people be so good and their government be so bad?"

I thought, *The same way the Chinese government can be so bad,* but of course, I said nothing. I felt honored that he accepted me so quickly.

Knowing that I would be meeting Father and Mother Yao, I'd brought small gifts— perfume for Mother and a folding Leatherman pocketknife for Father, because I knew he enjoyed woodcarving. His work incorporated the natural curves of roots and branches he gathered from all over China when traveling with Harvey and Xiaobao. "*Shay shay,*" they said softly, revealing no emotion. I knew that a sentimental display was inappropriate. Xiaobao assured me they would enjoy their gifts.

After breakfast, we toured the old folks' living quarters where Father exhibited his natural, unique carvings. Xiaobao translated. "Please accept a gift from parents." She offered me a carved root, a foot tall. It looked vaguely like a gryphon. Father had carved and polished the head of an eagle leaving the natural shapes of the root to form the body and legs of a lion. The symbolism of this carving, eagle and lion, offered by the old communist gentleman to the American woman, hung heavy in the air. The piece was exquisite, and I struggled to avoid inappropriate tears.

Stuart arrived late that afternoon. Because of the demonstrations, we couldn't travel to Chengdu to get the visa for Tibet. "Well, if we can't go to Tibet, let's go to Kathmandu," Stuart said. Xiaobao scheduled our flight and we left the next day. The government-organized demonstrations had subsided, but travel to Chengdu remained unsafe.

To most Americans, the Kathmandu airport would have seemed primitive, but it was far superior to what I'd seen in India. We took a beat-up taxi to the Yak & Yeti Hotel at Dubar Marg, the most Western hotel in the city. A familiar wooden frame held the four-inch thick foam mattress with clean sheets. I slept well.

The next day we took a small plane from Kathmandu to Pokhara, closer to the Himalayan foothills. I shot images of the plane's wing with "Buddha Air" painted on the turned-up wing tip, framed by the Himalayan peaks above the clouds.

I'm a long way from Ohio, I thought. *Another dream I never could have imagined.*

At an exclusive hilltop resort, we watched the warm, monsoon rain from the porch, their only guests that night. Our modern suite had Western furnishings, including a small coffee pot. I thought it seemed a little too lovely, considering our location, but Stuart liked comfort, and it was his treat. When the sun came out on day two, Stuart didn't want to hike, so I spent the morning trekking with the resort's guide. A panoramic view of the Annapurna Range entertained Stuart as he read a Dan Brown novel with his feet propped on a low, stone wall. He'd been working very hard in air-polluted Beijing and found rejuvenation just breathing clean mountain air in quiet solitude.

Before leaving Bellevue, I'd researched Thangkas or scroll paintings. They are meticulously hand-painted by monks and illustrate a contemplative experience or lesson. I was determined to pay a reasonable price for them, about $30 USD—still double what a local would pay and at least ten times less than the US price. Many incense-filled shops offered hundreds for sale, but as soon as the vendors saw my blond head and heard my American accent, the price more than quadrupled. I sorted through hundreds of paintings, feigning disinterest in the delicate work.

I felt the energy of one Thangka even before I tugged it from the wooden bin. I couldn't ignore it. The shopkeeper unrolled it. From three feet away, this Thangka looked like a square in a circle in a rectangle. The monk had painted the fifteen by twenty inch canvas with tiny strokes of muted rose, blue, brown, and shiny gold. At close range, however, detail emerged. Serpents and dragons framed the outer edge. Vignettes around the inner circle showed gods and goddesses in temples and gardens. Symmetrical scenes of Buddha sitting in various positions filled the middle of the square. Detailed. Exquisite. I began to barter as if I didn't care.

"This one is probably OK," I said. "How much?"

At first, the shopkeeper ignored me and tried to barter with Stuart, who held up his palms and said, "Not *my* wife, not *my* wife." Confused, the shopkeeper reluctantly talked to me. He would not go below $50 USD, so I headed down the wooden stairs into the muddy street with an astonished Stuart close behind. I would have happily paid more if the monk or his temple got the extra. During the rainy off-season, I knew we'd find many amazing paintings and a shopkeeper who would meet my price. Besides, bartering was part of the fun. The shopkeeper shouted from behind us, "OK, thirty dollar; it deal, it deal." He wrapped my Thangka in many layers of Sanskrit newsprint to protect it from the rain, and I gave him $30 in American currency, not rupees, which made him smile. At home, the Thangka hung on my wall for a year before I realized it represented a mandala, a circle of life.

In the western hills of Kathmandu, I photographed the eerie Buddha eyes painted on the Swayambunath Stupa, the Monkey Temple. Prayer wheels, filled with carefully written prayers, flanked the walkways. The Nepalese believe that when the wheel spins, prayers fly to the heavens, repeating many times, thus increasing the odds of being heard.

As Stuart and I walked around the stupa, I felt the energy of those prayers and dreams spew into the air. The muscles in my chest and throat tightened. A penetrating quiet filled me. I was relieved when Stuart, insensitive to the spiritual surroundings, wandered off to watch the monkeys eat peanuts and left me to contemplate thick emotion caused by the spinning wheels, fluttering prayer flags, and mystical currents.

A ten-year-old shop girl read my face and her black eyes smiled, as if she heard the muffled song of my spirit.

Incense permeated her dimly lit six-foot-by-six-foot shop filled with hand-carved stone Buddha statues. At first, I was more interested in a broken English conversion with this exotic, dark-skinned child until I touched a strangely familiar stone Buddha statue. It held the same pose as the huge Tian Ta Buddha I'd visited near Hong Kong—my first introduction to Buddhism.

I held it, and we began the obligatory disinterested bartering game, but a shrill yelp interrupted us. She ran from the small room, her face twisted with concern. I followed. The piercing sound originated from a table covered with trinkets. The girl crawled underneath to recover a puppy. It was probably six weeks old and weighed no more than three pounds. Someone had stepped on his tail. She nuzzled and stroked the ball of brown fur, softly whispering words I couldn't translate but understood. We returned to her shop to barter for the five-inch Buddha that had selected me before the shrill disruption. She started at five dollars. We agreed on three. She put the puppy on the table while she wrapped my statue in Sanskrit newsprint. I stowed it in my shoulder bag, then took a US $5 bill from my pocket. With two hands, I presented it to the girl and said, "This is a gift just for you."

A white, new-teeth smile covered her ten-year-old brown face. "You wait, you wait," she shouted as she entered the adjoining room where, every night, she slept on a straw mat on the floor. She came back with her hand completely closed around a tiny cloisonné pillbox. "This gift you," she said. I accepted with both hands and thanked her from a place in my heart I didn't know existed.

I scratched the soft ears protruding from the ball of fur she adored, then pressed my hands together with my elbows high. She put the puppy down and did the same. "Namaste," we said simultaneously.

Stuart's six-foot-two redheaded frame appeared, looking strange in the doorway. "You've gotta see these cool monkeys," he said. "It's called the Monkey Temple for a reason, ya know."

I followed him around the stupa and we watched foreigners toss peanuts to the sacrosanct brown monkeys that inhabited the sanctuary. He felt no hint of the temple's spirituality. I decided not to mention it.

The next morning, Stuart arranged for a car to take us to the Royal Chitwan National Wildlife Refuge, about a four-hour drive south of Pokhara on the opposite side of Nepal. English royalty had once hunted wild tigers there. Stuart and I didn't see the tigers, but one morning we saw footprints in the soft riverbank mud.

Hundreds of candles lit the dining tent. We were joined by ten other guests, all much older, mostly British. The handsome blond waiter, a zoology student at Oxford, asked if we wanted veg or non-veg, the only choice for our meal. I ordered veg. Stuart ordered non-veg. We both ordered Glenfiddich, no ice, from the well-stocked bar. When the tasty food arrived, I stopped the waiter to say, "This is delicious, but I ordered veg; this is chicken." In a British accent that would melt a schoolgirl, the young man said, "Yes, mum, this is tofu. I hope you enjoy it."

After dinner, Stuart and I sat in wooden lounge chairs on the mowed lawn and watched the rhinos in tall, hazy grass about a hundred yards away. "Granddad would have loved to photograph this," I told Stuart, who wasn't listening. That night, I lay awake while the rhinos foraged under our cottage-on-stilts.

A herd of captive elephants shared the resort, including two huge eleven-foot males weighing about ten thousand pounds each, several females, and a young cow about nine months old, born after a bull escaped and had his way with her mother. No one knew she was expecting until the calf appeared.

Handlers had cut the tusks short to keep everyone safe. The handlers led one of the elephants as close as possible to the porch of the cottage-on-stilts so Stuart and I could hop into the box-like saddle. Riding an elephant felt like riding a huge rocking chair high above the ground. I was euphoric. The next morning I rode again, while the air was still cool and damp. Stuart relaxed on the lawn, finishing his Dan Brown novel.

During the ride, a big rhino parted the tall, wet grass a few feet away. He bobbed his impressive single horn and gave a loud snort. I held on tight in the corner of the elephant saddle, bracing for what I thought would be a bloody battle, but the elephant made no obvious response to the exhibition. The trainers knew this bluff. An out-of-focus photo of the rhino's movements in the tall grass was my favorite image of the entire trip.

I also took evening rides when the dew had dried and the grass was noisy. The Nepalese handler, who spoke no English, and the British zoological student accompanied me on each ride. We crossed shallow rivers and saw countless rhino in the ten-foot grass. The handsome student told me the elephants ate seven hundred pounds of grass every day but not while on a ride; eating is their reward when they return to the elephants' corral.

We returned early from one ride when dark clouds and loud thunder made the elephant more nervous than the rhinos, so I joined Stuart in relaxation under the cottage-on-stilts.

After our first ride, Stuart and I waded into the Chitwan River to help the trainers bathe the elephants. Wearing shorts, a T-shirt, and Teva sandals, I stepped into the knee-high muddy water. The Tevas sank into the silty mud, which oozed between my toes. It was softer than creek mud in Ohio. I tried not to think about poisonous snakes, man-eating fish, or crocodiles. Certainly, they would stay away from a river full of elephants and their handlers. Stuart and I were the only guests who accepted the invitation to bathe the elephants. We took pictures of each other splashing and rubbing the muddy gray skin of the Asian elephants while older guests stood on the riverbank watching. I grinned and waved my enthusiasm to a blue-haired British woman standing onshore. She wore big, white earrings and carried a straw purse over her arm as if on her way to the mall. I whispered to Stuart, "At least she's not in a rocking chair on her porch."

The trip was a celebration of Stuart's retirement and pending return to Seattle, and for me, remarkably inexpensive. I used United Airlines frequent flyer tickets to get to Guangzhou, and Stuart paid for everything else.

In Chitwan, he talked about marriage again. He was very persistent. "I don't want to be a bachelor all my life. I want to be married."

I stuck to my decision to stay single.

After four days at the Chitwan Resort, we boarded a six-seat, single-engine plane for the short flight to Kathmandu. Resort staff chased goats from the airstrip for takeoff.

By the time he actually returned to Seattle two months later, Stuart had announced his engagement to a Chinese woman. She'd achieved a medical degree and practiced medicine in Hong Kong. They were married on the *Star Ferry* in Victoria Harbour, and she came to live with him in Bellevue, Washington. She was twenty years younger than Stuart, beautiful, and all the things I didn't want to be. She loved exotic vacations in fancy hotels, exercising her Nordstrom charge card, and wearing the beautiful jewelry he loved to give her.

I was happy for them.

Stuart and I remain friends.

Different lifestyles accompanied my relationships with Stuart and Ray: sequins, fancy hotels, and jewelry with one; polar-fleece, camping, and exercise with the other. *Training*, engrained in my bones, had taught me to create an identity to fit the situation, and I thought tolerating their idiosyncrasies was necessary. I had no idea which identity was really me or if I'd conjured a persona to please the man in my bed.

I'd worked hard to identify my Self in a business environment.
Spiritually I was discovering alternatives to explore.
It would take a lot more time to sort out relationships.

chapter twenty-three

That November, when I retuned from India, Jim, the VP of international business development, asked if I'd be interested in another overseas project.

"Sure, but there are two things," I said. "I need more responsibility. Setting up another call center would bore me to death. I'd be happy to take on the sales team."

"No problem; we need someone with your background. What else?" he said.

"I need a few months with my family and time to get healthy after India."

"India was hard on the whole team," he said. "We're negotiating licenses in Brazil and Taiwan. Until one is awarded, I'll keep you busy here in Kirkland," he said.

I arranged for work visas in both Brazil and Taiwan, just in case.

In December, the Taiwanese government awarded the license to our joint venture. Jim insisted I leave immediately, so I spent the night packing and flew to Taiwan on my birthday, the day before my grand-daughter turned four. My one-year assignment was vice president of sales. EastComm was our partner company. The chairman and vice chairman were among the richest men in the world. On my first day, the secretary told me, "Address him as 'Chairman,' not 'Mr. Wong' and never 'Robert.'" When I met Richard, I addressed him as "Vice Chairman," but he asked me to call him "Richard."

Jim picked the initial sales and marketing team from a group of stateside employees willing to do the one-year assignment in Taiwan—Pat, Sam, and Tammy. Pat, a twenty-seven-year-old prima donna marketing assistant, had worked for the corporate office for less than a year and had never been "in the field." At least she had traveled in Europe during her college years. Sam, a twenty-five-year-old retail salesman, had never been out of Texas. Tammy was a twenty-three-year-old Taiwanese-American retail clerk from Seattle. She spoke Mandarin and Taiwanese, and her grandmother still lived in Taipei. The other member of my team was Tina, the wife of the VP of finance. She had been a graphic artist for a bank and was happy to have something to do all day while her husband was at work. She was a great asset. They were all young and naïve but shared an excitement for the foreign assignment.

This project meant jumping onto a rocket—long hours and little time to enjoy the landscape, photography, or exercise. Occasionally, I took a short run around the block near my flat, all the time I could steal for exercise. I captured few images of Taiwan.

The candidate for VP of marketing decided against the position, and Jim asked me to handle both sales and marketing until he could find another candidate.

As a team, our overall objective was to establish cellular service within six months, as well as hire and train local staff to take over within a year. I began interviewing local candidates who would replace the expats and selected a local ad agency. We developed a strategy and a marketing look and feel. I even managed the filming of our first TV commercial. The position required twelve or more hours a day, six days a week, and five or six hours on Sunday. But every day I returned to my flat thinking, "I can't believe I get to do this!"

Another facet of womanhood complicated my life there. At the strangest times, I felt like crying, and it seemed that the tropical heat bothered me more than in India. I started sweating at the strangest times. One minute I felt happy, the next minute sad. I assumed stress and lack of sleep and exercise caused conflicting emotions. Then I found a huge black hair growing from my chin. "Ick!" I freaked and tweezed it. My intense job exacerbated the symptoms, but I didn't put them all together. I'd begun perimenopause. Fortunately, I didn't know that the emotional effects could last up to five years.

Our international startup projects usually included a local VP and an expat VP in each position, working concurrently until the local was trained and felt ready to assume total responsibility. However, every candidate Jim interviewed for expat VP of marketing decided not to interrupt his career for a temporary international assignment. I needed help to meet the planned August launch date. By the end of June, we'd hired the *local* VP of marketing, Barbara. I was looking forward to handing the marketing responsibilities over to her sooner than we normally would have.

One Sunday morning late in June, during a rare moment of stillness, I lingered over my coffee before catching a taxi to the office. I stared at the dazzling crimson bougainvillea outside my apartment window and reflected on my life. I looked at my business card. On one side my name was printed in English, with my title—VP Sales and Market-ing—printed below. On the reverse side, my name and title appeared in Chinese characters, something that sounded like "Baa ee shee." I remembered a high school teacher who, in 1965, suggested trade school because, she said, "You don't have what it takes to go to college," and I remembered my struggle to vanquish her words. I remembered days on the farm when I explored my earthly mission with the support of my grandparents. With the bougainvillea's reassurance, I thought *Training* was a distant memory. I still didn't grasp how deep the indoctrination had been or the extent of the retrieval that remained.

My cell phone's ring broke the silence. "I found someone to handle marketing," Jim said, "Charlene, from the Florida market."

I'd met her at national meetings and found her dull and forgettable, not the dynamic personality this environment required, and it seemed a little late since Barbara would be starting in mid-July. I didn't say so. We needed all the help we could get. He went on, "Charlene's significant other, Jerry, will be joining her and helping with sales."

I found out later that Jerry had never worked in wireless, and both had to get their first passport before they booked their flights. Jerry had sold cars in Kansas. Jim desperately wanted someone in the marketing position, and he assumed I could deal with whatever Jerry brought to the table. I wrongly assumed that Jerry would report to me.

Charlene and Jerry would arrive the second week of July. On the Fourth of July, Tina stopped me in the hallway. "Charlene sent a fax. She wants cards printed before they arrive. Is this right?" She showed me the fax. "Charlene is VP Marketing and Jerry is VP Sales? What are *you* going to do?"

At first, I just stared at the fax. Then I said, "Well … yes, well … Charlene is coming to handle marketing but … uh … I'm not sure what's going on with Jerry … I'll get back to you."

I went to my office and called Jim's cell phone in Kirkland, Washington. He said, "Can you call back tomorrow? I'm poolside with the twins." Then a little annoyed, "Don't you know it's a holiday?"

I never called him unless it was important, and he knew it. His insensitivity made me furious. "Well, I'd like to be by the pool with my family, too, but I'm halfway around the world. The Fourth of July isn't a holiday in Taiwan. Maybe your wife could keep an eye on the boys for a minute. This is important." My assertiveness surprised both of us. Hormones do strange things.

He called me back in less than an hour. He said, "Charlene wouldn't agree to come unless her boyfriend got the VP title."

"Don't you think it would have been appropriate for you to tell me that Jerry was getting my job?" I said. "What do you want *me* to do?" Then I added, "You need to tell me if I haven't measured up."

"No! No! You've done a great job, Marcia. We just need more help over there. You can focus on roaming or equipment or something. You're a team player, Marcia. I gotta go. I'll call you in a few days. I'm on vacation this week."

From my twentieth-floor office, I looked out over the city. I knew I couldn't stay. Mockingly, I repeated his words. "*You're a team player, Marcia.*" Big fucking deal. What did being a team player get me? A week later, Jim still had made no announcements, but most people knew. I called him. "I'll be coming home," I said. "It's difficult to be effective. I've lost face."

"What do you mean 'lost face'?" he said. "You're not Chinese." In spite of many international deals he had put together, he knew nothing about actually working in the countries where his projects grew.

I arranged to meet with Richard, the vice chairman, in his office filled with antiques from around the world. Richard was five-foot-two, but his presence was large. I had a great deal of respect for him, and we worked well together. Probably too well, but I didn't understand the politics until much later.

Since Jim hadn't been completely honest with our venture partners, I explained to Richard that Charlene would be taking responsibility for marketing and Jerry would be in charge of sales. "I'll do everything I can to assure a smooth transition," I said. I didn't tell him I'd be going home.

Rumors grew, and to keep the staff at ease, I tried to put on a front, as though this had been the plan all along. We met in the small conference room, and I confirmed the rumors. "Charlene and Jerry will be here next week and will take responsibility for sales and marketing."

My team sat in silence. Then Sam asked, "What are you going to do?"

I tried to be casual about the whole mess. "I'll be going home," I said, in a tone that fooled no one. I tried to ignore the big tears flowing down my face, and so did they. "Look, you guys, you've done a great job getting sales and marketing ready to go. This won't have an impact on your jobs. Jerry and Charlene will be counting on you," I said. "We need to plan a meeting to show them what we've accomplished."

My young team plus the locals we'd hired planned the "Hand-Over Summit," a play on the recent hand-over of Hong Kong to the Chinese. We arranged our presentation in the huge, well-appointed conference room on the forty-third floor with a view of Taipei. The room was rarely available to us. Chinese antiques filled the lobby, including a priceless seven-foot terra cotta warrior statue, one of the few that has ever left Xian, China. The conference table, constructed from beautiful *he-tao-mu* (Chinese walnut), gleamed in the morning sun, and the big rosewood chairs looked as if they belonged in a museum. Pat placed wooden easels with our advertising storyboards around the room and installed the PowerPoint presentation to project from the built-in audiovisual equipment, new and impressive technology in 1997.

I wore a dark suit, cream silk blouse, and a colorful hand-dyed silk scarf I'd found in a street market. Everyone on my team wore a suit. When Jerry and Charlene walked into the room, their attire surprised me. He wore a golf shirt and Dockers. She wore what my grandmother would have called a housedress. Everything you do in the business world has meaning, especially in Taiwan. They knew they were meeting with the sales and marketing staff, the people who would report to them. Whether purposeful, unconscious, or just ignorant, their choice of attire was condescending. I got the impression Charlene preferred polyester to silk and that Jerry always drank Bud, never wine.

I stood at the head of the long conference table with the remote in my hand, the new logo projected on a huge screen behind me. It was a gorgeous logo. The company name in black, red, and silver, very high-tech and classy. It was pronounced something like "wan twan" when the Americans said it. The look and feel clearly represented the strategic plan.

When I introduced my team, Pat, Tina, Sam, and Tammy, my voice caught in my throat. I handed the remote to Pat and sat down. The team easily took over.

As they proceeded with the presentation, I thought, *What's happening to me? Why am I crying all the time? I never cry about business stuff!* Of course, hormones exacerbated my sadness, but I still hadn't figured it out.

When the team introduced our plans for the retail locations in Taichung and Kao Chung, Jerry laughed. "That's the size of a closet. Who negotiated that crap?" I did and he knew it.

They'll eat him alive, I thought, but said nothing. Everyone in the room knew immediately how incompetent he was. Clearly, he had not walked the streets in Taichung or Kao Chung, where tiny shops provide goods within walking distance of the patron's apartments. Worse, he didn't know that he should.

After our Hand-Over Summit, I met privately with Jerry and Charlene in a small, glass-walled conference room to discuss personnel. Jerry watched the office activity around us. "They're all so cute! Who's that adorable little thing in the pink outfit?" he said. His inappropriateness felt like fingernails on a chalkboard.

I wanted to say, *She's wearing a suit, you idiot,* but instead I said, "That's Charlotte. She has a law degree from Vassar and a Harvard MBA," knowing he had never finished college. Poor Charlotte, she would be working with this buffoon.

After the Hand-Over Summit, I skipped the Friday morning staff meeting. Jerry and Charlene attended. My seat next to Richard stayed empty. That morning, I jogged from my flat to the Chiang Kai-shek Memorial Hall and Gardens. I ran up the huge concrete stairs like Rocky Balboa, but I had no feeling of triumph when I reached the top and slowly walked back down. I had been in Taipei for over seven months and never had time to tour the twenty-four-thousand square feet of well-groomed gardens in the Zhongzhen District, so I lingered there for over an hour, watching two-foot-long iridescent white and orange koi in the reflection pond. Several men dressed in navy blue Mao suits and conical hats used hoses to water the grass and flowers. While I ran back to my flat, I began thinking about my future. *Maybe I can find a job as a garden sprinklerer,* but I couldn't feel the humor.

Back in my flat, still sweaty, I jumped when the doorbell rang. I leaned down to look through the low peephole, surprised to see Richard. The Taiwanese business equivalent of Ted Turner stood at my front door. Wondering how he'd gotten past the building security, I said, "Richard! What a surprise. Please come in." He stepped in and looked around at the Western-style furniture.

I tried very hard to be normal but he could see the tension in my face and said, "You're planning to return home. Do you really want to leave?" I shook my head, unable to speak. I motioned toward the sofa. He sat down, but his feet barely touch the floor. In normal circumstances, I would have found that amusing, but there was nothing jovial about this day. I sat on the chair across from him.

"I didn't think so." He looked at me closely. "It's OK," he said, and I lost it! I hid my face in my hands and sobbed in front of Richard!

Through the embarrassing sobs and sniffles, I said, "This was not my idea, Richard. We needed more help, and Charlene wouldn't come without Jerry, and I can't stay if he has my job." My pain caused tears to well in his eyes, but they did not spill. His compassion and empathy were unusual among Chinese businessmen or, in my experience, men anywhere.

"I'd like for you to stay," he said firmly. "Charlene and Jerry won't last for long." Richard was about fifteen years my senior and very perceptive. We'd become friends, and he respected my contribution. Years later I learned that Charlene and Jerry lasted only three months.

"I'd love to stay, Richard. I can't tell you what an honor it's been to be part of this project, but it's time for me to go home," I said.

It *was* time. I had no patience for politics. I loved the start-up, the building of a new company. We'd scheduled the marketing campaign launch and the political maneuvering had begun.

"When do you plan to leave?" he said.

"I have a plane ticket for Sunday."

"You'll miss the launch event?"

We'd spent months planning a huge announcement for the end of July. Everyone that was anyone in Taiwan, from government officials to local celebrities, would attend. The advertising agency had helped to plan the banquet, write the presentations, and had nearly finished the audio visuals.

"Yes, that means I'll miss the big event," I said.

"Marcia, you must be there." It wasn't rhetorical—he wanted me there.

After he left, I arranged a return trip to Taipei just for the event.

After Richard left that Friday, I pulled my luggage out of the closet and put the two bags on the bed. I'd convinced myself that this was nothing more than the end of an assignment. I was thinking, *It's time to move on*, but my body knew better. When I leaned over to pull the smaller bag close to the edge, my lower back seized in pain.

Fifteen years of dedicated service, hours of self-sacrifice, frustration, sorrow, and anger compressed into a spasm that literally brought me to my knees. I buried my face in the bedspread, unable to stand. Eventually the spasm subsided just enough for me to crawl onto the bed and curl face down between the suitcases, with my knees under me. Never before or since have I felt such pain.

Finally, I managed to push the empty bags to the floor. Bent in half at the waist, I found some Tylenol and washed down four capsules with a bottle of warm water I'd left on the nightstand. I crawled into bed in my running shoes. I waited for relief but little came. During the night, I swallowed more Tylenol and removed my shoes. By morning, I could stand relatively erect. I took a hot shower, thinking it would help, but I couldn't hold the blow dryer to dry my hair. Haphazardly, I packed as much as I could but spent most of the day in bed. It was helpful knowing the flat was mine until after the launch event. The following morning, I managed to dress and wait by the door for my driver.

At the airport's passenger drop-off station, my driver helped me out of the car and put my bags onto a luggage cart, which doubled as a walker. Inch by inch, I rolled to the ticket counter. When the attendant pointed and said, "Put bags here," I could barely hold myself upright but managed to transfer the bags without moaning too loudly.

Before boarding, I left a voice message for my doctor in Bellevue so that a prescription would be waiting for me at a twenty-four-hour pharmacy near my home. The plane trip was fourteen hours of agony.

In Bellevue, I gave the taxi driver a big tip to stop at the drugstore drive-through. By afternoon the next day, I felt dizzy but somewhat relieved.

⁂

Dressing for business in Asia was very different from the US, so I needed the appropriate attire for the launch event. I went to an exclusive shop at Fifth and University in downtown Seattle, Helen's of Course. The shop reminded me of a scene from *An Affair to Remember*, with Cary Grant and Deborah Kerr. There were no racks to browse. As in the movie, the saleslady brought items from the back. We never discussed price. If you needed to ask, you'd be shopping at Nordstrom.

"I have a very important business event to attend in Taiwan next week," I told the helpful saleslady. "I need something business-like but elegant. It needs to be, well, stunning." This was the single most important piece of clothing I'd ever purchased. Whatever I wore had to represent *my* style—the woman I thought I was.

The event would be my grand finale.

After a few of my "No thank yous," the saleslady presented a classy, monochromatic, not-too-business-like silk suit and matching silk blouse in a pale, yellow-gold—a color that symbolized prosperity and wealth in Chinese culture and perfectly matched my intent. I had little time for minor alterations to make the thousand-dollar suit fit perfectly, but at that price, they accommodated my needs.

⁂

I'd arranged to meet Jim and the VP of human resources in the Kirkland office.

Beforehand, I stopped by to see my old boss, Rod. My presence made him uncomfortable, and he shut his door, which he rarely did.

"What are you doing here?" he said.

"I have a meeting with Jim and the HR guy in a little while. If I survive this, I'll be looking for something to do."

"After what happened in Taiwan, I wouldn't touch you with a ten-foot pole. Nobody would," he said.

"What have you heard?" I said as my insides tightened and my back straightened.

He told me about a management meeting he'd attended. "Jim told the powers that be that he wanted you to stay but you refused, that you abandoned the project."

"Well, that's not exactly what happened. You know I wouldn't do that."

"I wondered; it didn't sound like you," he said. "Still, I doubt you'll ever overcome it, especially with all the changes going on around here."

<hr />

Trembling, I sat down with Jim and the international director of HR in Jim's office. Drugs controlled the back pain, but the emotional pain was unbridled. Every measure of disappointment, disheveled hormones, and suppressed feminine tenacity boiled into a powerful broth that had simmered for nearly fifty years. My career was unable to survive the intensity.

They'd thought of me as an amicable team player, *just a girl,* who would do their bidding. The sad thing is they were mostly right. I always did whatever possible to make the company successful. I supported my staff, gave them credit where credit was due, but I didn't know how to position myself in the political structure as the men did.

"I worked my ass off over there," I said to the two men in polo shirts. "I negotiated the biggest distribution contracts *ever* in the history of the wireless industry. In less than seven months, the sales team is hired and trained, and the marketing campaign is ready to launch. Everything is ready to go!"

I was behaving like a "bitch" as far as they were concerned. I'd never been good at expressing anger, but I was confident now. No one could dispute my ability to do the job.

"If I were a man, the situation would be different, and you know it. If this is how you treat your people, then I want nothing to do with this company. This conversation is over."

My career was over.

From a small stage in the ballroom of the Plaza Hotel in Taipei, the chairman, wearing a handsome hand-tailored black wool suit, crisp white cotton shirt, and yellow silk tie, introduced me as the VP of sales and marketing. I was calm and confident, wearing my gorgeous suit. In Mandarin, Robert presented the company identity and marketing campaign to several hundred guests, mostly Chinese.

He introduced Jerry and Charlene without mention of their new titles. Charlene wore a long, matchstick skirt over her generous hips and a matching cotton blouse. Jerry, wearing a blue oxford shirt, solid navy tie, brown trousers and no jacket looked like the used car salesman that he was. At the celebration afterwards, I avoided Jim. He was shaking hands and making conversation in front of the four-foot, sculptured-ice dragon. Jim was six-foot-six, with black curly hair, pale skin, and bright blue eyes. He towered over the local celebrities and guests but looked distinguished in his dark, well-tailored suit and white shirt. I wondered if he noticed how his new sales and marketing executives represented the company.

Since taking the sales assistant job in 1985, I'd identified with my work. My career was my contribution to the planet, and my ever-increasing self-worth had a checkbook-scoreboard.

I thought, *Who am I now?*

Without a scoreboard, I had no reason to show up.

I still carried a stack of business cards that identified me as "Baa Ee Shee," VP Sales and Marketing for one of the largest telecom companies the world. Maybe now I'd carry a card reading: "Mom, Grandma, Aunt, Daughter, No One's Lover, No One's Wife." Not a pity-party, just reality.

Repatriation is difficult in normal circumstances. No one I knew could comprehend or cared about what it took to live and work in a country where I couldn't tell the difference between dish soap and cooking oil.

My severance package included outplacement. Even the word "outplacement" implies psychosis. The consultants at Drake Beam Morin were quite familiar with this sort of thing, i.e., losing identities with jobs. The consultant assigned to me, Carolyn, was more like a therapist than an employment agent. She helped me deal with the emotional debris while I wrote my résumé, found potential employers, and sought a target for my energy.

I gave myself six months to find a new career. I knew it would work itself out. I had the severance package to live on and most of my international salary had gone into savings. I remodeled my home in case I decided to sell and enjoyed Paige and Taylor with no pressure to decide my next career move.

Within a few weeks, however, a friend, Mick, asked me to join a small, wireless consulting firm he was forming. We fondly called ourselves "FOM"—Friends of Mick. About six months later, one of the clients we called on, a software company with roots in London, offered me a VP of product marketing position with a six-figure starting salary, a bonus, and stock options.

I took the job and almost immediately felt trapped by it. At the pinnacle of the software revolution, however, it would have been financial suicide to resign. The top brass prepared to sell the company, and if I could hang on for a year or two, I'd be in a position to receive a considerable amount of money.

I called Carolyn at Drake Beam Morin. I explained the situation. "I need a career coach," I told her. "I don't like the way this company does business. Some of their practices are less than ethical, and I've no way to release my frustrations. I'm afraid I'll quit or get fired before my stock vests. Do you know anyone I could consult?"

"I have a small private practice," she said. "We could meet by phone for an hour every month or more if you like." We agreed on a schedule and her fee—$150/hour and worth every penny.

The company kept adding more stock options to my compensation and gave me a raise after six months. A year later, a London-based conglomerate, Marconi, purchased the company, and my options would vest when the deal closed. They offered me another raise and twice the stock if I would stay. When I talked to Carolyn, I said, "We made it! The merger will close in a week or two."

She helped me compose my resignation letter, free of the emotions just under my skin, and we practiced how I would tell my boss, Geoff.

During our next meeting, I said, "This morning I told Geoff that I won't be staying after the merger."

"Congratulations," she said. "I never doubted you could do it."

To my surprise, the London president of the company called me at ten o'clock one evening, my time. "Geoff says you're planning to leave us. I'd like you to reconsider," he said. "We'll double your options and add another 20 percent to your salary if you stay."

I said, "Thanks, Karl, but I've made my decision."

It's not that I was so great at my job. The deal included retaining a percentage of the management staff, including women. If too many managers resigned, the deal would collapse, leaving me where I started.

Against the advice of my financial planner, I sold my stock for £15.00/share with a £1.50 strike price and wrote a huge capital gains check to Uncle Sam. Twelve months later, the stock value had dropped from £15.00 to 60¢ per share. The company laid off most of its US-based employees. I'd made the right decision and now had the financial means to do as I pleased for a while.

Unemployed again, I had plenty of time for exercise and decided to train for a marathon. I joined the Leukemia Society's Team-in-Training (TNT) Program. They helped runners train for a marathon in return for fundraising. We met every weekend for fundraising tips and together ran longer and longer distances. I sent letters to all of my friends, colleagues, and neighbors and raised five thousand dollars for leukemia research.

One Saturday morning, two weeks before the race, we did our longest training run, twenty miles. The coach said, "If you can run twenty miles, you can run 26.2." In near freezing temperatures and pouring rain, I found myself running my eleven-minute-mile pace with a woman about my age. Rain dripped from the bill of my baseball cap and my gloves were soggy. Her companionship helped make the time go faster and the cold less noticeable. Sometimes we ran in silence.

After we turned at the ten-mile post, I rhetorically asked, "Why are we doing this?" I didn't expect an answer. It was a joke really.

To her it was no joke.

"Because my twenty-two-year-old son has leukemia," she said. "Pushing myself makes me feel as if I'm doing something to help." I didn't know what to say.

Suddenly, the energy drained from my body. I couldn't put one foot in front of the other. As I slowed I said, "Sorry, I have to walk for a while." She slowed with me. We walked in silence for a few minutes. Then I said, "You've given me a new reason to accomplish this goal. I hope your son will be OK." We resumed our pace and hugged at the finish line. "Good job," we told each other. I never saw her again.

I peeled the wet gloves from each finger as I walked to my car. My hands were so cold I needed one to support the other to get the key in the lock. I started the engine and turned the heater on full blast. As the windows covered with steam, I sobbed. Not tears for this woman and her son, I cried out of gratitude, tears amplified by endorphins. My children and their children were happy and healthy. I knew how lucky I was. "Thank you," I said.

I ran the Honolulu Marathon on my fifty-third birthday. As we ran up Diamond Head, my TNT coach announced to the crowd, "It's her birthday!" About a hundred strangers began to sing, "Happy birthday to you, happy birthday to you ..." I was thinking how great I was doing for my age when a leathery-looking woman passed me on the steep hill. "It's my birthday too," she said. "I'm eighty-three today."

"Wow, happy birthday!" I said. "Is this your first marathon too?" straining to keep up with her.

"Oh no, honey, this is my fifty-third."

As she ran past, I said, "Congratulations—many more!"

After Hawaii, maintaining the training schedule was easy, so I ran the Portland and Seattle Marathons before my next birthday. The intense focus on the mental and physical exercise helped clear my mind.

I had a new identity: "Retired Grandmother Who Runs Marathons," a respectable identity, I thought.

chapter twenty-four

In Albuquerque, I rented a red convertible. I'd never driven a convertible. A baseball cap kept the sun off my face, and I didn't care if the warm wind tangled my hair. I'd been accepted into the Santa Fe Photography Workshop, led by *National Geographic* photographers.

Prior to class the first morning, high on freedom, fresh air, and early light, I drove into the mountains at sunrise. I found narrow trails into the Aspen groves, hiked the gentle incline, and fell into a trance. My mind became completely free with just enough analytical awareness to operate the camera and find my way back to the car in time for class at nine. Greedily capturing backlit yellow aspen framed by a brilliant, clear-blue sky, I wished the lens could catch the rustling sound and smell of fall.

The photographers in the seminar understood the riveting exhilaration I'd experienced that first morning. "It's why we do it," offered a middle-aged woman with long, wiry, gray hair, wearing Birkenstocks and heavy socks. "Something happens to your senses when you peer through the lens," she said. "No matter if you're shooting architecture, people, or landscape, it's a feeling of exhilaration." I wasn't alone in my respect for light, shadow, color, and composition, which we studied intensely during the one-week seminar.

On the flight home, I thought about how much I loved to travel and how much I loved photography. Why not travel photography? By the time the plane landed, I'd written a business plan. For years, my camera had been a constant companion. I knew I could do anything if I wanted it bad enough.

Back home, I took Granddad's Kodak out of the drawer. When I touched the aged brown leather case, a powerful sensation rushed through me. I knew Granddad was proud of me. I enrolled in more seminars and printed business cards. "International Photography" was born.

My brother Rob and I were middle children together. Maybe that's why I felt closer to him than the others. He never married nor had children because, as he said, "I don't want to pass on the neurosis."

He became a passionate and knowledgeable birder and kept meticulous records of the birds he saw. He also became an accomplished bird photographer using a new technique called digi-scoping.

I loved watching how animated he became when he added new species to his life list, exceeding 580 species in Washington State. His excitement was contagious.

"I'm going on a pelagic birding tour out of Westport," he told me on the phone. "You want to come along and take pictures?"

"Sure, I'd love to photograph an albatross and maybe a whale or porpoise."

Rob picked me up in his dark-green Subaru wagon, mid-afternoon on a Friday. It was one of those beautiful Northwest days, when you can't believe weather can be so perfect. Bright sunshine, about seventy degrees, and a sky so clear we could see the Cascades all the way north to Mt. Baker. Even the base of Mt. Rainier was clear. The 150-mile drive was gorgeous.

We checked into our rooms at The Alaskan, a modest and clean, AAA-approved motel in Westport, Washington. The little fishing town was on a peninsula between Grays Harbor and the Pacific Ocean.

"Where's a good place for dinner?" Rob asked the motel owner.

"The West Wind just down the road is my favorite," he said.

The hostess led us to a booth by the window. Before our pasta arrived, Rob opened his copy of *National Geographic Society: Field Guide to the Birds of North America* to prepare me. The list was short but Rob was eager to see them all. Besides albatross, we were likely to get Heermann's gull, parasitic jaegers, and pomarine.

After dinner, we toured the Red Apple Grocery Store for lunch and snack provisions, which we stowed in his cooler, then drove back the motel. I set my travel alarm for 4 a.m. and went to sleep around nine. To be sure I was ready on time, Rob knocked on my door at 4:10 a.m.

"I'm up," I said.

By 5:15, we were having breakfast at the Half Moon Bay Bar and Grill, where the coffee was strong, the eggs fresh, and the biscuits hot and buttery. No sissy lattes here. The place was teeming with salty anglers. Some were commercial fisherman, but most would be sport fishing. They looked old either because of the ungodly hour, the dim light in the tavern, or the need for a shave. Each man wore many layers of well-worn clothing that forecast the unpredictable weather we could expect on the open ocean.

I swallowed a Dramamine as we arrived at Float #8 just before six, ahead of schedule (of course; I was with Rob). We boarded the *Monte Carlo* in the pastel morning light. Twenty-three birders from all over the US trickled on board for the next half-hour: a short, stocky older woman and her daughter from the East Coast; a tall, thin, quiet man from Texas; a young couple, apparently students in love. Rays of sunlight broke the horizon as we cast off at exactly 6:30 a.m.

George, the director, made announcements. "We can expect clear skies, moderately calm water, and five-to ten-foot swells."

I popped another Dramamine, just in case.

"We're likely to see a whale or two and probably some porpoise along with albatross, Heermann's gull, parasitic jaegers, pink-footed shearwater, a fork-tailed storm-petrel, and pomarine."

When these birds appeared, I abandoned my telephoto lens in favor of Rob's extra pair of higher-power binoculars.

My 200-mm telephoto lens was inadequate, when, about thirty miles off shore, the albatross appeared with no landmarks to differentiate its eight-foot wingspan. Through the lens, an albatross looked like a plain old seagull—excuse me, a California gull.

When George spotted a targeted species, he announced the location as if the boat were a clock on fire. "Parasitic! Parasitic jaeger! Nine o'clock! … Heermann's! Heermann's gull! Four o'clock!" his voice boomed above the roar of the engine.

We saw a gray whale, a humpback whale, and a darting black and white Dall's porpoise. The Dall's porpoise produced rooster tails like a Jet Ski. Someone spotted a shark-like fin cutting through the water in the midst of a flock of floating gulls. The captain stopped the boat near the ten-foot ocean sunfish, or mola mola, usually found in much warmer water. It rolled onto its side like a flounder, probably allowing the sun to warm its skin. A single, bulging, pale eye stared at the sky within inches of the boat. Gulls landed on its white flesh. Then its large dorsal fin rolled out of the water like a shark's, and it dove under the boat.

The unusual circus-like antics of a huge northern fur seal delighted us for over thirty minutes. George guessed his weight close to seven hundred pounds. Even so, I was surprised that George spotted him in the vast, rolling ocean. When the boat stopped within six feet of the seven-foot, wild creature, the seal rolled to one side then the other while he rubbed his belly as if bathing. He turned backward summersaults in the clear water and shyly covered his face and whiskers with his flippers while he circled within ten feet of the boat. Several times his head pushed high out of the water, and he shook, showering sparkling seawater like a shaking dog. Even the seasick student and sleeping old woman came to life to watch his antics. Paul and the crew had never seen anything like it on their previous tours. Again, my lens was inadequate.

In all we identified thirty-one species of birds, twenty-three of them pelagic (not observable from land). Most were new to me, doubling my poorly kept records. Rob added two to his meticulous life list. As we docked in Westport, I photographed the boatload of pelagic birders, red-faced from the cold wind and sun, unstable from the swells, and all a-twitter with enthusiasm.

As always, Rob asked, "What's your bird of the day?"

"I'd have to say the mola mola," I joked. "It was amazing."

"OK, that's your favorite beast of the day. How about a bird?"

"You first," I said.

"The fork-tailed storm-petrel."

"Me too!" I laughed. "Oh, it's too hard to choose. I saw albatross in Patagonia, so these weren't my first, but wow, they are impressive."

The day's reward was spending time with my brother and people that loved and respected nature.

I felt alive. "Thank you," I whispered.

chapter twenty-five

"I saw your résumé on line," said a recruiter on the phone. "We have a position in India that perfectly matches your background. Are you available to return to India?"

"Thank you, but no, I'm not interested in returning to India." A few days later, the recruiter's manager called and pressed me about taking the job. Again, I politely refused.

The recruiter called again. "What would it take to get you back to India?" I gave him a figure I thought was outrageously high. To my surprise, he said, "Can you leave next month?" Reluctantly, I flew to Boston to interview for the position, and within a few weeks I'd accepted the position, and prepared to go to India. The money was just too good to refuse. Anyway, I'd become a nomad who longed for international adventure.

The plane landed in Delhi before daybreak. On the way to the hotel, the taxi's headlights barely penetrated the dirty, hot air. Men on bicycles appeared suspended in the dusty glare. Oxcarts blocked a street near the hotel. *What have I done?* I thought. To some it may have seemed exotic, but to me it was all too real. I'd be breathing this dirty air for twelve months. The next day I flew to Chandigarh, in the northern province of Punjab, near Pakistan.

Recovering from jet lag, I watched from my third-floor balcony as a fair-skinned man wearing a Speedo baked in suntan oil by the swimming pool while an Indian woman swam in black, floor-length, baggy pants and a long-sleeved top—sort of a "swimming burka," leaving almost no skin exposed in the intense heat.

Early the next morning, I stood by the window to watch the hot, April sun rise over the Himalayan foothills. A black koel, hiding in a sandalwood tree, announced the day with a annoying crack, ko-eel, ko-eel, ko-eel. A cacophony of melodious tropical bird songs, unfamiliar to my foreigner's ears, soon accompanied the distinctive bird. The sun warmed my face through the glass as the pale gray sky turned dark ruby, then rose, then yellow. *Can I be the same girl who played in the cow pastures in Ohio?* I thought.

I noticed women already working at a construction site next door. *What if these women were transported to sunrise on a farm in Ohio?* I thought. *The sound of the rooster's cock-a-doodle-do serenading the dawn, accompanied by robins and fragile-sounding chickadees, would be just as strange to them.*

The women would labor wearing brightly colored fabric from head to toe, but their work would be very different. They would milk the cows with a machine and cultivate the corn riding big, green tractors.

My bare skin would embarrass them, and they'd be confused when I ran the country road wearing shorts and a tank top. These women could not imagine why exercise was necessary. They carried bricks on their heads, shoveled heavy sand through a sieve to remove the rocks, and mixed mortar with sticks—all in the harsh 120 degree heat. They could barely afford enough food to survive.

These women could not imagine spring storms drenching the endless, flat Ohio farmland. As children, they dug miles and miles of irrigation ditches to carry muddy water from the Himalayan foothills to the Punjabi fields.

In Ohio, they would watch as the cows returned to the fenced pasture after milking rather than freely roaming village streets as cattle do in India. Their tent-like home on the construction site had no electricity, but an electric fence had contained the herd in Ohio for more than forty years.

In America, I still fought my secondary status as a woman, but these Sudras were socially below men, cows, and rats. Would they be as awed by an adventure in Ohio as I was by this Indian morning? Probably more so.

That first morning, my hairdryer burned up. When Ratna, a new colleague, arrived to take me on an assimilation tour, I said, "My hair dryer burned up this morning. Where can I get a new one?"

"There's a repair shop across the street," she said. Repair hadn't occurred to me. "A new one would cost a small fortune, about 650 rupees."

We crossed the dirt street to a dark, little cinderblock shop that offered dry cleaning and electrical repairs. I left my smoke-scented hairdryer in the hands of a young Sikh wearing a bright-blue turban. Rocking his head from ear to shoulder, he said, "Please be returning at 3:30; I will be having it ready." I did, paying him sixty rupees when he demonstrated the hair dryer's improved condition. (That came to $1.54, probably twice as much as he would have charged a local. I hoped the repairs would last. It was unlikely I'd find a new hair dryer to purchase.)

Coming back from the dry cleaner/hair dryer repair shop, I saw scooter traffic approaching, and for a moment I thought that most of the men in Chandigarh wore brightly colored helmets. Helmets had been unusual in Pune. When they came closer, I realized it was a swarm of Sikhs. They wrapped their long, never-cut hair inside their turbans, making a motorcycle helmet out of the question and probably unnecessary. They managed their long beards in various ways. Some hung free and split at the chin in the wind. Some men restrained their beards with hairnets or handkerchiefs tied under their chins, which looked like they were nursing toothaches. It all looked very uncomfortable in the heat. The most interesting beard treatment involved Dippity Doo. When a man jelled his beard to his face, his cheeks took on a weird glow and his dark skin distorted like a cartoon character's.

When I left the too-cold, air-conditioned hotel the next morning, the heat slapped my face like an angry hand. It was over 120 degrees at eight in the morning. My driver, in a hot car that smelled of spices, cigarette smoke, and body odor, drove me to the office, where there was no air conditioning. It was *hot*.

Still prone to the issues facing women my age, I sat in the stifling conference room with all-male colleagues discussing communication technology while experiencing a hot flash, like my hair dryer's power surge. *Do I smell like smoke?* I wondered. I could scarcely keep from laughing, although the subject of menopause was no laughing matter. *No more eggs and—oh my God—back to childhood?*

Menopause causes emotional traumas as annoying as the psychological issues of pubescence. We expect kids to be "wacko" at that age, but no one talks about the stress of going the other way.

At two-thirty in the morning, a rustling noise woke me. I turned on the light next to the bed and saw the contents of the dustbin moving under the desk. *A small vertebrate or large arthropod?* I wondered. In one swift jerk, I put on my bathrobe and stood on the bed. *Now what?* Soon a scruffy rat squeaked its way to the bathroom. I shrieked and picked up the phone. A sleepy voice answered in Hindi. No one in housekeeping spoke English. A very dark, heavy-eyed, friendly chap came to the door, but he had no idea what I wanted. As if it would help communicate, I wrote "RAT" on a yellow sticky note I found on the nightstand, gave it to him, and jumped back onto the bed until he returned. Moments later, he appeared at the door with a long pole. What did he think he could do with a ten-foot pole in a four-foot bathroom? The rat was gone but had left black droppings to prove it wasn't just a nightmare. I never slept soundly in this strange place. Night sweats didn't help. After the rat visit, I hardly slept at all.

Later I learned that Hindus believe humans temporarily inhabit the bodies of rats until rebirth. The hotel staff fed them in a closet. At least it was a sacred rat that disturbed my sleep.

We'd found only a few restaurants in Chandigarh, and they all served the same bad food—even bad Indian food. My Pune experience had made me aware of this eventuality, so I had packed cans of tuna, granola bars, dry soup, and a small 220-watt hot pot meant for boiling tea water. I anxiously waited for the box I'd shipped to myself, but it never arrived. *What a way to diet!*

There was absolutely nothing to do in Chandigarh, and even if there was, it was too hot to do it. Reading was the only pastime after work—TV was usually in Hindi. I soon finished reading the last book I'd brought from home and began trading with colleagues' wives. That summer I read almost everything Nora Roberts ever wrote, because those were the books they were reading. I couldn't figure out what the men did during the long, hot evenings. They had no books to share and nothing much to talk about except work.

One of the local VPs, Naveen, had been working on the customer service issues for over a year, but when I arrived, he refused to share the results. "I'm no one's understudy!" he shouted on my first day. On two occasions during my first week, he screamed, "You are not being productive!" He was so close to my face I smelled his vile, curry breath and wiped spit from my forehead. I was not his direct report, I had no deliverable, and I knew nothing about work completed to date. He was performing for his colleagues. He wanted me to scream and make a scene, but I didn't. I just waited.

During a senior staff meeting, Hemant, the local CEO, reminded Naveen and the rest of the management team that I was in charge of customer service. Naveen completely stopped talking to me after that meeting, but the others began including me.

Pankaj was Naveen's wife's sister's husband's brother. Naveen had hired him to set up the call center. Of course, the poor man had no idea what a call center was or what technology was required. He welcomed my help but talked to me only when Naveen left the office. Naveen managed everything in his life by intimidation. I shuddered to think what Naveen's wife must have dealt with on a daily basis. It was an arranged marriage; 90 percent of marriages in India still were.

Ray called my cell phone from Seattle. It was nice to hear his voice and to know he still thought of me. "I just wanted to be sure you were OK," he said.

"I'm fine," I said. "This isn't much different than Pune, except the food is worse and maybe it's even hotter."

"Have you heard about the nuclear testing?"

"No!" I said, "There's been nothing in the papers."

The Pakistanis and Indians were testing their nuclear prowess, and as a result, the Americans had issued trade sanctions. Ray described the angry mob that had picketed our old office in Pune. Raj, the CEO, had gone out to speak to them and pointed out that the company was Indian-owned. They went to the new Baskin-Robbins and burned it down.

I wondered how many local people lost their jobs because of the mob's misdirected anger.

I shared the news with my colleagues. Betty, an engineer's wife, called her friend at the American Embassy in Delhi. She described two disturbances but didn't mention the Pune incident. No one on the team seemed terribly concerned by either the nuclear testing or the rioting. I wanted to go home.

━━ ⌁ ━━

On the ride from the office to the hotel one afternoon, I watched from the relative comfort of my smelly, air-conditioned car as several naked Indian children played in a fountain in the middle of a roundabout. Their wet, brown skin glowed under the scorching sun. The temperature was over 130 degrees Fahrenheit. They splashed and laughed like children enjoying water-play anywhere in the world. I noticed one little girl, about six or seven years old, whose hair was matted and tangled, as if it had never been combed. I realized she was probably too poor to own a comb. She was a street orphan. The heap of sienna-stained rags near the fountain was all she possessed in the world. She ate what she could find in the streets.

At the hotel bar, I met a young German engineer named Rainer. Over our Scotch, we commiserated about the bad food and extreme boredom after work hours. "It's not so bad, I guess," he said and told me about Mother Teresa's orphanage just outside of Chandigarh. I arranged to go with him on his next visit.

Every American should be required to visit such a place. It would put perspective on our abundant lives. An English-speaking nun wearing the familiar habit of Mother Teresa's Missionaries of Charity, the white sari with blue trim, met us at the front gate. She stood next to a small wooden box wedged in an opening in the stone wall that surrounded the facility.

"What's this box for?" I asked. It seemed out of place on the wall.

"This is where they are putting the small babies," she answered, her head rocking from side to side, ear to shoulder.

"You mean the orphans?" I asked.

"Some of the babies are orphans, yes, but most are handicapped babies that the parents cannot be caring for. Many are healthy newborn girls, left by parents wanting a boy child."

As we entered the first concrete building, the nun looked at my camera. "Please do not be taking pictures." I couldn't have. The interior was too dark for photos.

Small windows offered dim light even on that bright, sunny day. I hesitated while my eyes adjusted. Small cribs filled with babies, mostly girls, packed the thirty-by-thirty-foot concrete room, but there was no newborn smell of powder or lotion, just a dank, musty stench. Jarring silence filled this room of infants.

In the next room, we slid sideways between larger cribs with older babies. Same stench. Same silence. However, many of these babies were standing. "Please do not be talking or touching the children." It appeared that no one ever did. Blank, little faces told the story of their solitude. Beyond despair. They knew no other life.

The tour went on and on and on, each room more depressing than the last. Many children were physically deformed and mentally handicapped. I asked the nun, "What happens to these children. How long do they stay here?"

"They will never be leaving. The ones that are able are helping, and the others just living out their lives here." We walked through the areas housing progressively older groups, some healthy children, others with hydrocephalus, cerebral palsy, autism, Down's syndrome, or spina bifida. Metabolic. Genetic. Infectious. Congenital.

My healthy American good fortune provided no clue for understanding what it was to live these lives.

We reached the geriatric area where we added Alzheimer's and dementia to the list. Skeletal old bodies held skin too abundant for the bones. These old people, probably not as old as we thought, sat in the dry, dusty dirt of the courtyard surrounded by concrete walls. Some sat out of the dirt in broken wheelchairs, their mangled legs twisted beneath them. The staring blank eyes, some cloudy with cataracts, revealed no inhabitants.

When the disturbing tour ended, I handed the nun a three-inch-thick brick of rupees worth about $300 USD, weekly expense money I'd received that morning. Back in the car, Rainer patted my hand, rubbed my shoulder, and offered a box of tissues. He had come prepared. "I reacted the same way on my first visit," he said in his German accent.

For months, unexpected tears trickled down my cheeks when I flashed on those ill-fated inmates and the nuns who cared for them.

At first, I thought my office frustration was due to being a female in a Punjabi company, but after three months, I suspected this project, construction of a hybrid wireless/coax network, would never reach fruition. Every day, the local VPs argued over insignificant issues while collecting paychecks from USA partners. I suspect the project manager fabricated progress reports, but I never knew for sure. I spent most days playing solitaire while receiving $300 a week for living expenses that cost nearly nothing. The company deposited 100 percent of my salary into my USA savings account.

Bob, the only colleague I befriended in Chandigarh, was an intelligent, pleasant man with a dark interior. I never learned his sad secret, but speculated it had something to do with his four sons, their photos he displayed on the desk in his room. A mid-1980s haircut and outdated clothing locked one son in time, whom I presumed had left him in one way or another.

I could have continued for months, but I called the Boston office and asked to be excused from the project. Once safely back in the US, I met with the human resources manager and explained my reasons. Months later, I learned that the US partners walked away from a multi-million dollar investment. My suspicions that the project would never be completed were confirmed.

Bob and I left the project on the same day, making travel more interesting and probably safer. We took a company car that reeked of tobacco and curry to the train station, then the overcrowded pungent train from Chandigarh to Delhi, followed by a stale-smelling taxi from the Delhi train station to the airport, and of course the planes to San Francisco and Seattle. As I gathered my luggage from the rotating carousel in Sea-Tac I'd never smelled worse and never felt happier to be on American soil.

chapter twenty-six

ack home, I spent time honing my photography skills. In January, as wanderlust returned, I decided to photograph the Chinese New Year celebration in Shanghai and visit with my brother, Craig, who taught English there. I used frequent flyer hotel coupons and checked into the Hyatt in Shanghai, paying for only one of five nights. I could have been in a Hyatt anywhere in the world. The furniture was lacquered black and the bathroom sink was a clear bowl, lit from below. The glass-brick shower stood before a floor–length, tinted window high above the city. I could see for miles. A multitude of cranes lurked, ready to build gleaming sky scrappers in place of what remained of the red-roofed ancient city.

Craig and I took an eight-hour train ride to the village of Long Yu for Lunar New Year's dinner, guests of his student, Pumpkin, apparently a phonetic pronunciation of her Chinese name.

We checked into a small hotel, and her father drove us to her grandfather's rural home. On the way, she told us about her grandfather. Orphaned young, he had been taught by his adoptive family to keep bees, and in the early 1950s, he became an apprentice beekeeper near Ningbo, south of Shanghai. After a year, he returned to Long You, where his bees pollinated tangerine blossoms. Soon, that changed.

In the early sixties, during China's Cultural Revolution, the communist party assigned Mr. Nan and his wife to migrant beekeeping. The Chinese government imported high-producing Italian honeybees to replace the pesticide-ravaged Chinese bee population. Mr. Nan's work unit loaded a train bound for springtime in the vast Chinese countryside.

We arrived at the farm before noon as the women finished cooking in the tiny rustic kitchen. I felt like I'd stepped one hundred years back in time. The one-story cinderblock and clay structure had a red tile roof like the ones I'd seen from the shower in the city. We entered through an open garage-like door, which filled the space with winter light. The large room filled, with utilitarian furniture, had four conical, sweat stained, hats hanging in a row on the lime-green wall. To the right, a door led to a long, dark bedroom with one small window and several beds. The kitchen was on the left of the big center room. The women had cooked beef, fish, duck, chicken, dog, snapping turtle, vegetables, and noodles over a fire-fed "stove." They built the fire through a big hole on the outside of the house under the "range top" on the inside. *I'll never complain about my appliances*, I thought.

We crowded onto very narrow benches around a three-foot-square, well-worn table with Mr. Nan, Pumpkin, her father, mother, and uncle. The table was set with chopsticks and small china bowls that fit in the palm of my hand. There were no serving spoons. Everyone ate from the serving bowls, which were slightly larger than our personal bowls.

We were at Pumpkin's mercy to know where we were, what was happening, and what people were saying. Mr. Nan, her grandfather, was proud to serve his homemade rice wine. He carefully ladled the brew from a large ceramic jug into an empty, green plastic Sprite bottle, which he put in the middle of the table. It reminded me of the Japanese sake bottle I used at home to serve coffee cream.

During the meal, his son, Pumpkin's father, frequently stood up, lifted a bowl filled with the clear fiery liquid, and said, *"Kung hei fat choi"* and a few other Chinese words, then, *"Gum bay!"* (bottoms up), toasting the New Year, family, and guests. In Hong Kong, when someone shouted, *"Gum bay,"* he expected everyone to swallow the entire cupful. After just a taste, I could feel my elbows tingle. With each new exclamation of *"Gum bay,"* I brought the bowl to my lips but scarcely took a drop. I wanted my wits about me in this unusual place.

Each entrée included the bones of the respective creature. Family members chewed on a piece of meat and spit indigestible bits onto the table. As the meal progressed, small piles of bones, gristle, and cartilage grew on the table next to each small bowl. "Leaving the bones in the meat," Pumpkin explained, "makes it possible to determine the origin of the meat."

A box of tissues materialized. Pumpkin knew we were accustomed to using a napkin. When we first sat down, Pumpkin's mother used her chopsticks to serve a few bites of meat to each of our bowls. We followed the family's lead, feasting on the spread before us, ignorant of the identity of most of the dishes even after we sampled a bite or two. Unfortunately, I couldn't recognize the bits of bone and had a problem separating the meat once it was in my mouth. We assumed the bites Pumpkin's mother served us were well-cooked beef, but Pumpkin eventually disclosed that it was dog meat. The family believed that eating dog meat in winter would help keep them warm.

In spite of my efforts to remain composed, surprised eyes, and paler-than-normal face revealed my horror. Pumpkin's mother exchanged the bowl of dog meat with a plate of green vegetables. My appetite for meat had significantly subsided. Even the rice wine could not dissolve the pungent taste of dog. I wanted to floss!

At the end of the meal, Grandma Nan pulled an old wool blanket off the electric rice cooker near the table. Eating the rice she offered would have implied I did not get enough to eat. I declined the hot white scoop.

The wool blanket reminded me of Grandma's ice cream freezer, draped with an old quilt. The cylinder, packed in a salty ice bath, waited in the hall after she removed the paddles. At the end of a big meal in rural Ohio, she offered the frozen dessert and no matter how full, I never refused a scoop of the cold white treat.

When we finished eating, the children ate while the aunts and grandmother stood behind them. The children were messy eaters, but the aunties were tolerant. Customarily, the men ate before the women and children, avoiding the mess. They'd made an exception for their foreign guests.

The small, wrinkled beekeeper always wore his fur hat, even at dinner. He seemed very old and feeble, slurping noodles and broth from his bowl, his mouth sinking where his bottom teeth once were. My blond hair fascinated him, and his small eyes twinkled as he stared at my head and fair skin. The rice wine caused a healthy, pink glow on his leathery cheeks.

The bent, little man transformed when he sat on the small wooden stool by his cherished beehives, now the more modern, rectangular boxes. He became strong and calm, his eyes widened, no longer small slits in his glowing, weathered face.

His calm was contagious. I remained undaunted as the air around my face, hands, and camera slowly came alive with buzzing honeybees. Captivated, I reminded myself to take photos. He slowly removed the burlap wrap, the outer lid, and inner cover. He gently lifted each brood board to expose the bees and the honeycomb. The cold, lethargic bees crawled up his fingers, others landed on his ears, face, and clothing, never distracting or stinging him as he calmly inspected the bees, honeycomb, and queen.

I realized the bees were crawling all over me as well, but I wasn't stung. I instinctively mirrored Mr. Nan's calm, and the bees sensed I was nonthreatening. My brother, I think because of his attitude, was stung three times. Like most men I was acquainted with, Craig tried to take control, wildly swatting around his face and head. Mr. Nan knew how to live in peace with the bees.

I remembered the rectangular beehives huddled in Granddad's small orchard where peach and apple trees lined the yard full of clover. I walked barefoot on summer mornings, summer's dew cooled my feet. The bees never stung me. Residents of the three old hives hummed from peach blossom to apple blossom to clover blossom, covering their bodies with fluffy yellow pollen and filling their crops with golden nectar. Fresh-from-the-hive honey and sweet butter dripped from the warm bread Grandma and I made together. In rural China, I could almost smell the baking bread from fifty years before.

My grandparents in Ohio kept bees because they chose to do so. Mr. Nan had little choice in becoming a migrant beekeeper. While our American family enjoyed unquestioned freedom in the wide-open fields of Ohio farmland from the 1950s to 1970s, China closed itself off to the outside world and nationalized businesses under communist rule. Mr. Nan's children were born on the train, as he and his wife chased spring from farm to orchard, the appointed pollinators of China. As China opened to the outside world in the early 1980s, Mr. Nan retired from nomadic beekeeping but retained some of the beehives for his family in Long You.

This holiday celebration reminded me of many holiday meals my family enjoyed in faraway Ohio when I was a girl. Grandma put extra leaves in the big wooden table. She used a white linen cloth and her best china and silver. The men, women, boys, and girls ate together, as many as fourteen. Like their Chinese counterparts, the women did the cooking. Grandma, Mom, and my aunts served turkey, ham, and beef, homemade bread and butter with honey, fruit salad, mashed potatoes and gravy, green beans with bacon, corn on the cob dripping with sweet butter, cold, fresh milk for the kids, steaming hot coffee for the grown-ups. Then they served apple, peach, pumpkin, or cherry pie and maybe a scoop of homemade ice cream.

That night, as I relived childhood memories of dinners with grandparents, a disturbing adult memory seized my mind. One very hot summer day, Niki, Matt, and I were visiting my parents in Ohio. Niki was about three years old and still a messy eater. My father came home for lunch as always, and we ate in the cooler daylight basement. Niki attempted to reach her mouth with each spoonful of rapidly melting vanilla ice cream, but the milky liquid ran down her elbow and dripped onto the table and floor. "Can't she get a goddamn bite into her mouth?" my father said. Then, looking down at Niki, as if she couldn't understand, he said, "If she can't stop making such a mess, she can't have any more ice cream." With his fingers, he snatched the melting scoop from her bowl and dropped it into his own. Then he went back to work. I went to the kitchen for a replacement scoop, hoping my three-year-old daughter's disappointment would melt as fast as the ice cream. *"You're not worthy of ice cream"* could too easily become *"You're not worthy,"* the message he'd imbedded deep into my bones.

Feelings of unworthiness still seeped out on occasion but could not ruin this trip to rural China.

The next morning, Pumpkin's father drove us to an ancient Buddhist temple. Inside, I walked toward the candlelight until my eyes adjusted to the dim illumination. A leathery old woman knelt at the altar, tightly holding smoking joss sticks in her bony, speckled hands. The intensity of her prayers silhouetted her bent frame.

A little boy, her great-grandson, laughed out loud and ran in circles on the packed dirt floor with his toddling baby brother. It surprised me that she allowed children to behave like children in this holy place.

The temple's spirit had outlived its wood and stone many times. The location was centuries old even before the current temple was built two hundred years before. A twenty-foot, sitting Buddha occupied 90 percent of the space. Genderless and wise, the huge Buddha tenderly smiled down on us with garish red lips, huge blue eyes, and bright gold skin.

The presence of ancient spirits made my skin tingle and my heart race, their presence as certain as the sun and moon. In those days, I knew nothing of spirits and had no way to learn about the old woman's life, but my chest ached with her memories.

I felt the spirits of her dead family members. I knew, somehow, that the old woman's mother, grandfather, and husband had been dead for decades. In this temple, they were alive as the day they had prayed here, and she came here to be with them.

Smoke generated by incense, candles, and joss sticks stained the walls and symbolized thousands of prayers. The smoke swirled higher, invisible except for the beam of light above the Buddha's head. Each curl of smoke held a prayer and embodied the pain, happiness, sorrow, or fear sent by centuries of visitors. The smoke rose to the ceiling, occupied the beam of light in the small window then vanished. It became the light.

This was my third mindful encounter with spirits. I'd felt them in Harvey and Xiaobao's studio in Guangzhou and at the stupa in Nepal. The spirits were so obviously present I could not deny them.

I could have absorbed the energy for hours, but Pumpkin had told her father that I wanted to take photos. As soon as the shutter clicked, he was anxious to move on.

chapter twenty-seven

I sold some Patagonia images and published an article about the migrant beekeeper in China, but travel photography wasn't lucrative. I didn't care. Peering through the viewfinder eased the clatter in my mind. I lived the solitary life of an anchoress as I shot landscape photos, wrote in my journal, and read the white fiery words of ancient goddess myths and female spiritual legends.

I'd been "aping men in power" to collect a paycheck since my first job in the lab in Kentucky. Workplace decisions came easily, and I coached my children to find their own conclusions, but I felt empty when I presumed to answer the question: *Who am I?*

What do I want to do now? How will I recognize it when it comes?

What do I prefer, mayonnaise or Miracle Whip?

Sequins or polar fleece?

Golf or mountain biking?

Hotels or tents?

Are physical life and spiritual life mutually exclusive?

I began to discover new alternatives: fresh store-ground, organic peanut butter, neither Skippy nor Jif.

In the same way, I began to discover a spiritual world quite different from the 1950s Sunday school religion I'd rejected as a child.

On a weekend trip to photograph the Oregon Coast, I traversed a steep slope to Arcadia Beach and left my running shoes on a driftwood log. My bare feet sank deep into the loose, dry sand, and I slid a half-step back with each stride forward until I reached the firmly packed ocean's edge. I set a pace toward a twenty-foot rock, shaped as if a heavenly chef had boiled multicolored stones into thick chowder then left a crescent glob to solidify on the sand. I slowly circled the calico rock and let my fingertips slide lightly over its odd-colored surface. I felt as if this rock knew me, strange as that sounds. I sat inside, facing the ocean, delightedly isolated. Transfixed by luminous, metrical waves, my mind quieted while this non-judgmental rock examined my soul. When time enough had passed, I thanked the rock for the sanctuary of its unusual aggregate walls and ran barefoot on the foggy beach until my stomach demanded breakfast. Turning back, I saw nothing but mist, as though my rock had been an illusion. Then, a light ocean breeze cleared the haze, exposing a covey of curious college students with notebooks. They swarmed the rock that had tendered shelter and serenity a few minutes earlier. Their scholarly attraction was very different from mine. I'd found what I needed, and so would they.

In the spring of 1996, my son, Matt, graduated from Colorado State with honors in physics and math. Several companies clamored for his attention and he received a signing bonus to work as a photolithographic engineer for a company in Colorado.

In 1998, he transferred to a company in Portland, Oregon, and brought his girlfriend, Julie, to meet me. Unlike our blond clan, she'd inherited curly black hair and green eyes through her Minnesota Norwegian heritage.

It may have been the sparkle in his brown eyes, the lilt of his long step, or the way he leaned over her five-foot frame, but I knew immediately that she'd be the one. They were married in the Rose Garden in Portland a year later. In spite of a patriarchal world, Matt had grown into a man who was sensitive, kind, and respectful of all people.

In 2001, Matt and Julie visited me in Bellevue to tell me they were expecting. We'd spent Monday afternoon with Craig and his family who happened to be visiting from Shanghai.

Early Tuesday morning, I was alone in the kitchen, making coffee when the phone rang. "Mom, turn on the TV," Niki said in a clipped voice.

"What's going on?" I turned on the coffee pot.

"There's been an awful plane crash in New York," she said.

Matt heard the phone, sensed something was wrong, and joined me in the kitchen. With the phone on my ear, I pointed to the TV and he crossed to the living room to turn it on. I said to Niki, "Thanks for letting us know. I'll call you later." Julie joined us as the smoking towers came into view. I switched to CNN. We sat in silence. The second tower crumbled.

The sensitive man I'd raised, slid onto his stomach on the carpet. He buried his face in his folded arms and sobbed. My son's child, my grandson, would be born into a world changed forever.

Although they had planned to leave early, Matt and Julie stayed most of the day. After they'd gone, around five, I decided to go for a run on the Marymoor Park trail, leaving the TV tuned to CNN as if it would keep me connected to the world while I was out. After a mile, I noticed I was walking. With no energy, I retuned to CNN and my journal.

Writing in my journal had been an on-and-off practice since 1979, when I sorted out married life. I loved writing, even in the corporate environment, although there was nothing exciting about writing articles for *Wireless Review* and *Billing World*. I found writing cathartic and entertaining, so I enrolled in a weeklong, nonfiction seminar at Centrum in Port Townsend, Washington. A mixture of amateur and semi-professional writers filled the room, all escaping daily lives to focus on writing.

Each morning, like homing pigeons, we found yesterday's chair and perched in familiar space. By the fourth day, the energy of the group had shifted, and only one remained in his original seat. When I entered the room, the American Indian history buff was in my former roost by the window. He was serious and pensive, and rarely spoke. I sat in his former perch in the back.

"The words were not words I would have written," said the man in my chair. "Still, there they were. I had written them." He didn't say he channeled the words, but the thought was in the air. He said, "Just write, get out of the way, and let the words flow onto the page."

The timbre of his voice and the intensity of his speech filled the room like vapor. Through the window above his head, a bald eagle ascended in a tight spiral. When the man had finished speaking, the eagle was gone. Most hadn't seen the eagle, but the energy was there, circling. Everyone tried to contribute, voices on top of voices, interrupting, edgy, each member reacting to or ignoring the intensity in his or her own way.

"I prefer a more controlled approach."

"Writers need to craft their words."

"Research is required for accuracy."

You need to get the facts straight, but a few of us smiled, instinctively knowing that what he said was true. The others expected the words to come from life experience, observing life, or reading about life, but some writers know that the words also come from the memory in our souls, our cells, our DNA, a source we understand no more than Moses could understand radio.

Just write.

We lingered after class, hungry to hear our famous classmate, Mark Pearson, sing his poetry and play his guitar, as he had promised. The first chord created a spark, igniting the emotional vapor. His heart filled the space like smoke, seeping beyond the walls and stinging our eyes. Thinking I was the only one moved to tears, I rushed from the room, choking back sobs. I tried to hide inside myself, a place once familiar but now odd.

Emotions, ideas, wisdom.

Past. Present. Primal.

Afterward, one student remarked, "Why am I crying? I never cry!" Everyone had.

That night, we built a fire on the beach and ate our dinner together. We knew the music and words to songs Mark had played, and we sang along. I wondered how it would feel to have strangers sing along with my own inner melody.

Near eleven that night, a long yellow path appeared across the wet sand and Puget Sound, leading to the full moon rising on the horizon. Leslie danced barefoot at the water's edge in the moonlight, her silhouette bowed, her arms raised, a knee bent. Her shadow looked like Kokopeli. I wanted to join her feminine waltz with the moon, but I was shy and still ignorant of the rising moon's power.

chapter twenty-eight

few weeks later, I attended an American Marketing Association networking luncheon at the Washington Athletic Club (WAC) in downtown Seattle. Malcolm Gladwell, with his wild, lopsided Afro-like haircut, presented his book, *BLINK, The Power of Thinking Without Thinking.* We were a group of marketing professionals listening to Gladwell explain how humans make decisions based on the first two or three seconds of an introduction using visceral, inexplicable knowledge.

During the lunch that preceded his talk, we passed business cards around the table—take one and pass it on. I chatted superficially with other attendees, including Deanna, who sat across from me. After the presentation, Deanna and I stepped into the hall at the same time. She was the only person at my table, or in the dining room for that matter, that I hoped to see again. Deanna had chin-length dark hair, hazel eyes, and wore appropriately casual business attire. Nothing about her led me to suspect that she was more than she appeared. We arranged to meet at a coffee shop in Kirkland a few days later. This is what you do when you're networking. I had no other expectation.

I settled into a padded wicker chair with my decaf, non-fat latte. Deanna arrived minutes later, ordered her coffee and joined me at the little table in the corner. After a few minutes of small talk, I said, "I brought my résumé, just in case you know of any consulting assignments.

I'm always open to finding something new." I opened the manila folder on the table.

Deanna looked it over briefly. "You've had a pretty interesting career, especially the international assignments. I've worked at marketing agencies most of my career." The conversation was going as I expected. Then Deanna revealed, "I'm also very interested in Eastern philosophy and spirituality." In the same tone she could have said, "*I like sugar in my coffee.*"

I fell back in the big wicker chair as if someone had hit me in the chest. I gulped air, as if I hadn't drawn a deep breath in years.

"How did I know?" I said. I was dizzy. For a moment, I thought that my decaf latte included double caffeine by mistake.

Something in the universe had shifted.

In my nearly conscious mind, I knew that the guides had sent Deanna to lead me on the next segment of my journey. Not the physical, nomadic sort of journey I'd often taken. This would be my spiritual journey.

Deanna smiled, pleased by my recognition. She had known all along that our connection would be spiritual. We huddled in the corner of the coffee shop as if sheltered by a protective pod. She told me more about her practice.

"I'm an energy healer," she explained. "I meet with clients on Sundays; it's the only time I have to devote to this part of my life." She recounted her work and the eight years of her spiritual education. "I'm trained in Reiki, Tachyon, and other methods of holistic energy healing. During private sessions, my clients learn to demystify their intuitive gifts. Rather than hide, they learn to live consciously, bridging mainstream life with spirituality."

Silently, without judgment, Deanna watched my face and body language. I felt that I could safely expose absolutely anything. "Sometimes I feel like a three-dimensional jigsaw puzzle," I tried to explain. "All of the pieces are there but out of place, and there's a peculiar shell that prevents getting close to people."

Events from deep in my childhood began to emerge. "My mother used to knit a lot," I told Deanna. "When she found a mistake in the fabric, I watched her unravel a sweater. I see myself as one of her defective garments, as if I've discovered dropped stitches in the first few rows of my life, but if I unravel and roll into a ball, a re-knit might be impossible." She nodded and smiled a knowing smile. Her eyes told me I was safe and not alone.

Deanna had no Web site, no brochure, and no marketing communication materials, unusual for a marketing professional of her caliber. "If someone is ready, he or she will find me, just as you did. When *you're* ready, you'll contact me."

Later, on the street by our parked cars, I was astounded to discover that two hours had passed. We hugged like old friends. I told Deanna, "I'll be in touch." For days afterward, I felt a tingling sensation where her hand had touched the center of my back.

I had trouble concentrating during the days that followed. Everything in my life seemed secondary to the journey. I sorted through the stack of cards I'd collected at the meeting. Then I realized I could have found her card with my eyes closed. It had a noticeable energy that the other pieces of heavy stock didn't have. I stared at it. *What have I stumbled into?* Via email, I arranged a Sunday morning appointment.

I'd been spiritually unconscious but giving thanks to something I called "guardians" or "guides" for most of my life. I was in my early twenties the first time I could remember saying "Thank you" to the guides. I was behind the wheel of our old, brown Pontiac with my babies safely strapped into their car seats. I'd stopped at a green light. I wondered, *Why am I stopped?* Then, a fourteen-wheeler raced through the intersection. I didn't sit there thinking about God. I just said, "Thank you," and waited for the next green light.

As a child, I'd rejected religion and all spirituality. From the pulpit each Sunday, mean and nasty Reverend Swinehart often damned those "Catholics down the street" and had few positive words to say about anything.

I didn't see the world that way. *Why not focus on the positive?*

I was living proof that positive visualization could manifest a better life.

Still, I'd dismissed auras that occasionally appeared and doubted mysterious familiarity.

With Deanna's help, I learned that contemporary human knowledge or vocabulary couldn't rationally explain every experience. Lack of explanation or words didn't mean what I felt or saw wasn't real. Radio waves, once just as mysterious, are invisible but no less real. I didn't understand how the guides had given me what I asked for, but years of evidence proved that, against all odds, I'd had a happy life.

Still, there was a lot of healing to do when the spiritual journey began. I remained unaware that I'd floated out of my body, untethered, safe from my violent father, encroaching sisters, and my mother, oblivious to it all.

I'd been living *out of body* since I was that frightened little girl, pinched between my sleeping sisters, watching my Self float near the ceiling. Deanna taught me how to recapture my splintered energy.

During our first session, Deanna said, "Stand up."

I did.

Then she said, "Where are your feet?"

"On the floor," I said while thinking, *This is weird.*

Then she said, "Where's your energy?"

Emotion swelled in me. My energy wasn't touching the floor, but I couldn't articulate where it was … just … out there.

"Close your eyes," she said. "Now, allow your energy to flow through the soles of your feet. Let it flow from your head, through your feet to the center of the earth." Before that moment, I never realized I *had* energy. It was odd to feel it flowing through the soles of my feet and beyond. I'd never felt so centered and safe.

chapter twenty-nine

$\mathcal{M}$om missed a tee time.

Even at eighty, she still shot under 50 on nine holes and never missed golf. Her friend, Lou, knocked and let herself in with a key usually used when my mother was out of town. She found Mom unconscious on the floor and called 911. If the paramedics hadn't arrived when they did, she would have died. A kidney infection had hit hard and fast. Our mother was in the hospital for several days and recovery took months.

My sister Lili insisted that our mother move to the Pacific Northwest to be near family, specifically in Edmonds where Lili lived with her husband. Without considering how Mom's meager fixed income could accommodate the inevitable increase in rent and living expenses, Lili flew to Ohio like a knight on a white horse, before anyone could ponder the possibilities. I had no intention of interfering and I was too busy with my job to get involved. Mom would be close enough to my sisters and me to use her subtle manipulation. I braced myself.

"Hi, Marsh, it's Lili. I tried your home phone. Where are you?"

"I met with clients in California yesterday. I'm at the San Francisco airport. What's up?"

"Well, we've been looking for a place for Mom to live here in Edmonds, and we're trying to figure out how she can buy a condo. The rent here is so high, and there's nothing decent in her price range."

No shit! I didn't say it.

"We were wondering if you could help. We were thinking if we all pitched in, we could buy a nice condo."

We, We, We! I wanted to shout, *"Why doesn't Mom ask me herself?"* but I knew—Lili liked being in charge, and Mom liked being taken care of. It was symbiotic.

"We found a brand new complex," she went on. "It's a community for over-fifty-fivers. It has a putting green, and the residents seem nice." She told me the price. "We made offers on two other units, but there was a bidding war, and both sold for more than the asking price."

"I'll do what I can." I said. "Can we discuss this after my flight? I can drive straight from the airport and be there by two-thirty or three. I'll call you when I'm closer."

During the drive from Sea-Tac airport, I called my friend Charley, a loan officer for Washington Mutual Bank. "With 20 percent down, we can set you up with a sub-prime ARM," he explained. "That way, the payments will be low. With real estate increasing like it is, this kind of a loan is a good deal."

I met Mom and Lili at the listing agent's office and followed them to the gated community. The condo in question was on the main floor, with a sliding glass door to a small, private garden. It smelled of fresh paint and new carpet. After the tour I said, "Mom, I can buy the condo and rent it to you, but I can't do it for $400 a month. Just the association dues and property tax add up to $400 a month. I'll need to discuss specifics with my banker before I can give you an exact amount, but…" I offered an estimate.

I gave the realtor a $5,000 earnest money check and the developer accepted the offer at 9 that night.

After I worked out specifics with my banker, I called Mom with the exact rent amount.

"Oh, well, that's more than I paid in Columbus. I just don't think I can do that," she said in a tone that scraped like sandpaper on my nerves.

I took more than one deep breath. "Mom, I told you how much I could put down, and you said you'd rather not liquidate anything in your investment account. We discussed what the rent was likely to be. Don't you remember? We were standing between the greenhouse and the putting green." I tried not to panic. "I'll lose the earnest money if you back out now." Then I added, "Mom, Lili said that before she called me, you made offers on two other units. You couldn't have offered that much less than I'm paying for this one. How were you going to do that?"

"Let me think about this," she said, avoiding my question.

A few days later, I called her at Lili's. "Mom, if you don't make a decision today, I lose the earnest money." I suggested a revised amount, leaving me with negative cash flow.

"Is that doable?" She agreed and I relaxed—a little. She'd have a new condo with stainless steel appliances and I'd have a good investment, I hoped.

"I'll finish the financing," I said.

Lili called the next morning. "Sounds like you and Mom worked out a good deal," she said, *almost* sarcastically. "If Mom helps you buy the condo, it will be part of her estate, right?"

"No, that's not how it works, Lili." I tried to stay calm. "Mom is paying for the use of my money and the risk, not for a portion of ownership."

She was silent.

"How long will Mom stay there?" I asked, "How long will the real estate market stay hot? What if she moves out and I can't rent it?"

"Well, I don't know!"

"No one knows. That's the risk." I tried to be patient. "With the mortgage payment, association dues, and property taxes, my expenses will exceed the rent. I'm counting on an increase in equity to balance it out in the long run."

"Well, fine then," she said.

I felt like I did when we were children and I got dirtier than Lili in the sandbox.

The situation reminded me of our childhood and Lili's craving to be in charge of everything, even Granddad's electric fence.

Being in charge was Lili's tool for surviving.

⚬

I drove to Edmonds on Mother's Day. During lunch, Mom said, "When I moved out here, Lili helped me get rid of so much stuff, but I still have the letters Granddad and Grandma wrote to each other just before they were married. I found them in Grandma's things when she died. That was more than fifteen years ago. I've never read them." As an afterthought she added, "Would you like to have them?"

"Of course I would!" I said. When we finished our homemade vegetable soup and ham sandwiches, we crossed the parking lot to the row of garages that still smelled like fresh drywall inside. Mom hopped into her old Buick as if she were in her fifties. As she backed out of the narrow space, I thought, *I hope I'm that spry at eighty.*

From a stepladder, I searched the metal shelves Lili had set up for her against the back wall. I found five, small cardboard boxes. One box was labeled "Marcia." I looked at Mom as I held the box.

"Oh. I keep forgetting to give you that. It's full of your old report cards and some photos." I carried the box across the small parking lot to my car.

As I walked, I remembered how upset she was that she'd lost "everything" when she left Dad. Clearly, she had exaggerated.

I rearranged the Bekins packing cartons until we found the one containing the rusty metal box.

"I think it's that one," she pointed. "Put it on the hood of my car." As I did so, Mom leaned on my shoulder, encroached on my space, and diverted my energy. As long as I could remember, I'd avoided her touch. Now that Deanna had introduced me to my energetic field, I could feel my mother suck it out of me. There was no space to retreat. I was reminded of the out-of-body existence I'd become so comfortable with and recognized the cause of my escape so many years before.

I opened the rusted, metal box and felt Granddad and Grandma's energy tingle all around us, as in *Raiders of the Lost Ark*, but this was a positive, happy glow. Mom didn't notice or, if she did, she ignored it. I touched the discolored envelopes and the tingle intensified. "I'll be careful. The paper is so fragile," I said as I stepped away from her vacuum to put the old box in my car.

On the way home that afternoon, I stopped at a restaurant, ordered coffee and collected my energy. I poured cream into my coffee and allowed the power back into my energetic field.

During the following Sunday's session, I told Deanna about the letters. "I haven't read them yet. I feel like I need permission."

"If it would make you feel better," she offered, "light a candle, a pillar of white light to fill the room, then make your request from a place of greater good, both yours and theirs." I agreed, though I felt a tinge of resistance. This sounded like a prayer. I didn't pray.

As we got further into the session, I told Deanna about my relationship with my Granddad when I was just three years old, before *Training*. I knew he loved me even though I was *just a girl*. There in Deanna's tiny, candle-lit room, I could feel his life force supporting my efforts to be happy and whole. "Do you realize how important he is to you even now?" Deanna asked.

I knew. I could feel him there with me, but the *concept* was still foreign and unnerving. "I always thought it was Grandma," I told her, not knowing where that thought came from.

Deanna said, "I smell something strange, like straw and mud with something foul. Do you know what it is?" I could smell it too, but I thought it was a memory. Could Deanna smell my memories?

I explained, "On Granddad's dairy farm, the cows tracked mud and manure into the stalls during milking. Granddad threw straw on top of the muck to make it easier to walk on. He helped me clean it from my boots with a hose. And I remember driving the John Deere tractor in the fields, pulling the manure spreader when I was only nine." The odor permeated the air in her candle-lit room. "It smells … so … so … safe."

There was no manure or straw in the room near Green Lake, north of downtown Seattle, but the feeling of safety was strong and sure. Where did the smell come from? I'd never mentioned to Deanna that Granddad lived on a farm.

At home that night, I arranged the letters on my dining room table and searched for a candle. I stood over the discolored envelopes in the candlelit kitchen and closed my eyes. "Please bless these letters and the greater good of our family, that I might know my grandparents and see the beauty of their lives together." Over fifty years had passed since the last time I'd prayed—the Lord's Prayer in Vacation Bible School.

Who am I praying to?

The letters contained the private thoughts and dreams that Granddad and Grandma had shared nearly one hundred years before. Grandma had saved them locked in a rusty metal box with the key hidden in her dresser drawer until she died. If Granddad and Grandma had known I would read these letters, would they have burned them? Was it OK for me to read them now? I left the letters on the table, went to bed, and slept soundly.

Granddad and Grandma appeared in my dreams. They drove a horse and buggy down a dirt road under an arch of spring green maples, laughing in the filtered summer sunlight and dreaming of their future children.

The next afternoon, I arranged the letters by date. I wanted to read them in chronological order. The TV mumbled in the background. I wasn't watching really. The news was over. Then I noticed the program featured an old man teaching children to play the harmonica. Granddad had played the harmonica. Of all his instruments, it was my favorite. I lost it—big-time, inside-out, gut-wrenching sobs. It was a sign. I didn't believe in signs, but there it was—a sign.

Each letter I read brought me closer to my grandparents' lives, Cecil and Edith, so important in my earliest memories. The letters revealed the loving hearts I'd cherished and known long after they fell in love with each other:

From a ranch near Wilder, Montana,

March 31, 1920

My Dearest Edith,

What better way to celebrate my birthday than writing to you. Of course being with you would be perfect but as that can not be, I will write. Just think I am twenty, makes me feel old. But I suppose it will seem young some day. When a fellow has a birthday he doesn't usually think anything about it much but today I thot about it all day. I suppose being so far away from you had a great deal to do with it. Remember where we were last March 31st?

I received my tripod and was tickled to death when I got it. I was just like a little kid. I wanted one and to think you sent it made it all the nicer. I played with it about all afternoon, I would of taken some pictures right away but have only one film here and I am saving it to get some pictures of the river when the ice goes out. The ice is breaking up now and may go out most any time...

...Please forgive this short letter but the mail goes out tomorrow and I am getting tired so will stop. But will send you all the love you will expect and I feel that you won't kick on the amount. So here comes a whole lot.

> *Forever Yours,*
>
> *Cecil*

She lived eighty-seven years. He lived eighty-eight. He was, forever, hers.

chapter thirty

I hurried in from the deck to answer the phone.

"You've become a recluse!" my friend Kara scolded. "What're you up to?"

"I'm writing a memoir," I admitted.

"You'll never get it published 'cause you're not Hanoi Jane or Hillary."

"It's not *always* about money," I said, a little too defensively. Kara personified my outgrown Self, always focused on results with no patience for the journey. "I can't talk now. Niki and Matt are here with their families. I'll call you tomorrow, I promise."

I went back outside to be with my family. My son, daughter, their spouses, and my four grandchildren, including Matt's seven-month-old second addition, Alex, blessed me with two rare and blissful days. Loving without smothering was a challenge. I wanted to hug and not let go ... to hold little hands, feed little mouths, cuddle growing bodies ... but my children were in their thirties.

They left Sunday afternoon, all eight of them. After one long, last hug, extreme stillness permeated my life again. Emotions gathered like the storm clouds over Lake Sammamish on that sunny afternoon, light-darkness, rain-drought, love-loneliness.

Pride. Isolation. Joy.

To soften the silence, I read from my old journal.

The entry I opened to recounted the single-mom apprehension and guilt I'd felt twenty years before when Niki and Matt, eleven and thirteen, began coming home from school to an empty house ...

Niki called at three today to let me know they're home so I was surprised when the admin pulled me out of a meeting at 4:30. "Your daughter's on the phone. She says it's important."

"Hello." I braced for bad news.

"Mom, there's a rainbow in the backyard! It goes right into the picnic table!" She considers herself grown up at thirteen. She no longer bounces out of her room to share the school day's events. I ask for details and she's reluctant—now she's sharing her rainbow.

I could imagine Matt bouncing like a pogo stick in the background, "Wow, it's so cool. I'm gonna look for a pot-a-gold."

"And, Mom, you can see each color," Niki went on, "blue and yellow and pink and violet!"

"I'm so glad you guys called me!" I turned my back so the nosey secretary couldn't see my mom-face.

Finally Niki said, "Oh no, it's fading, like the wind blew it away."

Like your childhood.

Reading the rainbow memory produced an echo of light and joy in my quiet, empty home and filled the dark shadows of a stormy beginning. Washed in the pride of motherhood, I noticed rain clouds gathering and absently wandered outside to retrieve the toys left behind by my grandchildren. To my amazement, a double rainbow reached from the peak of Mt. Rainier to the shadow of Mt. Baker. The bright colors completed their circular journey, reflected on Lake Sammamish. As if the past could foretell the future, the rainbow reassured me.

Light, color, and the echo of children's laughter.

❦

I met with Deanna on Sunday mornings. If anyone asked, I said I had a massage appointment. I couldn't begin to explain Deanna's ineffable talent. I was seeing an energy healer, a doctor of sorts that puts you back together without touching or a psychoanalyst that already knows your thoughts and past lives.

In the first few months of my spiritual journey, I was anxious to reach a conclusion. I discovered, however, this is not a lifetime journey.

This is the journey of my spirit, and it will last long after my physical body withers.

Until this journey began, my life's early misery was water under the bridge. *You can't change what has been.* My paycheck confirmed my identity. I refused to allow difficult memories to ruin my life. I began to understand that the unhealed wounds festering beneath thick girl-hood scars, needed to heal before I could reclaim my womanhood, my Self.

The swirl of my changing energy felt out of place in my Bellevue condo.

"We sold our place," my neighbor announced. "You can't believe how much we got. It was an auction in the end. If you've ever considered selling, now's the time—this is nuts! I got the number of a couple that really wanted ours but they didn't get their bridge loan fast enough. Maybe you should call 'em."

"What's the name and number?" I asked. As I wrote it down, I thought, *I don't have to call them*, but I did.

Dave and Janna arrived about five the following Sunday afternoon when Lake Sammamish and the Cascade Mountains were putting on a light show. Pink snow covered the mountains, and the lake reflected the deep blue sky. After a tour of the house, I led them to the deck where my planter-garden was at its peak with variegated vines, white lobelia, red germaniums, and a deep purple laceleaf maple next to a bubbling fountain.

I served a Washington chardonnay with assorted French cheeses and artisan bread. Sitting on the deck, they agreed to my outrageous asking price, and we worked out the timeline.

Where would I go?

I drove to Oregon to see my son and then to Cannon Beach to meet a realtor and look at property. For weeks, she sent new listings, but before I could get there, someone from California purchased each property, sight unseen.

A friend said, "How about Hood Canal? It's beautiful, and the weather's better than the Oregon Coast."

I called a realtor she knew on Bainbridge Island and explained I was looking for income-generating property, maybe a duplex where I could live on one side and rent the other, or maybe a B & B.

She said, "How about a farm?"

"I never considered a farm," I said.

"The previous owner raised llamas. The property's in Kitsap County, surrounded by horses and tree farms. There's a spectacular view of the Olympic Mountains, a great location for a B & B," said the realtor.

"Where did you say it was?" I asked.

"Near Poulsbo," she said.

"Where's Poulsbo?" I asked.

"It's less than thirty minutes from the Bainbridge ferry."

In September, I toured the three-acre llama farm and thirteen-year-old house. I began calculating the cost of converting the house to a B & B—beds, linens, light fixtures, window coverings, paint, furniture…

Fred Morgan had homesteaded the original property in 1921, about the same time my grandparents began dairy farming in Ohio. The property contrasted sharply with Ohio in every other way. Dairy cows versus yard art. Dry-flat farmland versus Hood Canal, Puget Sound, and mountains all around. Hot summers versus mild marine weather. Maple and oak versus cedar and fir.

I read about owning llamas and learned they're much easier to care for than horses or other livestock. During the second visit, I asked the realtor if I could walk the property alone. I inspected a fountain that needed repair. The waterfall was dry. Wild mallards floated on the pond while I sat on a rock. A great blue heron swept by, aborting his landing when he saw me. I stood with the curious llamas, who sniffed and stared. The smell of hay lingered as I opened the wooden doors in the hayloft, stood in the sunlight, and stared at the mountains.

Morgan Hill Llama Farm felt like the perfect place for me. I made an offer, llamas included.

I wanted to raise chickens on my new farm, but October was late in baby chick season. If I intended to serve fresh eggs in the spring, I had no time to ponder. "Are these really baby chicks?" asked the mail carrier, handing me the peeping perforated cardboard box containing the minimum online order—twenty-six chicks.

"Don't worry. I'm moving to a farm in a few weeks." Until moving day, the yellow, brown, and black chicks lived in a plastic bin under a heat lamp in an empty, walk-in closet.

chapter thirty-one

Trying not to bounce the basket of pullet eggs, I ran to answer the phone.

"Morgan Hill Retreat, this is Marcia." The B & B would open soon. It was late March.

"Hi, Aunt Marsh," said Jason, Kali's son. "At Christmas you said you needed help getting ready to open the B & B. I was wondering if I could come for a visit."

"Perfect timing, Jason. They just delivered a load of gravel. I'm going to spend the weekend spreading it on the path to the gazebo."

"I'll be on the four o'clock ferry," he said. It was that fast. We hardly talked at all.

When he came to the door he startled me at first. He seemed taller, about six-foot-four, and more handsome than I remembered. I realized what little time I'd spent with him since elementary school. He had gone to a small college in California, where he'd graduated with honors.

After a quick hug, he avoided eye contact by looking over the top of my head. His dilated pupils caused an eerie expression. His handsome face looked sad.

We superficially chatted, then I took him to dinner at my favorite restaurant, Molly Ward Gardens, just a few miles away. He told me about his job at his uncle's real estate development office. I shared stories about the llamas and comical chickens. After dinner, he went to his room, and I went to bed. I sensed something peculiar about the evening, but I thought I'd lost touch with the younger generation and dismissed it.

Up early as usual, I set a place for him at the table, then worked in the yard. At two-thirty, he was still in his room.

I called Niki. "Jason spent the night here, and he's still in bed. Should I be concerned? It seemed like he was in a weird mood when he arrived yesterday."

"Don't worry about it, Mom. He probably stayed up late reading or watching TV. It's so quiet at your place. He's probably really relaxed."

At three, he came outside. I said, "Good morning. I hope you slept well."

"I'm starved," he said.

I held up the basket of fresh little eggs I'd just gathered. "How about scrambled eggs and bacon? I have strawberries and yogurt I made myself."

"Great. I'll get started on the gravel after we eat." He had no idea what time it was. It didn't matter. I prepared breakfast while he sat on the porch, staring at the mountains.

Together, we spread gravel until dark, with very little conversation. While he took a shower, I fixed dinner.

"Wow, you did all this for me?" he said when he saw the table set with wine glasses, candles, and cloth napkins. "Is that a roast that smells so good?"

"You're worth it, Jason. Thanks for your help. Do you want a glass of wine with dinner?"

"No, thanks," he said.

After dinner, we sat in the living room by the fire and finally had a real conversation. He was frustrated with his dad and uncle. They controlled his twenty-three-year-old life. I tried to listen and be supportive. He fought angry tears, but there was more to his pain than he was telling me.

Finally he said, "I've been taking medication for schizophrenia, but it made me feel terrible. The doctor gave me a different prescription. I started taking it yesterday."

I tried not to disclose my shock. *Schizophrenia?* Could the new medication cause dilated pupils? I had questions but didn't ask. He needed to talk without judgment. "How do you feel today?" I asked, as if this was a normal conversation.

"Better, I think."

In high school, he'd been a rich-kid delinquent. His dad had bought him a new Acura before he turned sixteen, and he'd been given an allowance that any of us could live on, but he stole cars and sold the parts. He nearly went to jail instead of college, but his dad had hired expensive attorneys. That night at my place, he started talking about his delinquent days.

Not knowing the consequences of my words, I said, "Jason, don't beat yourself up about those high school days. How could you have learned limits and self-discipline when your parents were so inconsistent? Since the day you were born, your mom said no, your dad said yes, or vice versa. You were a smart kid and figured out you could get anything you wanted. You tested limits until the police caught up with you, and even then your dad fixed it all up."

"Yeah, I guess you're right," he said.

"Sometimes it's just hard to grow up," I said.

His silence told me he was out of words.

"Well, I've had a busy day in the cold air. I'm going to take a hot shower and go to bed. See ya in the morning. Oh—there are lots of DVDs on the shelf over there. Help yourself."

"Thanks—I read all the *National Geographics* last night," he said. "Oh, Aunt Marsh, thanks for dinner."

I gave him a hug and went to bed.

He slept until noon the next day. After breakfast, we worked in the yard. Suddenly at four, he pushed the shovel into the diminished pile of gravel and said, "I've got to catch the ferry."

"You can stay another night," I said. "It's great having you here."

"No, gotta catch the ferry."

He packed his things, and he was gone. As his car turned out of the driveway, I felt a sense of loss. I knew he had a difficult struggle ahead and nothing I could do would help.

A few days later Kali called around six in the evening. She had that I-hate-you tone in her voice. "Where do you get off telling Jason I'm a bad mom?"

"What?"

"Wasn't he at your house this weekend?" she asked.

"Yeah, he was very helpful." I waited for the rest.

"I know what you said—that I'm an inconsistent parent."

"Kal, that's not what I said."

"You think you're such a great mom?"

"Nope, not by a long shot."

She told me again how much she hated me and went through her *I-should-love-you-like-a-sister-but-I-don't* routine. She shouted, "I never want to talk to you again!" and hung up.

In an Adirondack chair in the cool March air, I sipped a glass of merlot. The clouds over Mt. Olympus changed from puffs of white to sweeping fuchsia while my mind twisted with her words.

Finally, I stepped back from the sting.

She *wanted* to think badly of me and waited for me to fulfill her desire. If we were closer, she would have asked what really happened. She would have appreciated my efforts to help her struggling son, but she focused every situation on herself.

I was learning to balance my emerging spiritual awareness with my new "normal" life. Living on the farm helped. I decided, that moment, I would never again give Kali the opportunity to unleash her negativity on me. Banishing her abuse was part of letting go of *Training*. People often say, "Family is everything," but not in our case. We shared bad memories and DNA, little else. It wasn't just that Kali had hated me for forty years; it's that she expected to hate me. I stopped blaming myself.

In late April, when I saw her name on caller ID, I let the call go to voice mail then checked messages when the red light flashed. "We've moved up the wedding to my birthday in May." She sounded like a different person. "Hope you can make it." The timbre of her voice was happy and light.

My liberal sister was marrying the conservative music teacher she'd met on Match.com. I tried to be happy for them but declined via email. I thought about calling her, telling her I would no longer tolerate her outbursts, that she was out of my life forever. Just the thought of it gave me a stomachache. Confronting her would serve no purpose, but pretending nothing had happened was equally pointless.

She told our family she didn't invite me to the wedding. My children attended. My siblings attended. Her children and even her ex-husband attended, and of course, our mother.

There was a Fourth of July party at Mom's condo. My children, their families, and my siblings attended. I wasn't invited.

I talked to Mom in late November. "Beth brought a great spiced carrot recipe to the potluck a few weeks ago." I assumed Beth was her neighbor. "She emailed it to me. Do you want me to forward the email?"

"Sure," I said. *For eighty-something, she's really getting good at email,* I thought.

When the message arrived, I found her note to Beth at the bottom: *I'm having family Thanksgiving at my place, and I'd love to serve your spiced carrot recipe.* She'd hosted Thanksgiving without me. I was hurt. Not that I wanted to go. She knew I wouldn't. She'd ignored me, as if I wasn't real, like the day she'd turned my doll-sized loaves of bread into hot dog buns. At nearly sixty years old, I still felt stunned when my mother ignored me.

The only thing I could change was how I reacted.

All my life I felt like an unreal shadow, an accidental assignee in our unhappy family. I spent years trying to conform, as if my natural tendency toward happiness was lazy, stupid, or inappropriate.

Maybe my assignment on this planet was to remember that happiness is a universal gift.

My family can't take it from me if I don't let them.

chapter thirty-two

*J*ust after I opened the B & B, I received an invitation to an open house at Chico Spa on Puget Sound's Sinclair Inlet, but I had decided the new lavender garden took priority. I wanted to finish putting in the two hundred plants I'd purchased. I was dirty, sweaty, and tired, with no motivation to clean up and drive a few miles to Chico. Around four, however, I found myself in the shower, as if I had no choice. In a stupor, I managed to find something appropriate to wear.

I parked the car and walked toward a group of mingling strangers holding wine glasses on the deck overlooking Puget Sound. I felt that familiar sense of dread I'd carried to every sales call and trade show throughout my career. I'd frequently joined such groups but ignored the uneasiness.

To steel myself, I hesitated under the massive pine trees adjacent to a series of concentric paths covered with long pine needles and marked by smooth stones no doubt gathered from the rocky Puget Sound beach below. I stood with my head cocked to one side, as if this formation of rocks spoke a strange mythological language.

"It's a Cretan labyrinth," I heard a woman's voice explain, the tone revealing she knew I had no idea. A tall woman with short gray hair and kind face introduced herself. "I'm Sandy."

"Nice to meet you. I'm Marcia." We shook hands. "I saw a similar maze in St. George, Utah, a few years ago," I told her. "What's it for?"

"It's a spiritual tool, symbolic of the journey to the center of your Self, an aid for learning about your spiritual path."

A breathy "Wow!" was the extent of my vocabulary.

"I'll walk with you if you like," she said.

She led me to the entry in the outermost circuit.

"The basic labyrinth design is prehistoric and found all over the world—some in ancient caves, some on church floors. The design even relates to a Hindu Mandala. It's characterize by wholeness and spirituality, not religion. Like most human lives, this is a meandering purposeful path. Some believe that walking a labyrinth can awaken the knowledge encoded in our DNA."

The concept of encoded memory had often occurred to me, but I had never really taken it seriously.

"I just finished a year-long labyrinth sabbatical," Sandy told me. "I walked labyrinths all over Washington." Her voice was full of excitement as she told me about her favorite walks. "One was built in a forest, and the paths twisted around trees and up and down a hill."

"You mean they don't have to be as mathematical as this one?"

"No, but a labyrinth always winds to a center and then back out again. You can't get lost in a labyrinth like you can in a maze."

"Didn't that Greek guy need a magical thread to find his way out? I can't remember his name."

"Yes, you remember your mythology. It was Icarus." Sandy said. "The magical thread in the myth represents a connection to higher self, the ability to trust your own consciousness."

"I want to build one," said a voice. I looked up to see who had spoken, but the words were mine.

"There's a good book by Melissa Gayle West, *Exploring the Labyrinth*. She gives easy-to-follow instructions for building your own." When we reached the bench in the center, she tugged a small pad and pen from a pocket and demonstrated how to draw a labyrinth, starting with a plus sign in the center. She made it look simple.

As we wound out of the labyrinth, at times it seemed the two of us walked in opposite directions, but we were actually still on the same path. I got goose bumps.

We walked to the deck where Sandy introduced me to Cathy, the owner. "She wants to build a labyrinth like yours," Sandy said.

"Great. You're welcome to borrow the stakes and rope we used to mark and measure this one. There's no sense starting from scratch," Cathy said.

The next day I ordered Melissa's book from Amazon.com and began planning. I called Cathy and arranged to stop by for the stakes and rope she'd offered. Obsessed with my labyrinth, I surfed the Internet to learn about the history of labyrinths and how to build one, studying size, shape, maintenance, budget, etc.

Where should I build the labyrinth? Moving a bench around the yard and pasture, I sampled each perspective, experienced each possibility, and sensed the new labyrinth's life. It chose its place between the babbling rustic fountain and my new lavender garden where fragrant culinary varieties would permeate the summer air. I stretched and adjusted a circle of garden hose around the bench to emulate the future circumference and decided an eighteen-foot radius would be ideal. I knew from gardening that there were plenty of rocks in the soil. Residual piles still waited at the corners of the lavender garden.

Connecting to the earth during each labyrinth walk was important, so I began searching for a surface suitable for walking barefoot. I visited garden stores to research low maintenance plants that would tolerate being walked on. At Vern's Topsoil, I danced barefoot from one warm pile of mulch to the next, testing each product. That night, I soaked and scrubbed for an hour, removing dirt and splinters from my feet.

On a misty Monday morning in September, the rototiller lurched and pitched under the drip line of the cedar tree, unearthing rocks. I tossed them into piles outside the circle I'd marked.

Mark, a local gardener, arrived with his wheelbarrow and pitchfork. We removed the sod and paraded our wheelbarrows to the far corner of a pasture where the chickens began scratching as if we'd built them a playground.

On Wednesday, Vern's dump truck delivered ten yards of wet, sifted sand. Load by load, Kyle, a high school student, moved the heavy sand while I smoothed each wheel barrowful over the dirt. Then we firmly packed the sand with the riding lawn mower, dragging a "come along" we had rigged from chicken wire and chunks of discarded concrete.

Thursday's foggy morning brought Vern's dump truck filled with ten cubic yards of warm, steaming playground mulch, the softest I could find. Earthy aroma filled the damp air I as raked a thick layer into place to create a spongy surface.

On Friday, I began marking the circuits using the numbered stakes and measured rope I'd borrowed from Cathy, methodically following the comprehensive instructions in Melissa's book. That night, after my B & B guests checked in, I slept like an exhausted three-year-old.

I prepared a gourmet breakfast for my guests on Saturday and leisurely served each course as though I had nothing to do but attend to their satisfaction. When they left for a day of sightseeing, I finished the dishes and raced outdoors to arrange rocks. The design quickly consumed the piles I'd collected.

After the guests checked out on Sunday, I positioned more rocks and circuits emerged.

That evening my good friends, Kevin and Kathleen, owners of the Purple Goose B & B, stopped by. They placed a few rocks and told stories of labyrinths they'd walked at Chartres Cathedral in France, built in 1200, Grace Cathedral in San Francisco, officially dedicated in 1964, and San Vitale in Ravenna, Italy, constructed in the sixteenth century.

We toasted the nearly completed creation in Poulsbo, Washington. The labyrinth in Chico was the first I'd ever walked. Soon I'd walk my own.

With no guests to serve, I began early on Monday. I filled the wheelbarrow several times with smooth round rocks from the edge of the lavender bed, from the pasture, and from the beach of the trout pond, exposed by summer's drought. I spent the day bowing and stooping, placing the gathered rocks. I planted woolly thyme so powdery green, walk-able vines would grow into the path. Over time, the scent of thyme would blend with lavender. At dusk, I contemplated my labyrinth but found myself strangely unable to walk the path. Subsequent days brought my artistic admiration and the same peculiar hesitation. Through a nearly unconscious sense of the labyrinth's power, I knew that walking its circuits would open an awareness I'd longed for but still feared. If I allowed my Self to go to that place of serenity, I might not be able to come back.

Finally, at sunset on the first of October, I walked. A hardy fuchsia held its final dripping blossoms next to the path where I paused before entering. I expected to clear my mind and eliminate the noise, but my thoughts took charge.

If I plant a tree over there, the neighbors can't see when I walk," I thought. *When the woolly thyme gets bigger and spreads over the path, I'll be able to walk barefoot.*

"Be still!" I said aloud.

I sat on the bench in the center of the labyrinth, facing east, the cedar tree, the fuchsia, and the trout pond beyond. I rolled a cold, flat, amber-colored stone in my palms until it warmed. Then, as if something had bumped my hand, I suddenly dropped it. "OK," I said aloud, "I don't need to fidget."

I sat quietly for a few seconds.

I feel like I'm perched in the middle of the yard, and people driving by think I'm nuts, I thought.

"It doesn't matter," I said aloud.

Several moments of stillness passed. Tears welled. My chest felt heavy. Finally.

A flock of argumentative crows broke the silence. *Maybe the eagle's back,* I thought and twisted westward.

Rose and fuchsia brush strokes swept past tufts of steel wool clouds and sharp mountain peaks. The flock of crows flew out of the sunset. I wondered what they saw as they circled the labyrinth, the house, and the barn as if inspecting the inn before booking. They'd returned to their nightly home in the tall cedar trees that surrounded my farm.

A blessing?

Shamans believe Crow is a sign of change.

At last I knew, *I'm home.*

epilog

The champagne cork pops, and bubbles spill onto the porch.
"Ah, my favorite sound," I say. I pour two flutes of our favorite treat.

Kathleen and I toast the end of the busy season. "Was it always your dream to run a B & B?" she asks.

My answer surprises us both. "More like a nightmare." We laugh.

A bed and breakfast owner herself, she knows the intensity of the *busy season*, fresh in our bones.

"I don't mean it like it sounds. It's sort of like being a housewife, but I'm married to my business. I knew I'd have to clean toilets and make beds, but the volume of laundry is astounding!" I say. "Most of my guests are wonderful, but if I get a bad one, it's a brief encounter, not a divorce."

We laugh again.

"I know what you mean," she says. "I'm happy when they check in, and no matter how great they are I'm happy when I'm alone in the house again."

The rainy horizon clears, exposing snow-dusted mountains. As we watch in silence, crimson captures the pewter clouds then rakes the cedars and Douglas fir. Even the llamas blush with color.

As the lightshow fades, I say, "I never even dreamed of a place like this."

Early on a misty February morning, with no guests to care for, I walk the property with my companion, Howard, the Bichon Frise. The llamas *kush* on the uppermost corner of the pasture, guarding every inch. It's their job. They watch us but don't move. Tillie and Ted Toulouse-goose honk their morning greeting, and the Khaki Campbell ducks quack softly, all anxious for their bath in the pond. The blue-and-white bantam rooster squeaks like a leaking balloon, warning his mates of a lurking predator. I search the treetops, sure that the eagle is waiting for a breakfast of chicken or duck. I hear a high-pitched chirping whistle and see the silhouette of a big bird perched on the top branch of the cedar by the pond, his identity uncertain in the mist. Then the osprey spreads its narrow wings, exposing his white underbelly, and disappears into the fog. I wonder where he came from and where he's going in late February.

The raven's prehistoric call announces her approach. She scolds, hoping I'll offer the duck eggs as I did when the snow was deep. "You'll need to look elsewhere for breakfast today, sweetheart."

In the distance, I hear honking, but the domestic geese are in their pen. "The Canada geese are back!" I tell Howard. They arrive in February, hatch their goslings in May, and leave in July. I'm told it's their eighth season.

I hear her stride on the pavement before I see her. My neighbor, Jan—tall, thin with short dark hair and long legs, a runner who usually covers five miles a day. As she passes on the road by the cedar trees, she says, "Nice outfit."

"Thanks," I say as she runs out of sight. I look down at my Christmas-red polar fleece bathrobe and mukluks. When I opened Morgan Hill Retreat, I traded business suits, high-heeled shoes, and a briefcase for flannel shirts, elastic waist pants, and spotted yellow boots.

A career perpetuates its own necessity. The accouterments must match. The car. The clothes. The haircuts and highlights. Makeup and manicures. The gym membership and massages to relieve stress, and for some of my friends who still compete, facelifts to maintain the façade of youth.

I traded the gym for farm chores. I traded latte lines and the fast track for herbal tea and labyrinth walks. I traded expensive restaurants for homemade yogurt and farm-fresh eggs. I traded international travel for the joy of knowing animals and pondering the sunrise.

In this place, my feminine spirit rediscovers the saturated light of childhood.

Training dallies like an inconsequential shadow.